Mitra-Varuna

HAU
Books

Director
Frédéric Keck

Editorial Collective
Matthew Carey
Deborah Durham
Casey High
Nora Scott

Managing Editor
Hannah Roberson

HAU Books are published by the
Society for Ethnographic Theory (SET)

www.haubooks.org

Mitra-Varuna

An Essay on Two Indo-European Representations of Sovereignty

Georges Dumézil

Translated from the French, *Mitra-Varuna. Essai sur deux représentations indo-européennes de la souveraineté* by Derek Coltman

Critical Edition with New Introduction by Stuart Elden

Afterword by Veena Das

HAU Books
Chicago

© 2023 HAU Books

Initially published as *Mitra-Varuna. Essai sur deux représentations indo-européennes de la souveraineté*

© 1940 Presses Universitaires de France, first edition
© 1948 Éditions Gallimard, second edition
© 1988 Zone Books, English translation

Mitra-Varuna. An Essay on Two Indo-European Representations of Sovereignty, critical edition with New Introduction by Stuart Elden.

Notice to Readers of the Electronic Edition:
All rights reserved. No part of this publication may be reproduced, distributed, or transmitted in any form or by any means without the prior written permission of the publisher, except for brief quotations in reviews or other noncommercial uses permitted by copyright law. Access to the Electronic edition is for private use only. Any violation of these conditions constitutes an infringement of copyright law and the rights of the Proprietor, Author, and Publisher.

Cover design: Daniel Meucci
Layout design: Deepak Sharma, Prepress Plus Technologies
Typesetting: Prepress Plus Technologies (www.prepressplustechnologies.com)

ISBN: 978-1-912808-97-7 [paperback]
ISBN: 978-1-912808-99-1 [e-book]
ISBN: 978-1-914363-04-7 [PDF]
LCCN: 2022944238

HAU Books
Chicago Distribution Center
11030 S. Langley Ave.
Chicago, IL 60628
www.haubooks.org

HAU Books publications are marketed and distributed by The University of Chicago Press.
www.press.uchicago.edu

Printed in the United States of America on acid-free paper.

HAU Books would like to thank the Dumézil family for their gracious permission to publish this critical edition.

Contents

Mitra-Varuna: A Re-Introduction to Georges Dumézil

Stuart Elden

This Introduction does three main things. First it provides a background to understand where Georges Dumézil was in his career when the first edition of *Mitra-Varuna* was published in 1940. It then discusses the years between the first and the second edition in 1948, including some political questions about his work.[1] Finally it says something about Dumézil's writing on these topics after 1948, concluding with some brief thoughts about why *Mitra-Varuna* is a particularly apposite book to reintroduce Anglophone readers to Dumézil's work. The enduring importance of Dumézil's ideas is further explored in the Afterword by Veena Das.

Georges Dumézil was born on March 4, 1898, and began his linguistic studies with Latin, Greek, and German at an early age. He studied in Paris, meeting Michel Bréal, who was the grandfather of a classmate, and Antoine Meillet. Bréal had been a professor at the Collège de France, both a philologist and mythologist, and, among other things, a translator of Franz Bopp's *Comparative Grammar*.[2] Meillet ranged across the Indo-European languages, working particularly on Slavonic languages and Armenian, and was the co-compiler of a dictionary of Latin etymology.[3] Dumézil's notes to the present work attest to his importance. Dumézil entered the prestigious École Normale Supérieure in 1916, where he studied Arabic and Sanskrit. Breaking his studies because of the First World War, when he served as an artillery officer, he passed the *agrégation* in letters in 1919.[4] With this teaching qualification in hand, he taught at a *lycée* just north of Paris for six months before being advised his future career lay outside of France.

Dumézil's first overseas post was for six months at the University of Warsaw as a lecturer in French literature; there he also studied both Polish and Russian.[5] He then received a bursary to undertake the research for his theses, published as *Le Festin d'immortalité* (The Feast of Immortality) and *Le Crime des Lemniennes* (The Lemnian Crime), for which he received his doctorate in 1924.[6] In 1925 he moved to the University of Istanbul to teach history of religion, though he transferred to literature after a year. He travelled extensively in Turkey, Russia, and the Caucasus, learning Turkish and several other languages, including Ossetian, Armenian, and Abkhazian. He would describe these as "happy years," crucial to his life-long love of the region.[7] Between 1931 and 1933 he taught French at the University of Uppsala, where he also worked on Scandinavian languages, including Old Norse. Finally in 1933 he returned to France as *chargé de conférences* in comparative religion at the École Pratique des Hautes Études, fifth section. With the exception of some visiting posts, his future career was all in France; he was elected to the Collège de France in 1949 to the chair in Indo-European civilisations, after having been defeated for a chair in the history of religions in 1933 by Jean Baruzi.[8] The linguist Émile Benveniste was crucial in his successful election, writing the reports both for the creation of the chair and Dumézil's election to it.[9] Dumézil retired in 1968 and spent parts of the next three years in visiting posts at the Institute for Advanced Study in Princeton, the University of Chicago's Divinity School, and the University of California, Los Angeles. Elected to one of the forty chairs at the Académie Française on October 26, 1978, he was inducted as one of the "Immortals" by Claude Lévi-Strauss.[10] Ill health limited his travel in his final years, though not his prodigious work-rate. He died on October 11, 1986 at the age of 88.

Dumézil's Work Pre-1940

As Dumézil indicates in the "Preface to the Second Edition" of *Mitra-Varuna*, his earliest works had been in comparative Indo-European mythology, and he particularly notes his principal doctoral thesis, which was published as *Le Festin d'immortalité*, and his third book, *Le Problème des*

Centaures (The Centaur Problem), in 1929.[11] In each study he looked at examples from three cultures—in the first, magic drinks which gave the gift of immortality in Indian, Roman, and Norse mythology; in the second, Indian Gandharva, Greek centaurs, and Roman Luperci. Looking back, he suggests that some of these early works lacked "sufficient philological preparation."[12] Yet the focus on the Indo-European tradition, the approach of comparison, and the pairing of mythology with philology indicated in these works laid the foundation for subsequent studies.

In 1934 Dumézil published *Ouranós-Vāruṇa*, a short book comparing the Greek and Vedic gods, closely followed by *Flamen-Brahman*, which compared the priesthoods of India and Rome.[13] These are the most obvious forerunners to the present study. In the analysis of the sovereign gods of two mythic traditions, and the etymological and structural relation of the priestly class, he was already beginning to sketch out some key themes of his later work. Seen from the perspective of his later career though, there are certainly limitations. Apparently the sociologist and sinologist Marcel Granet told Dumézil in 1935: "Until now you have only talked nonsense [*bêtises*], but it is intelligent nonsense."[14] Granet encouraged the development of Dumézil's work, and Dumézil attended Granet's lectures on Chinese thought and culture. Lévi-Strauss says when Dumézil first had the courage to knock on his door, Granet said "Come in, I've been waiting for you for ten years."[15] Granet's approach was important to Dumézil, who pays tribute both in the present work and in a preface to a re-edition of Granet's *La Religion des Chinois*.[16]

The fundamental breakthrough, however, came in Dumézil's 1938 article entitled "La Préhistoire des flamines majeurs."[17] In this article he presented his twofold claim that there was a relation between the Vedic, Latin, and Celtic names for a king—*rāj-*, *rēg-*, *rīg*—and the Vedic and Latin names for a priest, *brahman* and *flāmen*. He makes the point that these are not two distinct claims, but two parts of a whole: "In both India and Rome, the two names designated two connecting bodies [*organes solidaires*], more precisely the two inseparable halves of a single body [*organe unique*], the body of *Sovereignty*."[18]

This leads Dumézil to outline what would become his most important and influential idea, that mythological traditions and social divisions in quite different contexts are structured around a divide between priests, warriors, and producers. This is his tripartite, or trifunctional, hypothesis. In India, the king and brahmin were set apart from the warrior class, *kshatriya* or sometimes *rājanya*, and a third class of the farmers and producers of the *vaishya* group. The three *varna*, or castes, have parallels in several different traditions, notably Roman legends, with the *flamen*, the military, and the farmers, or the division between gods in Vedic, Roman, or Norse mythology. In Rome this social divide maps onto the gods Jupiter-Mars-Quirinus; for the Norse gods it is Odhinn-Thor-Freya; in Vedic mythology Varuna-Indra-Nasatya. Dumézil draws some parallels with other traditions, especially ancient Iran, but recognises that Greece is not as clearly divided as Rome, and that Welsh and Slavic traditions are often too fragmented to be thematised in the same way. Broadly speaking the first function is sovereign; the second, martial; the third, productive. Daniel Dubuisson suggests that this 1938 piece shows that "the conceptual and theoretical mechanism upon which the initial hypothesis and first broad analyses of Dumézil's work were built is itself based on fragile notions and daring generalizations."[19] But as a foundation it is important, since it gives the spur to so much that follows in his work.

His first book-length study to explore the trifunctional hypothesis was *Mythes et dieux des Germains*, published in 1939.[20] Dumézil later indicated that it was largely written in 1936, but reformulated in 1938 in the light of his insights into trifunctionalism.[21] The structure of the book is indeed threefold. After an introductory chapter, Dumézil devotes three sections to Myths of Sovereignty, Myths of Warriors, and Myths of Vitality, each with three chapters. This is a study which I will return to later in this Introduction.

In the 1938–39 academic year, Dumézil gave two courses at the École Pratique des Hautes Études. In the course records, these were described in the following way:

> In one of the two courses, the collection of ritual myths attached to the name of Vritrahan in India were studied, homologous facts were noted and analysed in the religions of other peoples speaking Indo-European languages, notably among Germanic people.
> The second course was devoted to examining the two complementary representations of sovereignty in several Indo-European mythologies (Varuṇa and Mitra, Romulus and Numa, Odhinn and Ullr, etc.).[22]

These courses are preserved in the Georges Dumézil archive, held at the Collège de France.[23] As Dumézil notes in the Preface to the Second Edition to *Mitra-Varuna*, the second course "provided the material for this book." The first, on the warrior function, and especially Indra, who bore the name Vritrahan as the killer of the serpent Vritra, was developed in later lectures in the early 1950s, which became *Aspects de la fonction guerrière chez les Indo-Européens* in 1956.[24] The course manuscript is the best source we have for the development of the present text, as unfortunately, unlike many of his books, the archive does not contain a draft manuscript for *Mitra-Varuna*.[25]

The course which became *Mitra-Varuna* was delivered between November 15, 1938 and June 8, 1939, with breaks for Christmas and Easter, but also a break of five weeks in February and March 1939, where instead Roger Caillois presented his views on the idea of the sacred.[26] This was a theme Caillois treated in his book *L'Homme et le sacré* (Man and the Sacred), published in 1939, in the series in which Dumézil had published *Mythes et dieux des Germains*.[27] Its original preface is dated to March 1939, just as he gave the final lecture to Dumézil's class. In that text, Caillois said that it was "impossible for me to indicate my debt to Mr Georges Dumézil precisely. So great is my appreciation of him that, if I tried to specify it, I would wrong the mentor who, in the history of religions, has directed me from my very first steps, and, still more, I would wrong the friend whose suggestions and guidance have contributed so much to this little volume."[28]

While *Mitra-Varuna* is a study of the first function of sovereignty, this is not to say it is a simple analysis of a unified god across different traditions. Importantly Dumézil also recognises that the divide does not cut simply three ways, but the first function, concerning sovereignty, is itself split. Thus in analysing the role of Varuna, Mitra also needs to be considered; if Jupiter is examined, then Dius Fidius, the god of oaths, must also be questioned, as Dumézil indicates in the Preface to the First Edition.[29] Sovereignty is, in this analysis, divided between a more legal, contractual, reasoning side and a terrible, magical, and warlike basis. As Dumézil says at one point in the book, "Mitra is the sovereign under his reasoning aspect, luminous, ordered, calm, benevolent, priestly; Varuna is the sovereign under his attacking aspect, dark, inspired, violent, terrible, warlike."[30] How this split in the first function might operate, with similarities and differences between traditions, is the focus of the present book.

As the table of contents indicates, each chapter looks at a contrasting pair of gods, mythical figures, or concepts. Sovereignty therefore has both a worldly, juridical form and a magical, supernatural form. The king–priest relation is therefore important to understand political power. Dumézil ranges widely in the book, from Rome to India and Iran, from the Norse myths to the Greeks and Celts. He provides, in particular, discussions of the early kings of Rome, noting that while Romulus founded the city, Numa founded its institutions. For Dumézil, in a way which would be controversial with more conventional Latinists, early Roman history was effectively mythology.

From 1940 to 1948

France had declared war on Germany in September 1939, after the invasion of Poland. Initially there was a period of uneasy and limited conflict, known as the "phoney war," until May 1940, when France was invaded. Dumézil dates the first edition preface of *Mitra-Varuna* to June 1939, and Gallimard indicates it was published in a limited run in May 1940,[31] which helps to explain why copies are so hard to find today. Paris was occupied in mid-June, and Marshal Philippe Pétain became leader with the formal French surrender on June 24. The Vichy regime was established in July. At the time, Dumézil was in Turkey, where he had been posted as part of the French military mission in the initial mobilisation.[32]

Dumézil lost his teaching post in November 1941 because he had been a Freemason in the 1930s. He regained the authorization to teach in January 1943.[33] Nevertheless he continued publishing through the war and after the Liberation, with three volumes of the *Jupiter, Mars, Quirinus* series and three of *Les Mythes romains* published between 1941 and 1947.[34] As the footnotes to the second edition of *Mitra-Varuna* show, in those works he developed several themes of the present book and corrected some of its claims. He would continue to revisit, revise, and develop his work throughout his career.

After the war Dumézil returned to *Mitra-Varuna*, producing the second edition—its preface is dated to January 1947—in part because the first edition was inaccessible and in part because it really was the foundation of so much of the work he was doing. The second edition was published on March 11, 1948.[35] The changes are relatively minor for the most part, with the most substantial alterations made to Chapter IX and the Conclusion. Shorter passages from the first edition which were replaced in the second are included and translated in endnotes below, while the two longer passages appear as Appendices I and II. A reader of this book therefore has all the material Dumézil published between the two editions. Given the inaccessibility of the 1940 edition, the French text of the variants is also included. A Francophone reader with the more readily available 1948 text and this edition would thus be able to reconstruct the 1940 version.

The year 1948 also saw a fourth volume of *Jupiter, Mars, Quirinus* and a book on the Norse god, Loki.[36] Lévi-Strauss would describe *Loki* as Dumézil's *Discourse on Method*, indicating the rules of his approach.[37] One further book from this period is worth noting, *L'Héritage indo-européen à Rome*, conceived as an introduction to both the *Jupiter, Mars, Quirinus* and *Les Mythes romains* series.[38] This book was initially planned with Harvill Press for an Anglo-Saxon audience, but it was not translated and was instead published in French.[39]

Alongside these works on history and mythology, Dumézil was running an almost parallel career producing a series of works in linguistics. Dating back to his time in Turkey in the 1920s, he had published books on northern Caucasian languages in 1932 and 1933.[40] Part of the reason for the early work on this subject was his distance from Paris and its libraries, which made research on mythology more difficult.[41] His work in the area of linguistics was controversial, leading to a furious exchange with the Russian linguist, Prince Nikolai Sergeyevich Trubetzkoy. Trubetzkoy wrote a critical review of Dumézil's books in 1934.[42] Trubetzkoy confessed to his friend, Roman Jakobson, that the reason he was so harsh on Dumézil was that Dumézil was dismissive of Russian scholars working on the topic, but that he felt Dumézil could not "hold a candle" to them.[43] Dumézil's angry response was published as a rather peculiar, limited print-run text, using a cursive script (not Dumézil's own handwriting).[44] The debate continued for a few years until Trubetzkoy's death in Austria in 1938.[45]

Dumézil did especially important work on Ubykh, a language of the northwest Caucasian family. In 1931 he produced a study with a grammar and translations of texts.[46] This early work was done in the belief that there were few native speakers alive, and that after the war there were none left. But in 1953 Dumézil learned that a few did still survive, now living in Turkey.[47] As a result, Dumézil worked closely with the last native speaker, Tevfik Esenç. This led to further studies in the 1950s through to a major work in 1975.[48] Dumézil was joined in this work by his student and colleague, Georges Charachidzé, and there were plans for a French-Ubykh dictionary between Dumézil, Charachidzé, and Esenç. In 1963 the Norwegian linguist, Hans Vogt, published a dictionary dedicated to Esenç and Dumézil. Dumézil had asked Vogt to work with him on such a project, but Vogt went ahead on his own and produced a volume which, while extensive, contained many errors.[49] Dumézil provided extensive corrections in a section of one of his own later studies.[50]

In his interviews with Didier Eribon late in life, Dumézil indicated that his subsequent work would be on Caucasian linguistics. This was partly because illness prevented him leaving home to conduct library work on mythology, but he could do much linguistic labour with his existing notes. Dumézil was said to have made thousands of index cards in preparation for the dictionary. But he died before he could bring this work to completion. Esenç died in 1992, and as a result, Ubykh is now considered extinct. Nor was the project's planned continuation by Charachidzé ever completed.[51] Although some of Dumézil's work in this register has been criticised, it has equally been suggested that "it is certain that knowledge of Ubykh would be extremely impoverished were it not for Dumézil."[52] This comment comes in the introduction to a recent grammar of the language in English, using a lot of Charachidzé and Dumézil's work, as well as an extensive archive of recordings of Esenç.[53]

Politics

Dumézil described himself as a "man of the right," and there is no question that his views were always conservative rather than liberal. But shortly before his death, and by some accounts helping to precipitate it, he was accused of darker political sympathies.

The initial charge was made in a single comment by the historian, Arnaldo Momigliano, in 1983, suggesting that the 1939 book, *Mythes et dieux des Germains*, "reveals clear traces of sympathy for Nazi culture," even though he recognises that Dumézil "almost always kept his politics separate from his scholarly activity."[54] Momigliano also recognises the importance of Sylvain Lévi and Émile Benveniste, both Jewish, to Dumézil's work.[55] Marcel Mauss was another significant mentor in Dumézil's earlier career, and his later friendship with Lévi-Strauss is well known. In making this charge, Momigliano conveniently obscured his own politics. Despite being from an assimilated Jewish family, Momigliano had joined the Italian National Fascist Party, swore an oath to Benito Mussolini, and unsuccessfully used this to try to avoid racial exclusion.[56] Dumézil responded to Momigliano's criticisms in 1984, forcefully denying any affinity with Nazism.[57]

The accusations were developed in a 1984 piece by the Italian historian, Carlo Ginzburg, which also focused on *Mythes et dieux des Germains*.[58] Ginzburg indicates some of the connections Dumézil draws between German mythology and the contemporary situation in Germany. He gives two examples of passages in which Dumézil's analysis connects to the contemporary moment. One concerns the connection between mythology and political power:

> Wagnerian names and Wagnerian mysticism animated German combatants in 1914–1918 in hours of sacrifice and failure even more than in hours of triumph. The Third Reich has not been obliged to create its basic myths; on the contrary, it is German mythology, revived in the nineteenth century, which gave its form, its spirit, its institutions to a Germany rendered miraculously malleable by unprecedented misfortunes; perhaps it is because he had first suffered in trenches haunted by the spirit of Siegfried that Adolf Hitler could conceive, forge, and practice a sovereignty that no German overlord has known since the fabulous reign of Odhinn.[59]

The other concerns the interrelation of police and military violence:

> The preceding considerations may explain some of the more recent German social phenomena: the development and success of the paramilitary brigades, the *dura virtus,* and the privileges of the Assault Units, the particular kinds of policing that uniformed youth have sometimes been tempted to practice.[60]

Dumézil's "particular kinds of policing" is rightly described by Ginzburg as "highly euphemistic."[61] Ginzburg also highlights a passage about the book in C. Scott Littleton's study of Dumézil: "It was perhaps ironic that it was in 1939, the year Hitler's legions began their grisly march, that Dumézil first focused his attention upon the Germanic branch of the I.E. speaking world."[62] This is a passage which Ginzburg describes as "scandalously shallow."[63]

However even Ginzburg recognises that Dumézil's wording is ambivalent: "There are no words of criticism or of condemnation, but praise or enthusiasm are equally lacking. At first glance, the tone seems consciously sober and neutral."[64] Ginzburg also recognises that *Mythes et dieux* had been reviewed by the *Annales* historian, Marc Bloch, in 1940,[65] who in Ginzburg's view saw it rather as "an enlightening and critical contribution on Hitler's Germany."[66] Lucien Febvre had also included *Mythes et dieux* in his survey of recently published books in *Annales* in 1941.[67] Dumézil had published in *Annales* in 1938, and his links to that historical movement remain to be fully explored.[68]

As Dumézil himself said of the accusations: "It's not a misunderstanding, it's a load of rubbish [*C'est n'est pas un malentendu, c'est une saloperie*]."[69] But instead of ignoring the attacks, he forcefully defended himself from Ginzburg's accusations in an article in *Annales* in 1985.[70] There he confines himself to four remarks, though he indicates he will provide a more detailed response.[71] In brief, he says he barely knew Marc Bloch, and that his links with the *Annales* school were more with the unrelated Jules Bloch and, through him, to Lucien Febvre. He was grateful Marc Bloch had reviewed his work, but no more.[72] Second he says that *Mythes et dieux* was the first book of his post-1938 period, and that the reader should not lose sight of the fact it was a preliminary sketch which was developed over the next half-century. In 1938 he felt he had the right key, but that it still required a lot of further work.[73] Third he draws a distinction between analysis of a society and support for it, between the descriptive and the normative.[74] Finally he rejects any real links to the Collège de Sociologie, though notes that Georges Bataille attended some of his seminars and that Caillois was "the most brilliant of my students," who became a trusted friend. He rightly dismisses the idea that Caillois had any sympathy for Nazism. However he insists that his friendships were because of people's characters, not their opinions. By way of political contrast, he mentions Pierre Gaxotte and Michel Foucault.[75] It does seem Dumézil indeed planned to do more by way of response, but ill health and his death in 1986 prevented this.

After Dumézil's death, Ginzburg's claims were supported by other historians, including Cristiano Grottanelli and Bruce Lincoln.[76] These accusations were disputed by Eribon in *Faut-il brûler Dumézil?* and to an extent by Dean Miller.[77] Eribon challenges any idea of Nazism and claims Dumézil was opposed to anti-Semitism. There is also a thorough analysis in the book by García Quintela.[78] Ginzburg's reading is described by Dumézil's bibliographer, Hervé Coutau-Bégarie, as an "inane article."[79] There are other complexities to explore.

Like *Mitra-Varuna*, *Mythes et dieux des Germains* had exhausted its initial printing, and Dumézil returned to it later in his career. But with *Mythes et dieux*, he did not simply produce a lightly edited new edition. Rather the 1959 book, *Les Dieux des Germains: Essai sur la formation de la religion scandinave*, used some of the earlier book's ideas and developed its claims. This was a common practice for Dumézil, who continually amended and updated his books. But here, he also removed the more problematic political issues.[80] It was this later book which was translated into English as *Gods of the Ancient Northmen*, again developed with some additional essays and some revisions by Dumézil.[81] This practice of revision, while the norm for Dumézil's work, and showing his continual wish to update and correct his analyses, has led to accusations of a coverup. Ginzburg suggests that it is a challenge to find the 1939 *Mythes et dieux des Germains*, even in good libraries, seemingly insinuating that it has been hidden.[82] Coutau-Bégarie rightly dismisses this, as a search of libraries proves.[83]

Dumézil wrote and published articles under the pen-name of Georges Marcenay in the journal *Le Jour*.[84] *Le Jour* was a newspaper of the right, opposed to the Front Populaire in the years immediately preceding World War Two. García Quintela indicates that part of Dumézil's reason for writing these pieces was to supplement his limited salary as a junior and temporary lecturer.[85] Eribon did important work in unearthing these pieces, but there is a debate about whether they should be seen as part of Dumézil's overall literary corpus. Coutau-Bégarie, for example, chooses not to list these pseudonymous pieces in his otherwise comprehensive bibliography. His approach is to only include pieces signed in Dumézil's own name.[86] But these articles are significant in understanding Dumézil's views. What emerges from these pieces is a royalist who is critical of parliamentary democracy, a French nationalist, who is pro-Mussolini but anti-German.[87] As Eribon most prominently has argued, the defence against charges of Nazi sympathies is that he was a nationalist, perhaps even a fascist. But the lines quickly become blurred after France's defeat. As noted above, Dumézil was suspended from teaching by the Vichy regime because he had been a Freemason, but he was allowed again to teach before the end of the war. This led him to be suspected of collusion with the regime, but he was exonerated after the Liberation.

Dumézil also had links to Action Française until 1925. He had dedicated *Le Festin d'immortalité* in 1924 to Pierre Gaxotte, the historian of the French Revolution, who was also a journalist close to the movement. Gaxotte in turn dedicated *La Révolution française* to Dumézil in 1928.[88] Through Gaxotte, Dumézil met the author and politician Charles Maurras in the mid-1920s.[89] Maurras was a key figure in Action Française, and Gaxotte had served as his secretary since 1917.[90] Maurras's biographer, Stéphane Giocanti, indicates that Dumézil also briefly served as a secretary to Maurras and the journal, working in shifts with Gaxotte.[91] This was in early 1925, before Dumézil moved to Turkey. Giocanti cites two letters from Dumézil to Maurras, one from May 1925 telling him of his engagement and a wish to resign and the other in September thanking him for copies of his books.[92]

Mitra-Varuna, in either its 1940 or 1948 versions, does not contain explicit references to the contemporary political situation in Europe. But this is not to say that the political is entirely absent from this book about sovereignty. Bruce Lincoln has suggested that lines about enemies, treaties, and ambushes, ostensibly applying to classical Rome and the ancient Germans, have a contemporary resonance with the Munich agreement of September 1938.[93] However, the course which was developed into the book did not begin until November; the related material was not discussed until May–June 1939, after the invasion of the rest of Czechoslovakia; and the book did not appear until May 1940, after the war had broken out.

Dumézil's references appear simply scholarly, drawing on work in several languages. As well as a wide range of classical references, it includes work by some leading figures in French sociology, anthropology, and linguistics, including Lévi, Granet, and Mauss. Some of his sources, however, deserve further attention. For one, his work on *Männerbund*, male societies or bands, owes much to the Swedish philologist and Indo-Iranian scholar, Stig Wikander, but also to the Austrian philologist, Otto Höfler.[94] Höfler was affiliated with and later a leader of the *Ahnenerbe* historical institute, associated with the SS and set up by Heinrich Himmler to promote racial doctrines. Höfler's ideas, though grounded on historical research, had a contemporary resonance.[95] He was dismissed from the University of Munich in 1945 and initially banned from teaching as part of the denazification process. But as Courtney Marie Burrell notes, he was "declared only a *Mitläufer* (follower) of National Socialism," which allowed him to return to teaching, leading to his reappointment in 1954 to Munich and then a chair in Vienna from 1957 until his retirement.[96]

Ginzburg criticises the way Dumézil uses Höfler's book in *Mythes et dieux des Germains* "without expressing the slightest critical detachment from it."[97] Dumézil's use in *Mitra-Varuna* is similar. Wikander's work was influenced by Höfler, and Dumézil had got to know Wikander, and through him Höfler, while based in Uppsala in the early 1930s. Mircea Eliade also uses Höfler's work in his analysis of shamanism.[98] Burrell indicates that it is Dumézil and Eliade's use which has led to the enduring importance of Höfler.[99] Equally Dumézil references the work of the Dutch scholar, Jan de Vries, who, as well as being an eminent Germanist, was a collaborator with the Nazi occupiers. He was imprisoned at the end of the war and lost his academic positions and accolades.

Dumézil also references Eliade in *Mitra-Varuna*. While they had been reading each other's work before the war, their correspondence began in 1940, and they met in November 1943 and again in September 1945, and became friends.[100] In the 1930s Eliade had supported the Romanian fascist organisation, the Legion of the Archangel Michael, later known as the Iron Guard, and had expressed admiration for Mussolini. His own nationalist views, and potential support for Nazism and anti-Semitism, are much debated.[101] Eliade worked for the Romanian cultural legation in London from April 1940, but in February 1941 was posted to Portugal for the rest of the war.[102] From 1945, unable to return to Romania with its new communist government, he lived in France. He taught at the École Pratique des Hautes Études and then at the Sorbonne, in positions partly arranged with Dumézil's support, before moving to the University of Chicago in 1956. Dumézil's friendship and support during Eliade's decade in Paris is well attested, from teaching opportunities, introductions to publishers, help with translation, reference letters and support in funding applications. Dubuisson, who is very positive about Dumézil and sees his politics as nothing more than those of a conservative nationalist, recognising a separation of his politics and academic work, is strongly critical of Eliade's politics and the ways this influences his academic research.[103] As Robert A. Segal puts it, "Dubuisson sees Eliade's theory of myth and of religion as a whole as a cover-up—a cover-up for a fascistic, racist, and anti-Semitic political ideology."[104]

Dumézil does not, with the revision of *Mitra-Varuna*, remove references to these sources. The 1948 text, even with what was then known about the SS and Höfler's work with the *Ahnenerbe*, de Vries's collaboration, and Eliade's connection to Romanian fascism, retains all these references. The links continued: Dumézil supported Eliade's career in France for some time, wrote prefaces to his books, and was invited to Chicago by Eliade after his retirement from the Collège de France.[105] Dumézil and de Vries kept up an extensive and friendly correspondence.[106] Dumézil's *Loki* book, in its revised 1959 German publication, has a preface by Höfler.[107] Dumézil also thanks both Höfler and de Vries for helping to bring this book into German.[108] Seventeen years later, both he and Eliade contributed to a *Festgabe* for Höfler's 75th birthday.[109] If the references alone might be seen as part of an academic exchange of ideas, their correspondence expresses a long-term friendship.

Some of the criticisms of Dumézil were based on the people who used his ideas, including Alain de Benoist, Jean Haudry, Michel Poniatowski, and Roger Pearson. While the uses made of his work by others is largely outside of his control, he did allow his name to be associated with these extreme-right figures. A particular moment of controversy came when *Nouvelle École*, Alain de Benoist's journal linked to the Nouvelle Droite, devoted a double issue to Dumézil in 1972–1973.[110] Dumézil had previously been interviewed by the journal in 1969.[111] The Dumézil issue was reprinted in part in 1979, without Benoist's preface but with some additional material.[112] As Stefan Arvidsson has noted, this issue, in such a prominent right-wing outlet, led to French press speculation about Dumézil's sympathies. As a consequence, Dumézil withdrew his support for the journal. But this controversy was a prelude to the examination of his earlier work for its politics.[113]

Yet even his strongest accusers recognise that there are distinctions to be drawn, often distinguishing his academic work on ideologies from support for those positions in the present. For Ginzburg: "To be sure, the recent endeavour by the *nouvelle droite* to coopt the work of Dumézil, interpreting it (especially the tripartite Indo-European ideology) as an exemplary archetype, has frequently been repudiated in no indefinite terms by Dumézil himself."[114] In one of the sources Ginzburg indicates, Dumézil is indeed explicit: "I take responsibility only for what I write or expressly approve."[115] Equally Dumézil wanted to stress that the object of his study was distinct from his wish for a different society. "What is the 'Indo-European mind'? I can only tell you that everything I have discovered of the Indo-European world would have horrified me. I would not have liked to live in a society which had a *Männerbund*... or druids."[116] Indeed he indicated the parallels between the diagnosis and the structure of contemporary dictatorships.[117]

After 1948

The second edition was far from the end of Dumézil's work on the questions explored in this book. His election to the Collège de France in 1949 marks a break in some ways, but his courses and publications continue to develop, deepen, and sometimes correct his earlier work. His inaugural lecture was in part a summary of where he was at the time, and less a programme of future work than an indication of possible lines of inquiry.[118] Then in 1952, based on lectures first given in London in May 1951, he published a short introduction to key themes in his work *Les Dieux des Indo-Européens*.[119] Around this time he also began to distance his work from the claim that the three functions appeared in direct social forms but rather often constituted a deeper ideological understanding in societies.[120] These developing views required revision of some of his earlier claims. Although he never published another formal revision of *Mitra-Varuna* after the 1948 text, his 1977 book, *Les Dieux souverains des Indo-Européens*, might be seen as a third edition, with the first chapter of the first part having "Mitra-Varuna" as its title, while much of the remaining chapters explore related themes in different mythologies.[121]

Before that book, however, he had produced his masterwork, *Mythe et épopée*. Published in three large volumes in 1968, 1971, and 1973, this was designed as a kind of summation of his research career. Volume I was entitled *L'Idéologie des trois fonctions dans les épopées des peuples indo-européens* (The Ideology of the Three Functions in the Epics of the Indo-European Peoples) and was planned for English translation under the title of *Earth Unburdened: Mythic Infrastructure in the Mahabharata*, edited by Jaan Puhvel, though this never appeared.[122] Volume II was titled *Types épiques indo-européens: un héros, un sorcier, un roi* (Indo-European Epic Types: Hero, Sorcerer, King), and was published in English as three separate books—*The Stakes of the Warrior*, *The Plight of the Sorcerer*, and *The Destiny of a King*.[123] As the title of the sections of the French and the English translations show, Dumézil here focuses on two parts of the trifunctional analysis, the sovereign and the martial, treating the first in the two aspects he discusses in *Mitra-Varuna*. The third volume of *Mythe et épopée* was *Histoires romaines*, of which one part and two appendices are included in the English collection *Camillus: A Study of Indo-European Religion as Roman History*.[124]

Dumézil initially intended the *Mythe et épopée* series to be his crowning glory. Published in the years immediately after his retirement from the Collège de France, it was largely written while Dumézil was in visiting posts in the USA. In another 1969 work, he described this as a process of consolidation:

> This unitary publication of revised studies constitutes part of the general updating in which I have been engaged for the past five years, in an effort to prepare for the inevitable autopsy as proper a cadaver as possible, that is, to deliver to the critic of the near future, in an

> organized and improved form, the results of the endeavors, of varying success, carried out over the past thirty years. The book thus takes its place in what will be my last series of publications, neither program nor *Vorarbeiten* but a balancing of accounts [*bilan*]...[125]

This *bilan* period was multi-faceted. Broadly it can be seen as beginning with *Archaic Roman Religion* in 1966 and moving to an outline or general overview in the first volume of *Mythe et épopée*, with discussions of the magical and juridical aspects of sovereignty and the warrior function in the second volume. As Udo Strutynski indicates, there is no equivalent study for the producer group, treating the question of agriculture or labour. Dumézil did apparently plan to complete a volume of studies on this theme, making use of previously published papers, and Strutynski describes this as "a yet-to-be-assembled collection of previously written articles, properly revised and commented on, for the third prong, which is diffused throughout the spectrum of concepts relating to welfare."[126] Dumézil himself indicated in April 1973 that a fourth volume of *Mythe et épopée* was planned but late in life confessed to Eribon that it was "broken down or abandoned [*en panne*]" rather than still in progress.[127]

Strutynski suggests that Dumézil's planned work on literature was "complete," and to *Mythe et épopée* should "be added the volume *From Myth to Fiction*."[128] Dumézil's late work was also concerned with a consolidated set of studies of the traditions of the different Indo-European peoples. For Rome this can be found in the third volume of *Mythe et épopée*, in *Archaic Roman Religion*, along with *Idées romaines*, *Fêtes romaines d'été et d'automne*, and its concluding "Dix questions romaines," and the appendix to *Mariages indo-européens*, entitled "Quinze questions romaines."[129] This long list already shows that the treatment is more extensive for Rome than for other societies. For the Caucasus, there is the book *Romans de Scythie et d'alentour*, to which can be added the posthumous collection of source materials in *Contes et légendes des peuples du Caucase*, which includes articles and parts of earlier books.[130] For the Indo-Iranian people, the definitive study is *Les Dieux souverains des Indo-Européens*, although Strutynski adds that "a collection of essays is foreseen to complete that dossier," which never appeared.[131] For the Germanic people, there was *Gods of the Ancient Northmen*, which extends the French edition, the essays in *From Myth to Fiction*, posthumously supplemented by the collection edited by François-Xavier Dillmann, *Mythes et dieux de la Scandinavie ancienne*.[132] In that book, Dillmann suggests that he was to edit a further volume, bringing together the 1939 and 1959 books *Les Dieux des Germains* and *Mythes et dieux des Germains*, but this was never published.[133] Strutynski notes that "in Dumézil's view, the panorama in Celtic and Greek tradition—and presumably in Baltic and Slavic as well—is too mutilated to repay the effort of a separate study for each of them."[134]

Despite the many books he did publish, Dumézil also abandoned several ideas. As well as the Ubykh dictionary, in 1969 he had also promised "a definitive *Jupiter, Mars, Quirinus* and a *Théologie de la souveraineté*," but neither appeared in quite that form.[135] The latter is, however, a good description of what was published as *Les Dieux souverains des Indo-Européens*. Indeed in 1970 Dumézil describes the *Théologie* as a book where "my early essays on Mitra-Varuna, Aryaman, and the 'minor sovereigns' will be revised and partially changed."[136] *Les Dieux souverains des Indo-Européens* also covers some of the ground intended by a revised *Jupiter, Mars, Quirinus*, being both an overview of the three functions and a detailed analysis of the first.[137] There were plans for a posthumous collection of his prefaces and introductions, but this never appeared either.[138] Perhaps the most significant absence from Dumézil's many planned projects is the consolidated study of the third function. Despite the absences, this was nevertheless a hugely impressive programme of consolidation, updating, and extension for a writer who was seventy when he retired in 1968.

Yet this was not the end. *Les Dieux souverains des Indo-Européens* was published on Dumézil's seventy-ninth birthday,[139] he was elected to the Académie Française two years later in 1979, and he continued publishing for several more years. Right at the end of his life, he produced *Esquisses de mythologie* (Sketches of Mythology), four volumes of twenty-five short papers each on topics or questions intended in part to spur work by others. The last of these volumes was published posthumously, edited by Joël Grisward. As noted above, some other collections of texts were also published posthumously, while the separate volumes of *Mythe et épopée* and *Esquisses de mythologie* were collected as integrated texts in Gallimard's Quarto series. Dumézil's interviews with Didier Eribon appeared in 1987, and are as close as he ever came to a memoir.[140] Unfortunately the majority of his books are out of print in France, as are almost all of the English translations.

Such was the breadth of his short works that it took another book by Coutau-Bégarie to catalogue them.[141] When his books were republished, Dumézil often added new prefaces, afterwords, or notes incorporating new research by himself or others. These further show his wish never to stand still and his approach of publishing interim reports rather than waiting for the whole to become clear. But not all these changes are immediately obvious to readers, particularly if they only have access to the later edition of a text. To understand the development of his ideas often requires the comparison of editions, as was done in the preparation of this critical edition of *Mitra-Varuna*. Dumézil also used the opportunity of translation to update works, with these changes often being incorporated into later French editions. *Loki*, for example, was updated in 1959 for the German text, before appearing in a new edition in French in 1986, shortly before Dumézil's death.[142] The 1970 English translation *Archaic Roman Religion* updated the French *La Religion romaine archaïque* from 1966, which was itself republished in 1974, incorporating these and other changes.[143] The Spanish *Los Dioses de los Indoeuropeos* included additional notes updating *Les Dieux des Indo-Européens*.[144] Given the challenge of locating some of his works, especially in first editions, readers can find it difficult to see the development of his ideas. The text presented here helps to show how one of his works changed, as well as bringing an important work back into circulation.

Les Dieux souverains des Indo-Européens deserves more attention. One of the reviews of the original English edition of *Mitra-Varuna* bemoaned the lack of a translation of *Les Dieux souverains des Indo-Européens* and suggested many readers would await it rather than turn to this book. According to various reports, a translation was considered, but it never appeared. Littleton reports that the anthropologist, Rodney Needham, planned to translate it for Oxford University Press, but that the press abandoned the idea.[145] Other reports, including from Dumézil himself, say it was considered by University of Chicago Press.[146] Over forty years since its publication, no translation has been made. Indeed there have been no new translations of his work since the atypical *The Riddle of Nostradamus: A Critical Dialogue*, in 1999.[147] This followed the Johns Hopkins University Press paperback edition of *Archaic Roman Religion*, in 1996, first translated for the University of Chicago Press in 1970. Until now the only English edition still in print is *The Destiny of a King*. Making available again works which *are* in translation is perhaps a first step towards getting more of his work into English.

In another review, N.J. Allen characterised *Mitra-Varuna* as "a period piece, in some parts superseded by Dumézil's own later formulation."[148] He elaborates:

> In what respects is the 1948 book superseded? Some themes (e.g. *nexum* and *mutuum* in Roman law) simply lose salience or vanish, but usually Dumézil's changes of mind are explicit. Thus, the Irish gods Lug and Nuadu cease to be homologised with the Norse Odin and Tyr (DSIE [*Les Dieux souverains des Indo-Européens*] 199), and the full complement of first-function Indo-European deities comes to consist of four sovereigns not two (which largely explains the change of title from *MV* [*Mitra-Varuna*] to *DSIE*). Because the Mitra-Varuna opposition is encompassed within a triadic structure, the comparison with the Chinese *yang* v. *yin* needed qualification (DSIE 78–80). More generally, Dumézil came to distrust the structuralists' emphasis on dualities, and his later criticism of Hegelian habits of mind tends to undermine his own 1948 formulation of the varna schema.
> In sum, this book needs to be read in the light of the author's self-criticism. A propos of the Norse figure of Mitothyn he remarked that "one of the joys of research [is] to correct a false solution or a half-solution". It is also a joy to watch a great mind boldly deploying massive erudition to envisage unexpected types of order, but doing so with humility before the evidence and with willingness to admit error.[149]

Dumézil encountered strong criticism, often from specialists. But this was not simply because of the undoubted errors he made, which he often corrected in later works.[150] It was, in part, because he was a comparativist, trespassing on their land. He reserved some strong criticism for their defences, mocking the way that all manner of work was accepted as long as "traditional forms are respected," but research from outside was condemned if it neglected existing literature or made a minor translation error. "One can imagine under such conditions what sort of hearing a comparativist could hope for: obliged to work with a score of languages and to orient themselves in their philologies, how could they be, for each one, as complete, agile, and as informed of the most recent developments as the scholars who devote all their time to it alone?"[151] As Dubuisson expands:

> Although he was one of them—and among the most gifted—Dumézil opposed the "classical" philologists. Disagreements arose from all sides regarding their respective foundations; we must not forget that these thick-skinned adversaries represented a very powerful and rigid force—the very model and heart of the university institutions of the time. Its members, sure of their humanist mission and of the

superiority of their discipline and its traditional tools, never listened to the lessons of the comparativists.[152]

The question of Dumézil's influence lies beyond the scope of this Introduction, but he was important to, among others, Lévi-Strauss, a range of classicists including Jean-Pierre Vernant, and a significant mentor to Michel Foucault, who read and discussed his work for thirty years.[153]

Editing this text has been both a pleasure and a challenge. In following up Dumézil's references to check, complete, and sometimes correct them, I have begun to get a sense of how he worked. Consulting some of his papers at the Collège de France has opened a further window into his approach: continually working and reworking ideas, adding more and more references and examples, testing ideas in the classroom before publication. His lecture notes seem to have begun with text tightly written in a right-hand column, with additions in the left. With his tiny and difficult-to-decipher handwriting, and the number of additions and replacements, texts are often very hard to read. He often pastes slips of paper onto the side of these sheets with more material. He frequently used these lectures as the basis of his subsequent books, and, as the revision process of his publications indicates, these then provided the basis for further development, refinement, and revision.

In 1943 in *Servius et la fortune*, Dumézil suggests that he had come across the problem he addresses in that book at the intersection (*carrefour*) of four paths. These paths were his previous work on connected themes: on the conception and practice of royal power, particularly the contrast between terrible and benevolent power; on social order, and in particular the tripartite division; on the beginnings of Rome, especially its early kings, institutions, and religion; and on religious, juridical, and political vocabulary.[154] As Georges Canguilhem says in his 1967 review of Foucault's *Les Mots et les choses*, *The Order of Things*, "by virtue of their meeting at the Dumézil intersection, these four paths have become roads."[155] It is not difficult to see how early steps along all these paths can be found in *Mitra-Varuna*. It is therefore an entirely appropriate book to re-introduce Dumézil's pioneering, influential, and important work addressing sovereignty to Anglophone audiences.

Editorial Note

The original English translation by Derek Coltman has been used as the basis of this edition. Coltman translates Dumézil's text accurately and with judicious choices. Reviews at the time ranged from the lukewarm—"the quality of the translation is acceptable"—to the more positive—"the translation is very good and the production is beautiful."[1] I have reviewed the entire text but made relatively few changes to the translation itself. In particular, we have tried to standardize the transliteration of words. The footnotes, on the other hand, generally follow the inconsistent French.

In almost all cases Coltman simply copied Dumézil's references, not checking their accuracy and only on odd occasions providing English equivalents. Dumézil's references are, however, neither complete nor entirely accurate. He uses abbreviations, especially for journals but also for monographs published in series, misses volumes or years, and sometimes makes simple mistakes. The editions of texts he used have sometimes been superseded. I have verified and completed Dumézil's references to secondary sources, and have been defeated only by a reference to a book which seems never to have been published and may instead be an article.

Dumézil does not generally provide details of editions he used of classical texts. I have neither tried to identify the editions or translations he used, nor provided a modern English equivalent in the notes. Given the standard referencing style for almost all these texts—with book, chapter, and section—correct references should allow readers to find cited passages in any good edition. But Dumézil's references, though usually precise, are not always accurate. I have therefore verified all the references, and have amended those which are incorrect. With some texts, such as Pliny's *Natural History*, Dumézil's references do not match the editions with widest circulation in English. I have therefore amended the references but noted the ones he gives in endnotes. Some of Dumézil's Sanskrit references are taken from texts which are not translated in full in a Western European language, but these usually come from John Muir's *Original Sanskrit Texts*, and there I have identified the source.

Simple typographical errors corrected in the second French edition are not noted. In the standard way, an asterisk before a word signifies a reconstructed form.

Dumézil's cross-references are often missing from Coltman's translation. They have been reintroduced here. References are to the French 1948 edition/current critical edition. The original translation removes the section numbers but they have also been reintroduced here.

Footnotes (Roman numerals) are Dumézil's own references added to the second edition, with some of his lengthier in-text references also moved to these notes. Any editorial interpolations, particularly to expand Dumézil's sometimes abbreviated references, are placed in brackets.

Endnotes (Arabic numerals) are the editor's, either providing textual comparison between the two French editions or giving additional references, including English translations when available. The original translator did not provide any notes or expand references, and on only a few occasions, notably the references to Marcel Mauss's *The Gift*, did he provide an English equivalent. I have done much more, which I hope readers will find useful.

I am grateful to Alex Gil Fuentes, Kai Frederik Lorentzen, John Russell, Christopher Smith, and J.R. Velasco for suggestions with some of the reference queries; and to Sheldon Pollock and Kyoto Amato for checking and correcting some Sanskrit passages. I thank Frédérique Pailladès and her colleagues at the Collège de France for providing access to the Fonds Georges Dumézil; staff at the British Library, Warburg Institute, and the Bibliothèque Nationale de France; and librarians at the University of Warwick for help with inter-library loans. It has been a pleasure to work with Catherine Howard, Nora Scott, Anne-Christine Taylor, Frédéric Keck, and their colleagues at Hau books. The Dumézil family made a series of critical comments on the Introduction, and the revised text attempts to present the controversy about Dumézil's political positions in an objective way.*

* The Dumézil family makes the following points: 1) Georges Dumézil had long abandoned any form of active political engagement by the time he embarked on the trifunctional program toward the end of the 1930s; 2) there is absolutely no evidence that the friendship relations of Dumézil with Eliade, or the mutual academic homages between Höfler and Dumézil mentioned in the introduction by Stuart Elden contained elements of political nature, nor that the reasons for quoting some authors known for or suspected of authoritarian politics went beyond the needs of normal scientific debate.

To my teachers Marcel Mauss and Marcel Granet

Preface to the Second Edition

The first edition of this work, which was published at the beginning of May 1940, formed Volume LVI of the *Bibliothèque de l'École des Hautes Études, Section des Religions*. The printing was a very small one, and soon exhausted. In my mind, however, *Mitra-Varuna* was to be merely the first in a series of studies devoted to a comparative exploration of the religions of Indo-European peoples, to the ideas those peoples had formed of human and divine society, and to a social and cosmic hierarchy in which Mitra and Varuṇa occupy only the uppermost level. Despite historical circumstances, this sequence of studies did in fact appear, at regular intervals, from 1941 through 1947, thanks to the devotion of Monsieur Gallimard and to that of my lifelong friend, Brice Parain.[1] Today, however, those works find themselves severed from their roots, as it were, since many English-speaking, Scandinavian, and even French readers, unable to refer to the 1940 edition, must experience some uncertainty with regard to certain essential points in my arguments. A second edition therefore seems necessary.

It contains few changes. Material errors have been corrected, some paragraphs removed or changed, facts updated [*l'information mise à jour*]. These revisions have been most extensive in the eighth section of Chapter IX ("Nuada and Lug," titled "Nuada and Balor" in the first edition), which has been entirely rewritten and given a different thrust, and in some pages of the conclusion.[2] I have also added to my notes a large number of references to books I wrote after *Mitra-Varuna*, which have made use of, clarified, or corrected some of its arguments. (The reference code, designed to facilitate the printer's task, is: *JMQ I* = *Jupiter-Mars-Quirinus*, 1941; *Horace et les Curiaces*, 1942; *Servius et la Fortune*, 1943; *JMQ II* = *Naissance de Rome*, 1944; *JMQ III* = *Naissance d'Archanges*, 1945; *Tarpeia*, 1947.)[3]

There has been occasional criticism – some of it meant kindly, some not – of the decision I made over ten years ago to publish in this fragmentary fashion a work whose overall configuration and final conclusions still remain to be fixed. To some, the trust thus required of the reader betrayed a lack of either discretion or patience on my part. Others warned me that I was risking repetitions, regrets, and all sorts of awkwardnesses that would produce an extremely bad effect. Still others suggested that I was simply leaving room for subsequent, and possibly fraudulent, maneuvering. It was felt, in short, that I would find it easier to convince my readers if I presented them with my work at a later stage, finished, coordinated, and fully equipped with all its offensive and defensive weapons, rather than associating them with the hesitant process of my research. Nevertheless, I am persisting in my original plan, and for three reasons. First, the longer the work goes on, the further off the moment of a harmonious and satisfying synthesis appears. The next generation of workers in this field might be in a position to attempt this, but I know only too well that I shall no more have completed even a first exploration of this domain in ten years' time than I have today, since the area to be covered is the whole vast province of Eurasian pre-history, and the research needed must necessarily be based on a massive quantity of very diverse material.[4] Second, I have found that this fragmentary form of publication is of use to me personally: at each stage, criticism and discussion have kept a tight rein (or so at least I hope) on the part played by arbitrary inventions or fixed ideas, both dangers of which I am well aware, but against which external control alone can prevail. Finally, we live in an age unfavorable to grand designs. In the course of what was once referred to as a lifetime, one's work is repeatedly at risk of being interrupted and destroyed. Cities and libraries disappear. University professors, as well as mothers and children, are lost in the tidal waves of deportation or the ashes of an oven; or else evaporate, along with bonzes and chrysanthemums, into dangerous corpuscles. The little each of us discovers therefore ought to be paid into the common account of human knowledge without too much delay, without any thought of first amassing a great treasure.

As for the methods, both comparative and analytic, that I am attempting to employ and also to perfect, there is little more to be said than can be found in the prefaces to my most recent books. One common – and very present – weakness of sociological work is multiplying preliminary rules and a priori definitions from which it later becomes impossible to break free; another is drawing up dazzling programs that one is prevented from fulfilling. As a consequence, many hours of work are lost each year in facile and flattering speculations that eventually prove somewhat unfruitful, at least from an intellectual point of view. I shall not add to this mental frittering.

From the two masters to whom this book is dedicated, I learned, among other things, a respect for the concrete and for the ever changing material of one's studies. For, despite unjust criticism, nothing was more foreign to the thinking of those two great men than apriorism and exclusivism. Marcel Mauss once said to us, "I call sociology all science that has been done well"; and none of us has forgotten Marcel Granet's quip about the art of making discoveries: "Method is the *path*, *after* one has been along it." This does not mean that I have no conscious method. But to do is better than to preach. In young fields of study, whether comparative or otherwise, isn't everything ultimately governed by those classic rules of Descartes and John Stuart Mill, the rules of common sense? To make use of all the material that offers itself, no matter which particular disciplines share it for the moment, and without subjecting it to arbitrary categorizations of one's own; to examine what is given at length, with all its obvious facts, which are often less than facts, and also its mirages, which are sometimes more than mirages; to be wary of traditional opinions but also, and equally, of outlandish opinions and fashionable novelties; to avoid trammeling oneself with premature technical language; to regard neither boldness nor prudence as "the" virtue above all others, but to make use of both while continually checking the legitimacy of each step and the harmony of the whole. This "pentalogue" contains everything essential.

The most useful thing I can do here is to recount the various stages that make up the labor which has preoccupied me for almost a quarter-century. I embarked upon the comparative study of Indo-European religions at an extremely early age, with many illusions and ambitions in my baggage and, of course, without sufficient philological preparation. To cap that misfortune, the subject I first encountered, in 1924, was among the most wide-ranging and complex: *Le Festin d'immortalité*.[5] In 1929, with the Indian Gandharva, the Greek centaurs, and the Roman Luperci, I found myself tackling a topic more amenable to definition and interpretation; but I was still unable to confine myself to the essential thrust of the facts or to the truly telling and useful parts of my exegesis.[6] Yet I regret nothing, not even those early errors, those first tentative gropings. If at the outset, before attempting to wrestle directly with the new type of problems I had glimpsed, I had aimed at mastering any particular philology, the central focus of my thinking soon would have been displaced, and I should have merely become a more-or-less respectable specialist in the Roman, Greek or Indian field. But I felt that the undertaking was worth the effort, and that my tasks were to improve my knowledge of three or four domains simultaneously (always in particular relation to the same type of problems), and to keep my sights fixed "between" those specialities, at the probable point of their convergence. In this way, I hoped to achieve a kind of mental accommodation that would enable me, eventually, to whittle a somewhat too-inclusive interpretation down to a more precise, austere and objective analysis. It took time, and some freedom.[7]

In 1930 the undertaking appeared to have foundered. One of my teachers, who had originally encouraged me without gauging any more clearly than I had the difficulties involved, was aware, above all, of the uncertainties apparent in my first two results, as well as sensitive to the criticisms that certain young and brilliant flamines did not fail to make of my Lupercalia. Was I going to compromise the prestige of the entire comparative method that was then establishing itself with such acclaim in the linguistic field by employing it in a lateral, clumsy, perhaps illegitimate way? Fortunately, at that very moment, others came to understand the scope and richness of this field, and, to put it simply, they rescued me: Sylvain Lévi, Marcel Mauss and Marcel Granet were to be the guardian deities of this new discipline.

It was not until 1934, in a short study devoted to Ouranós-Vāruṇa, that I felt I had succeeded for the first time in dealing with a theme in the field of "comparative Indo-European religious studies" in a proper way, that is, in a very few pages aimed directly at the heart of the matter.[8] That publication contained all the worthwhile results of the first lecture course I was asked to give, under the auspices of Sylvain Lévi, at the *École des Hautes Études* in 1933-1934.

During the following years, I continued my attempts to deal with a series of precisely defined questions in the same way. Then, quite suddenly, during a lecture in the winter of 1937-1938, almost as a reward for so many failed but constantly renewed attempts, so much tentative but unremitting research, I glimpsed the fact that dominates and structures a large part of the material: the existence – at the very foundation of the ideology of most of the Indo-European peoples – of a tripartite conception of the world and society; a conception that is expressed, among the Arya of India and Iran, by a division into three classes (priests, warriors and herdsmen-cultivators) and, in Rome, by the most ancient triad of gods (Jupiter, Mars, Quirinus). During the next academic year (the last before the war), I used both my lecture courses to begin an investigation of the fundamental myths of the first and second cosmic and social "functions," which is to say, the myths of magical and juridical sovereignty and the myths of warrior-power or, to put it in Vedic terms, the myths of Mitra-Varuṇa and those of Indra Vṛtrahan.[9]

The first of those lecture courses provided the material for this book. The other, to which I have returned several times, has not yet provided results clear enough to permit the publication of anything other than fragments;[i] but I do not despair of succeeding fairly soon.[10]

Since that time I have made every effort, no matter the topic, to highlight the numerous links that make it possible to keep one's bearing within the given religious structures, without falsifying their perspectives or proportions by emphasizing individual details. Hence my attempt, on two or three occasions, to deal with the most general problem, that of the underlying mythic and social structure of Jupiter-Mars-Quirinus. Hence, too, my somewhat unexpected discoveries relating to the origins of Roman "history" and to the field of Zoroastrian theology.[11]

I shall always retain a particular fondness in my heart for the year 1938-1939; but it is a memory peopled by ghosts. Both at Sceaux and in Paris, Marcel Granet followed with his kindly eye the progress of an endeavor already so much in his debt. Every Thursday in the lecture hall, beside Roger Caillois, Lucien Gerschel and Elisabeth Raucq, I would greet our gracious colleague Marie-Louise Sjoestedt, whose pupil in turn I became on Wednesdays when she taught me Welsh and Irish; she was not to survive France's first misfortunes.[12] Pintelon, an assistant professor at the University of Ghent, was destined to perish in uniform while on guard in Belgium, even before the invasion of the West.[13] Deborah Lifschitz, from the Musée de l'Homme, so kind hearted and intelligent, was doomed to the horrors of Auschwitz.[14] Other young faces were destined for other ordeals…

Georges Dumézil
Paris, January 1947

i Specifically: "Vahagn" in *Revue de l'Histoire des Religions*, CXVII, 1938, p. 152ff. [152–70]; "Deux traits du Tricéphale indo-iranien", ibid., CXX, 1939, p. 5ff. [5–20]; *Horace et les Curiaces*, 1942 [note moved from text].

Preface to the First Edition

This essay investigates a certain bipartite conception of sovereignty that appears to have been present among the Indo-Europeans, and that dominated the mythologies of certain of the peoples who spoke Indo-European languages at the time of the earliest documents. In my earlier work, mostly devoted to the mechanisms and representations of sovereignty, I had already encountered some of the elements that interest me here; but I had previously understood their relations only very imperfectly. In this work, it is the broad system of those relations that I try to elucidate.

Let no one object, before reading this book, that it is always easy for a mind dialectically inclined to subject facts to a preconceived system. The system is truly inherent in the material. It may be observed, always the same, in the most diverse sets of facts – in all those sets of facts, one might say, that fall within the province of sovereignty. Further, it reveals regularly recurring links within those sets of facts that will provide the reader with a constant means of checking the probability of the whole and, should it be the case, of discerning any illusions or artifices on my part. In matters of pure speculation, coherence is merely one elementary quality of the reasoning required, and in no way a guarantee of truth. The same is not true, however, for the sciences of observation, where one is required to classify numerous and diverse objective data in accordance with their nature. I hope the reader will also take due note that, in the majority of the areas touched upon, there has been no need for me to reconstruct or to interpret anything whatsoever: those who used the myths, rituals and formulas were quite conscious of the system; my sole task has been to make clear its scope and its antiquity.

I trust, too, that there will be no complaint that I have exaggerated the clear-cut nature of the system. In practice, it is true, classifications are always less distinct than in theory, and one must be prepared to encounter a great many overlaps and compromises. But this conflict, if it is a conflict, is not between myself and the facts; it lies within the facts themselves, and is inherent in all human behavior: societies spend their time forming an ideal and simple conception of themselves, of their functioning, and sometimes of their mission, which they also constantly alter and make more complex.

Finally, let no one reproach me with having accorded excessive importance to elements that in later stages of a religion are secondary and, as it were, fossilized; it was precisely my task to throw some light upon the old and superseded states, by means of internal analysis and, above all, by the use of comparison. It is certainly true, for example, that as we approach the threshold of our own era, both the Luperci and flamines had lost almost all their importance in the life of the Roman state; the newly emerging empire was to prove grudging, indeed, in the status it granted to the former, and was not always able to find even a single candidate for the chief *flāmonium*; but that in no way contradicts the fact that Rome's whole primitive "history" was built upon coupled notions, of which the Luperci and the flamines are merely the priestly expression.

I reproduce here, almost without alteration, a series of lectures given at the *École des Hautes Études* in 1938-1939. I increasingly take the view that, given the field's present state of development, the comparatist shouldn't aspire to the "finish" rightly demanded of the philologist; that he should remain flexible, unanchored and ready to make good use of any criticism; that at all times he should keep firmly to the broad paths of the subject he is investigating and never lose sight of the general plan. I didn't even wish to burden myself with notes. Parentheses are sufficient for any references; discussions at the foot of one's pages are inappropriate in an exposition that is no more than a program.[1]

The importance of the subject itself first became apparent to me in 1934, during a conversation with Sylvain Lévi. That great and kindly mind, having welcomed my *Ouranós-Váruṇa* had raised one question: "What about Mitra?" Early in 1938, during a Société Ernest Renan discussion of a paper in which I compared the Roman hierarchy of the three major flamines with the Brahmanic tripartition of society (see *Revue de l'Histoire des Religions*, CXVIII, 1938, pp. 188-200),[2] Jean Bayet pointed out a similar difficulty relating to the actual title of the *flāmen dialis*: "What about Dius Fidius?" The reader will soon perceive that these two questions are the whole question. The very fact that they occur symmetrically in India and in Rome, and in relation to divinities who are among the most archaic, led me to think that I was dealing, here again, not with a fortuitous coincidence, but with the vestiges of one of those religious mechanisms that are particularly well preserved in the extreme western and eastern reaches of the territory [*domaine*], among the Indo-Iranians, the Italiots and the Celts.[3] My efforts have been directed at isolating that mechanism.

Naturally, I began by investigating Vedic India and Rome, since those two areas provided the first clues, and this constitutes the material in the first two chapters. By the end of Chapter II, I was in a position to set out an exploratory program still confined to Rome, India and Iran; the next four chapters attempt to carry out this program. In Chapter VII, certain reflections on the work accomplished thus far enabled me to move on to a set of homologous facts in the Germanic field; and those facts, partly because of their new form, posed a series of problems that had hitherto escaped me, and in which Rome, India and the Celtic world are all equally involved (Chapters VIII, IX, X).

When this province of comparative mythology becomes better known, there may well be some advantage in following a different order, and, more particularly, in selecting a different starting point – just as textbooks in mathematical analysis dealing with, let us say, derived coefficients or imaginary numbers do not present the various parts of the theory in the same order as it was constructed historically, but move, as swiftly as possible, to its most convenient or most widely accepted points, so that their deductions may then proceed without hindrance over the same ground that early workers in the field had to toil over with such effort. We have not yet reached that stage; and it seemed to me more instructive to let my exposition follow the same paths as the original research. Constructive criticism will also be made easier by this method, to my great advantage. Indeed, criticism has provided me with powerful assistance already, during discussions with some of those present at the École des Hautes Études when the lectures themselves were first delivered. It was Roger Caillois's criticisms that led to the observations in Chapter VIII; and it was Elisabeth Raucq, from the University of Ghent, who brought to my attention that Odhinn's mutilation could bear importantly on my subject (Chapter IX). This trusting, generous and public collaboration is one of the characteristics and, I hasten to add, one of the privileges of our school, and it is with joy that I offer yet further testimony to it here.[4]

I wish to thank Jules Bloch and Gabriel Le Bras, who were kind enough to read and improve this essay in manuscript, and Georges Deromieu, who helped me to revise the proofs.

G.D.
Paris, June 1939

CHAPTER I

Luperci and Flamines

In the course of earlier research I discovered a parallel between the *rēx-flāmen dialis* and the *rāj(an)-brahman* (*Flāmen-Brahman*, *Annales du Musée Guimet*, *Bibliothèque de Vulgarisation*, vol. LI, 1935), and in an even earlier work I compared the band of Luperci who wield the *februa*, with the mythical group of Gandharva (*Le problème des Centaures*, *Annales du Musée Guimet, Bibliothèque d'Études*, vol. XLI, 1929).[1] At that time, however, I did not draw sufficient attention to the relationships between the Luperci and the flamines in Rome and between the Gandharva and the brahmans in India. Such an investigation is very instructive.[2] Let us first review some of the facts.

I. *Rex-flāmen, rāj-brahman*

Even as late as the Republican era, the hierarchy of Roman priests was headed by the *rēx sacrorum* and the *flāmen dialis*, who were not two independent priests but a priestly couple. This also must have been so in the very early state when the Roman *rex* was at the height of his power; and the legend of how the office of *flāmen dialis* was established does in fact make it clear that this personage is merely a subdivision of the *rex*! Numa created it so that "the sacred functions of the royal office might not be neglected" during those absences that wars inevitably imposed upon the *rex* (Livy I, 20). Previously, the *rex*, including Numa himself, had concentrated in his own person what was later split between the essence of the *rēgnum* and that of the *flāmonium* (cf. Plutarch's theory in number 113 of his *Roman Questions*). Religious practice confirms this legend: the insignia of the *flāmen dialis* and of his wife the *flāminica* were the insignia of the *rex* and the *regina*. The dialis had a royal cloak, a royal throne, and, on set days, passed through the city in a royal vehicle (*Lex Iulia Municipalis*, 62; cf. Livy, I, 20).[3] His wife sacrificed *in rēgia*, "in the royal house," and he himself appeared ritually with the *rex*[4] (*Pontifices ab rege petunt et flamine Janas, quis veterum lingua februa nomen erat.* "From king and flamen the priests seek the thongs, which in the old tongue were called *februa*," Ovid, *Fastes*, II, 21-22). Lastly, the *rex* and the major flamines were all "inaugurated"; and it was the same social organ, the very ancient *comitia curiata*,[5] that inaugurated them.

In India, in the very earliest times, *rāj* (or *rājan*) and *brahman* existed in a true symbiosis in which the latter protected the former against the magico-religious risks inherent in the exercise of the royal function, while the former maintained the latter in a place equal to or above his own. As Indian society, at a very early stage, solidified the Indo-European tripartite division of social estates into "castes," and *brahman* and *rāj* became the eponyms of the two highest castes (*brāhmaṇa*, *rājanya*), so the same interdependence is to be observed, broadened in its scope but just as clear in its mechanism, between the *brāhmaṇa* (member of the priestly caste) and the *rājanya* (or *kṣatriya*, member of the warrior caste). This interdependence, a commonplace in the literature of every epoch, is defined in numerous texts. Sometimes (Manu, IX, 327) the third caste, that of the *vaiśya*, the herdsmen-cultivators, "to whom the Lord of Creatures gave charge solely of cattle" is contrasted with the *brāhmaṇa* and *rājan* "bloc," who are in charge of "all creatures."[6] Sometimes (*ibid.*, 322), in an internal analysis of that bloc, we read that the *rājanya* cannot prosper without the *brāhmaṇa* nor the *brāhmaṇa* "increase" without the *rājanya*; but that by uniting or "overlapping" (*sampṛkatam*), the essences of the two castes (neuter *brahman* and neuter *kṣatra*) will "increase" both in this world and in the other world. As early as the Vedic texts, which precede the classical caste system, the reduced solidarity of *rāj* and *brahman* is stated clearly (*Ṛg Veda*, IV, 50, 8): "He lives prosperous in his abode, to him the earth is prodigal of all its gifts, to him the people [*viśah*, literally, the groups of herdsmen-cultivators; *viś* is the word that produced the derivative *vaiśya*, the name for the people of the third caste, and, alongside the neuter terms *brahman* and *kṣatra*, denotes the essence of that third caste] are obedient of their own accord, that *rājan* in whose house the brahman walks in first place (*yasmin brahmā rājani pūrvaḥ eti*)."

I attempted to establish what the structure of this interdependence was during those very early times, why the *rāj* wished to maintain within his household a personage to whom he yielded precedence. Evidence from ritual and legend led me to believe that this brahman "joined" to the king was originally his substitute in human sacrifices of purification or expiation in which royal blood itself had once flowed.[i] The simulated human sacrifices still performed in the purificatory ceremony of the Argei in Rome, and the major role played in that ceremony by the *flāminica*, with her display of mourning and grief,[ii] seemed to me to confirm this interpretation of the Indian evidence. However, all that is distant prehistory. By the time Indian society becomes observable, the *brahman* is already far from that probable starting point. It is not with his sacrificial death that he serves the *rājan* but with his life, each moment of which is devoted to the administration and "readjustment" of magic forces. In historical times the same is true in Rome, where the *flāmen dialis*, "*assiduus sacerdos*", "*quotidie feriatus*", constantly robed and solely "*ad sacrificandum constitutus*", assures the magic health of the *respublica*, heir of the *rēgnum*.

II. The statutes of the *flāmen dialis* and the *brahman*

It also seemed of interest to compare the lists of positive and negative obligations that constrained these two "magic instruments," these two living palladiums. Let me briefly recapitulate their similarities (apart

i Cf. the approval of this suggestion, which I was particularly heartened to receive, from P.W. Koppers, *Anthropos*, XXXII (1937), pp. 1019–1020, and *Mélanges van Ginneken* (Paris, 1937), pp. 152–155. [Note added to second edition. The complete references are P.W. Koppers, "Flamen-Brahman by Georges Dumézil," *Anthropos* 32, 1937: 1019–20; Wilh. Koppers, "Das Magische Wetschöpfungsmysterium bei den Indogermanien," in *Mélanges de linguistique et de philologie offerts à Jacq. van Ginneken* (Paris: C. Klincksieck, 1937), pp. 149–55.]

ii See A. Körte, *Argei*, in *Hermes*, LXXVII (1942), pp. 89-102. [Note added to second edition. Dumézil's reference is inaccurate. It seems to be a reference to Luigi Clerici, "Die Argei," *Hermes* 77, 1942: 89–100. Alfred Körte wrote a short note immediately following this article: "Zu Terenz Haut," *Hermes* 77, 1942: 101–102.]

from penal immunity, and apart from the singular gravity of brahmanicide and the crime inherent in *flamini manus iniicere*).

The *flāmen dialis* cannot be made to swear on oath (Plutarch, *Roman Questions*, 44; Aulus Gellius, X, 15; Livy, XXXI, 50); and the brahman can never – any more than the king, the ascetic, the madman or the criminal – be cited as a witness (*Code* of Vishnu, VIII, 2).[7]

The *flāmen dialis* must not so much as look upon armed troops (Aulus Gellius, X, 15); the brahman must suspend his sacred knowledge – that is, his reason for living – whenever he hears the hiss of arrows, or is in the midst of an army, and so on (Manu, IV, 113, 121…).

The *flāmen dialis*, apart from being forbidden any journey outside Rome, must neither mount a horse (Aulus Gellius, X, 15; Plutarch, *Roman Questions*, 40) nor, even for the purpose of sacrifice, touch one (Pliny, *Natural History*, XXVIII, 40); the brahman must not study on horseback nor, it seems, sit on any animal or in any vehicle (Manu, IV, 120).[8]

The *flāmen dialis* must not approach a funeral pyre (Aulus Gellius, X, 15); the brahman must avoid the smoke from a funeral pyre and cease his sacred studies in any village where a funeral procession is passing (Manu, IV, 69, 108).

The *flāmen dialis* must avoid drunkenness and abstain from touching fermented substances (Aulus Gellius, X, 15; Plutarch, *Roman Questions*, 109, 112); the brahman must not consume alcoholic drinks (Manu, XI, 94, 96, 97; cf. *Śatapatha Brāhmaṇa*, XII, 9, 1, 1).

The *flāmen dialis* must not anoint himself with oil in open air (Plutarch, *Roman Questions*, 40); the brahman "after having rubbed his head [with oil] must not touch any part of his body with oil" (Manu, IV, 83; cf. 84, 85, III and V, 25).

The *flāmen dialis* is forbidden to touch raw meat (Aulus Gellius, X, 15; Plutarch, *Roman Questions*, 110); the brahman must not eat any meat that has not first been offered in sacrifice (Manu, IV, 213 ; cf. 112: V, 7, 27, 31, 33, 36, 48, 53), and he must never accept any thing from the owner of a slaughterhouse (*ibid.*, IV, 84-86), of a distillery, of an oil press or of a house of prostitution.

The *flāmen dialis* may not touch or even name a dog (Plutarch, *Roman Questions*, 111); the brahman may not read the Vedas when he hears a dog bark (Manu, IV, 115) nor eat food that has touched a dog, or has come from people who breed dogs (*ibid.*, 208, 216).

The *flāmen dialis* may not, even at night, completely divest himself of his priestly insignia (Appian, *Civil War*, I, 65; Plutarch, *Roman*

Questions, 40) and his wife must retire only by way of an enclosed staircase so that her undergarments might never be seen (Aulus Gellius, X, 15); the brahman must never strip completely naked, and he must never see his wife naked (Manu, IV, 45, 144, 43).

The *brāhmaṇī*, the wife of the *brahman*, and the *flāminica*, wife of the *flāmen dialis*, are no less important, in a religious context, than their husbands. In Rome and India alike, it is the couple, the husband *with* the wife, who performs the expected magic function. This is natural, given that their role is essentially to provide stable prosperity and regular fecundity. Theoretically, in both cases, the strictest decorum[9] and fidelity are required. One of the most solemn of the eight modes of marriage in India is termed "brahman marriage" (*brāhmaṇavivāha*); similarly, the *flāmen* and *flāminica* must be married in accordance with the most religious of such rituals, the *confarreatio* – a ritual, moreover, that they must themselves preside over (see my *Flamen-Brahman*, pp. 60-63).[iii]

The *flāmen dialis* is "taken" or "seized" (*captus*) by the State and removed from his father's jurisdiction. The high pontiff, having seized him, presents him to the god and, with the help of the augurs, requests the god's assent (*in-auguratio*). The Indian legend of Śunaḥśepa, which legally establishes the superiority of brahmans over all other men, likewise depicts the young brahman as being bought by the king from his father and then presented for the god's assent (*Flamen-Brahman*, pp. 45-46).

The list of coincidences could be extended even further, but I shall add only one here. The color of the brahman is white (a constant doctrine in accordance with the Indian theory of the *varnāh* or "castes" – more literally, "colors"), and he consequently wears white clothes (Manu, IV, 35). Similarly, the distinctive headwear of the *flāmen dialis* is termed *albogalerus*, and Ovid, upon seeing a procession of the *flāmen quirinalis*

iii Cf. [Paul] Koschaker, *Die Eheformen bei den Indogermanen* (Berlin-Leipzig, 1937), p. 84, quoted by H[enri]. Lévy-Bruhl in *Nouvelles Etudes sur le très ancien droit romain* [(Paris: L' Institut de droit romain], 1947), p. 67. Also, P. Noailles, "Junon, déesse matrimoniale des Romains" (in the *Festschrift Koschaker*, I, p. 389); suggesting that the *confarreatio* might even be a form of marriage reserved solely for the flamines and rex. [Note added to second edition. Koschaker's article was published in Ernst Heymann ed., *Deutsche Landesreferate zum 2. Internationalen Kongreß für Rechtsvergleichung im Haag 1937* (Berlin: Walter de Gruyter, 1937), pp. 77–140b. Pierre Noailles, *Festschrift Paul Koschaker*, three volumes (Weimar: Böhlau, 1939), Vol. I, pp. 386–400.]

on its way to the feast of the Robigalia (*Fastes*, IV, 905ff.), describes it in two words: *alba pompa*. This coincidence, like several others, extends to the Celts, among whom the Druids wore white during their priestly duties both in Gaul (Pliny, *Natural History*, XVI, 95; XXIV, 62) and in Ireland (see the texts collected in Arbois de Jubainville, *La Civilisation des Celtes*, 1899, p. 112n.).[10] That white is the color of both brahman and *flāmen dialis* becomes even more significant when we recall that red is the color of the Indian *rājanya* and also the mark of the Roman *rēx* (Plutarch, *Romulus*, 26) as well as the Irish *rî*. (A Pahlavi text [translated by G. Widengren as *Hochgottglaube im alten Iran*, Uppsala, 1938, p. 247] also extends this social symbolism of white and red to Iran.)[iv]

The Sanskrit *brahman*, to judge by the Avestic *barəsman* (the bundle of sacred rods held by the officiating priest) must derive, with reverse guna, from **bhelgh-men-* or **bholgh-men-*. The Latin *flāmen* must derive from a neighboring form, **bhlagh-men-*, which, along with forms having the radical *-el-* or *-ol-*, presents the same shift (still obscure, but doubtless capable of interpretation by means of Benveniste's theories on root structure) as that evidenced, within Latin itself, by *flāuus* as opposed to *fel*, *lāna* as opposed to *uellus*, and *prāuus* as opposed to the pejorative *per-* (*perfidus*, etc.).[11]

III. *Februus*, fecundation and Gandharva

Once at the end of every year, on the *dies februatus* in the middle of the month of *februarius*,[12] the great purification called *februatio* took place. It was celebrated with the aid of various accessories termed (in the neuter plural) *februa* and ensured by divinities about whom the Roman historians no longer knew a great deal: Iuno Februa (Februata, or Febru(a)lis) and Februus.[13] The rites were performed by a brotherhood that played no other role in Roman life but which, on that one day alone, threw aside all restraint. Two groups of *Luperci*, made up of young men from the equestrian order, ran through the city naked except for leather belts

iv *JMQ I*, p. 66ff. [" 'Tripertita' fonctionnels chez divers peuples indo-européens"] *Revue de l'Histoire des Religions*, CXXXI, 1946, p. 54ff [53–72]. [Note added to second edition. The text referenced is in Geo Widengren, *Hochgottglaube im alten Iran: eine religionsphänomenologische Untersuchung*, Uppsala Universitets årsskrift 6 (Uppsala: Lundequist, 1938), pp. 247–8.]

striking females with thongs of goatskin in order to make them fertile. We do not know what the concluding rites of this violent scenario were, although we do know that goats were sacrificed before the race through the city, that the bloodied sacrificial knife was wiped on the foreheads of the bands' two young leaders, and that they were expected to laugh at that point. We also know that the Luperci sacrificed a dog.[v]

There are "historical" accounts that claim to explain the origin of these rites. The Luperci, they say, were imitating the *pastoralis iuventus*,

---

v From the two lines of Ovid's *Fastes* (II, 21-22) I quoted, G[eorg]. Wissowa (*Rei. u. Kuitus der Römer*, 2nd ed., 1912 [*Religion und Kultus der Römer*, Münich: C.H. Beck, 2nd edition, 1912], p. 517 n. 6; cf. Unger, "Die Lupercalia," *Rhein. Museum*, XXXVI, 1881 [G.F. Unger "Die Lupercalien," *Rheinisches Museum*, XXXVI, 1881: 50–86], p. 57) has concluded that it was the rex and the flamen dialis who distributed the magical *februa* to the Luperci. It has been objected, however, that in Ovid's lines *februa* could refer to purifications other than the Lupercalia, since Varro (*De Ling. lat.* [*De Lingua latina*], VI, 3, 34), followed by Festus and Lydos, said that *februum* means *purgamentum* in general, and *februare* "to purify" in general. The objection is a weak one. This general meaning must be an extension, as when we speak of "carnival" nowadays when referring to any kind of masquerade. In fact: (1) there is no trace of any use of *februum*, or of words derived from it, outside the Lupercalia; (2) the fact that the month of the Lupercalia is distinctively called *februarius* confirms that it was to those particular lustrations, indeed, that *februum* and its derivatives applied; (3) another passage from Varro himself (ibid., VI, 4, 34) established the equation: *ego arbitror Februarium a die februato, quod tum februatur populus, id est Lupercis nudis lustratur antiquum oppidum Palatinum gregibus humanis cinctum* ("But I think that it was called February rather from the dies februatus, 'Purification Day,' because then the people, *februator*, 'is purified,' that is, the old Palatine town, girt with flocks of people, is passed through by the naked Luperci"); (4) when Servius (*Commentary on the Aeneid*, VIII, 343) says *pellem ipsam capri veteres februum vocabant* ("the ancients called that goatskin *februum*"), he cannot be referring to anything but the Lupercalia. Therefore, it seems that Ovid's lines, which occur, moreover, at the beginning of that book of *Fastes* devoted to February, do indeed refer to an early stage of the Lupercalia: at the outset of the rites, those responsible for social order perform a sort of "transmission of power" to the representatives of sacred violence. [Note added to second edition. In the Loeb edition of Varro, the references are VI, III, 13 and VI, V, 35, the opening phrase of which reads: *ego magis arbitror Februarium.*]

the young men who had gathered around Romulus and Remus. Their name, like that of the *Lupercalia*, was an allusion to the two brothers' foster mother, the she-wolf, and to their childhood in the wilderness, during which their hearts became hardened and the seeds of their harsh future were sown. Moreover, the race through the city was said to commemorate a particular episode in the brothers' lives: one day, when Romulus, Remus and their companions were lying naked, lazily watching their meat roast, they were warned that strangers were stealing their cattle. The two bands threw themselves into action without taking the time to dress. The group led by Remus had the good fortune to rescue the cattle and to return to the encampment first, where they tore the barely cooked meat from the spits. "The victor alone," Remus declared, "has the right to eat of it" (It is reasonable to hazard that this singular feature had some corresponding moment in the rites that has not come down to us.) Finally, we are told that the flagellation of female passers-by referred to another, more scabrous[14] incident in the Romulus story: having kidnapped the Sabine women for his men, the young leader discovered, to his annoyance, that they were sterile. He consulted an oracle, which replied: "Let a he-goat penetrate the Roman women!" An augur then rendered a somewhat more decorous interpretation of this robust injunction: the women were struck with goatskin thongs, and they conceived.

The type of feral and brutal brotherhood featured in this episode of Rome's religious life has already been illuminated by ethnography. It is one of those "men-only societies" – societies characterized by disguises, initiations and extraordinary magical powers – such as can be found among almost all so-called semi-civilized peoples – societies that merit, at least in part, the description "secret," and which do not surface in public religious life except to oppose (and then overwhelmingly) the normal mechanism of that religion.

The early Indo-European world could not have failed to possess this essential organ of collective life, an organ of which the Germanic world, in ancient times and even into the Middle Ages, certainly provides more than mere vestiges, and of which the winter and end-of-winter "maskers" of modern Europe are, in part, a bastardization. It seemed to me that the *februatio* of the Lupercalia must have been the Roman adaptation of such scenarios, and I supported this opinion with comparative arguments drawn principally from the Indo-Iranian world.

In India, where the earliest literature is entirely sacerdotal in nature, one can nevertheless discern the existence of at least one such brotherhood. Though transformed into a band of supernatural beings, somewhat divine and somewhat demonic in character, called Gandharva, it can be recognized by one typical characteristic: *men may join it by initiation*. Moreover, just as the Luperci and the Lupercalis are mythically underwritten by the childhood, feral upbringing and early adventures of Romulus and Remus, so, too, the Gandharva educate heroes (Ayus, Arjuna and so on). In the *Ṛg Veda* the outward appearance of the (singular masculine) Gandharva is left vague, but in later writings the (masculine plural) Gandharva are beings with horses' heads and men's torsos who live in a special world of their own. As early as the hymns, moreover, they already stand in a precise relationship to horses and to the harnessing of chariots, those of the Sun and those of men alike, and they retain this feature throughout the epic literature. They are drinkers who steal the *soma* and other intoxicating drinks, who carry off women and nymphs (*Apsaras*), and who cheerfully live up to the ribald adjectives applied to them. Some ritual texts also claim that every woman's first mate, before her husband, is a Gandharva. The initiation scene to which I just alluded is found in the touching legend of the two lovers Purūravas and Urvaśī. The earthly king Purūravas is united with the nymph Urvaśī, who lives with him on the condition – as in the Psyche and Melusine stories – that he never show himself naked to her. The Gandharva, impatient to recover Urvaśī come by night and steal the two lambs that she loves like children. Without taking time to dress, the king rushes out in pursuit, whereupon the Gandharva light up the sky with a flash of lightning. Urvaśī sees her lover's naked body, and she vanishes. Purūravas laments, so pitiably that in the end Urvaśī allows him to find her. He meets her on the last night of the year (*saṃvatsaratamīṃ rātrlm*), and the next day the Gandharva grant him a wish. Upon Urvaśī's advice he chooses "to become one of the Gandharva." The Gandharva then teach him a particular form of igneous sacrifice (the accessories of which are made from the wood of the *aśvattha* tree, which contains the word *aśva*, "horse," in its name), which allows him to "become one of the Gandharva." Furthermore, while among the Gandharva, Urvaśī bears him a son named Ayus (literally, "vitality").

Finally, is there any need to point to the numerous analogies, both in form and behavior, that link the Gandharva to the Greek centaurs? The centaurs have horses' bodies and male human torsos; they are prodigious runners; they live in a land of their own, as wild as one can imagine; they are great drinkers, sensual, ravishers of women (especially of young brides), and also include among their number at least some artists, scholars, and *educators of heroes*. In particular, Peleus, the beneficiary and victim, like Purūravas, of a "melusinian" marriage, delivers his son, the young Achilles, to the centaur Chiron, who nurtures him for several years with the right amount of bone marrow and wisdom.

IV. Phonetics and sociology

Several of these resemblances were recognized very early on, and, as the two names sounded well together, the "*Kentauros-Gandharva*" equation was one of the earliest proposed. But the question was badly defined: time was wasted on reducing these strong personalities to naturalistic symbols. What is actually involved in both cases is the transposition into myth of an ancient society with animal disguises and initiations, a society that "educates heroes," a society linked with horses, and one that certainly had a monopoly on the Indo-European "masters of horses" just as the society of the Luperci still belonged to the *iuniores* of the equestrian order.[vi]

The similarities among these three groupings – *Gandharva*, *Kentauroi*, and *Luperci* armed with *februa* – are quite clear, even though they appear at different levels of representation. Luperci, in a ritual practiced at the end of every year, centaurs, in fabulous narrative, and Gandharva, in legends in which we glimpse a ritual (year-end) reality, all display the same fundamental features. Like the *flāmen* and the *brahman* they either form or recall a religious instrument, one that is impossible to define in today's languages with a single word, but that sociologists, alerted by those secret societies found among the majority of half-civilized peoples, are able to classify without difficulty. We are therefore justified in regarding the identity of the three names *Gandharva*, *Februo-*, *Kentauro-* – give or take a few articulatory nuances – as a probability. From the phonetic point of view alone, it is true, they can be explained in several divergent ways, but a convergent explanation is also possible: *Gandharva* by Indo-European *G^uhondh-erwo-, *Februo-* by IE *G^uhedh-rwo (for the ending cf. *-ruus* from *-rwo in *patruus*), *Kentauro-* by IE *Kent-ṛwo-. The differences between the first two can be explained by quite normal shifts (different vocalic stages, presence

vi Need I add that I have never claimed – as one critic inadvertently wrote – that the Roman Luperci were, in the first place, half-equine, half human monsters? [Note added to second edition. Dumézil has in mind his earlier book *Le Problème des Centaures*.]

and absence of "nasal infix"). As for the third, its unvoiced occlusives (*k-t-*), contrasting with the voiced aspirate occlusives (g^u*h-dh-*) of the other two, insert it into a set of doublets collated by Vendryes (*Mémoires de la Société de Linguistique*, XVIII, 1913, p. 310; *Revue Celtique*, XL, 1923, p. 436), and this consonantal shift, appearing precisely in roots that indicate a swift or expressive movement of hand or foot ("seize," "run," "recoil"), as well as in names of animals ("he-goat") and parts of the body ("head"), would be appropriate on more than one count in the names of beast-men, Indo-European maskers, swift runners, and great ravishers.[15]

I have already replied on several occasions to another objection; but I want to repeat that reply, since it concerns an important methodological argument that I still hope will bring all linguists over to my position.[vii] Some writers have argued, against this etymology of *februo-*, that initial *f* and internal *b* in Latin can derive not only from *g^u*h-* and **-dh-*, but also from many other Indo-European phonemes or phoneme groups (four for Latin *f-*: IE **bh-*, **dh-*, **ghw-*, **dhw-*; two for Latin *b-*: IE **-b*, **-bh-*), so that *g^u*hedhrwo-* is only one of fifteen equally imaginable and credible Indo-European prototypes for the Latin *februo-*. Agreed. But such indeterminacy is possible only if one refuses to take meaning into account. A totally similar theoretical indeterminacy does not prevent linguists from recognizing in the Latin *feber*, *fiber*, for "beaver [*castor*]," the equivalent of the Gallic *bebro-* (French *bièvre*), the Cornish *befer*, the Irish *beabhar*, the Lithuanian *bêbrus*, and the Old Slavonic *bobrü*, all meaning "beaver." In other words, they are quite happy to select from the large number of possible prototypes for *feber* the one that enables them to link it with the Celtic and Balto-Slavonic words, to wit, **bhebhro-*, cf. **bhebhru-*. In short, the identity of meanings seems to them here, quite rightly, a sufficient ground for decision. Yet the same is true in the case of the Latin *februo-*, with the one difference that the beaver can be denoted exhaustively by a single word and recognized at a glance, which gives linguists who are not sociologists the reassuring impression of a simple and concrete concept, whereas "brotherhoods of men-animals characterized by initiation, purificatory violence, and periodic fertility rites, and so on" cannot be denoted today without a long description. Yet, for all that, such brotherhoods are clear-cut, more or less constant social groupings among semi-civilized peoples.

vii Cf. the argument sketched out in the "Introduction" to *Servius et la fortune*, pp. 15–25 [note added to second edition].

As for the formation of the word, it clearly presents some obscurities, which is hardly to be wondered at. Ten years ago Antoine Meillet urged me to see in it the Indo-European root *$g^{u}hedh$ (Greek πόθος, etc.) "to have a passionate desire for." In any case, the suffix would have to be complex. It is better to give up all attempts to analyze a word that probably no longer had any clear formation in the various Indo-European regions.

CHAPTER II

Celeritas and *Gravitas*

I. Luperci and flamines, Gandharva and brahmans

If the analyses of the preceding chapter are correct, then in both the Roman and the Indian cases – that of Luperci as opposed to flamines and that of Gandharva as opposed to brahmans – we are dealing with two sets of representations that are not merely different but antithetically opposed to one another.[i]

They are opposed first, and most obviously, in the duration of their "social presence [*actualité*]." The brahmans, like the flamines and the priestly hierarchy they head, represent that permanent and constantly public religion within which – except on one lone day of the year – the whole life of society and all its members is set. The Luperci, as with the group of men the Gandharva seem to represent in mythic transposition, constitute precisely that one exception. Both these groups belong to a religion that is neither public nor accessible, except during that one fleeting appearance (in Rome on February 15, in Vedic India on "the last night of the year"). It is a religion that in fact does not exist, in its later

i At the very moment the first edition of this book was being published, M. Kerényi was making an observation of the same kind in *Die antike Religion*, 1940, pp. 199–200, with reference to the flamen dialis, who is always clothed, and the naked Luperci. [Note added to second edition. The full reference is Karl Kerényi, *Die antike Religion: Eine Grundlegung* (Leipzig: Pantheon Akademische Verlagsanstalt, 1940).]

Roman form, other than in that one irruption, and that could not, in any case, in any earlier forms be anything other than constantly secret, apart from on the day of the Lupercalia.

They are opposed also in their innermost purpose: flamines and brahmans are the guardians of sacred order, Luperci and Gandharva are the agents of a no less sacred disorder. Of the two religions they represent, one is static, regulated, calm; the other is dynamic, free, violent. And it is precisely because of its inherently explosive nature that the latter cannot remain dominant for anything more than a very brief period of time, the time it takes to purify and also to revivify, to "recreate" the former in a single tumultuous irruption of energy. The activity of the flamines and brahmans, in contrast, is coextensive with social life by its nature; they are the guarantors, and to some degree the embodiment, of the rules, of those sets of religious and, in a general sense, social prescriptions which are symbolized in Iran by one of Mazdaism's great archangels and which elsewhere led in two different directions – in India to an unlimited proliferation of ritualistic knowledge and philosophy, and in Rome to a new art, that of human law.

They are opposed, lastly, in their mythic resonance. Even the Romans, unimaginative as they were, recognized in the Luperci something of "the other world." One of the gods of the Lupercalia, Februus, is vaguely related to a god of the infernal regions, or else his name is regarded as another name for the feral Faunus. More over, the "guarantor legends," the stories about the birth, childhood and early companions of Romulus and Remus, are fabulous: the first Luperci grew up apart from human societies; before founding Rome they represented, for the Albani or the "city dwellers," the brigands of "the bush," given to sudden appearances, raids, incursions. There is nothing of this in the tradition accounting for the origin of the flamines: it was a considered act, a calculated social innovation in which there was no room for the slightest hint of the supernatural. The Indians, albeit always inclined to add mythic overtones to any reality, did not add a divine component to the brahman until quite late; and even if, as I believe, the myth of Brahmā creating the world by self-immolation is in fact only a transposition onto a cosmic scale of an early and savage scenario of human sacrifice, it is incontestable that the personification of Brahmā is philosophic above all, and that the neuter "brahman" contributed as much, if not more, to it as the masculine "brahman." The Gandharva, in contrast, even before the earliest documented evidence, were consigned wholly to the realm of the imagination. They are not even known to us other than in their mythic transposition; they are not "*equites*" – a human social class – but half-human, half-equine monsters; as part god, part demon, they inhabit a world of their own, "the world of the Gandharva," and so on.

By the late Roman Republic, the Lupercalia – as we know from the attempts undertaken by the early emperors to restore them – had declined in importance. Even so, evidence of that importance still persisted in the ritual itself: the consuls joined in the run as Luperci; and it was during the Lupercalia, during the race itself (undoubtedly with reference to a tradition that has not come down to us in any other form), that Julius Caesar and Mark Antony planned to restore the monarchy.[1] Lastly, the fact that Rome's justificatory legends are all situated within the exploits of its founder, and indeed constitute their essential elements, is sufficient indication that the festival, at least before its decay, carried equal weight, both as to solemnity and efficacity, with the religion that prevailed the rest of the year, and also that it related to sovereignty.

In India, all the early documentary evidence we have concerns the "brahman religion." Since a "Gandharva religion" could never be expressed in these writings, neither the singular nor the plural "Gandharva" are mentioned, except within their mythical transposition. It is only later, in Buddhist works or in a less occlusive state of Brahmanism, that the word "gandharva" came to be used to denote a category of humans, beings who certainly retained some element of the Gandharva of prehistory but who were by now chastened, impoverished, neutralized: these later "gandharva" are "musicians." As a whole, moreover, the early hymns and rituals are not hostile to either singular or plural Gandharva. They regard them not as demons but as genies, who have their own life and customs and with whom it is best to maintain good relations. The fundamental opposition between brahman and Gandharva surfaces on occasion, however; for example, in the lines of the *Ṛg Veda* (VIII, 77, 5) in which Indra is celebrated because "he has smitten the (singular) Gandharva into the bottomless darkness," and has done so "on behalf of the brahman so that they may prosper" (*abhi gandharvam atrnad abudhnesnu rajassu ā Indro brahmabhyah id vrdhe*).[2]

II. Antithetical rules of conduct

Both in Rome and in India, moreover, we have a simple and sure way of testing whether or not this antithesis actually exists. The *brahman* and the *flāmen dialis*, as we saw earlier, have certain features in common, and are constrained, in particular, by a certain number of identical or analogous obligations and interdicts. If I am correct, it is likely that Gandharva and Luperci will be characterized by features, by freedoms or obligations, diametrically opposed to the pair – brahman and *flāmen dialis*. This is easy to establish.

In Rome, for example, all Luperci belong to the *equites* or knightly order (see the conclusive evidence collected by Wissowa, *Religion und Kultus der Römer*, 2nd ed., 1912, p. 561, n. 3 and 4);[3] whereas the *flāmen dialis* is forbidden either to ride or touch a horse.

As *equites*, each of the Luperci wears a ring, and it is with a ring on his finger, holding the *februa* in his right hand, that the Lupercus of the *Ara Pacis* is represented beside the flamines (Domaszewski, *Abhandl. z. rom. Religion*, 1909, p. 92n. etc.);[4] whereas the *flāmen dialis* is forbidden to wear a ring unless it is open and hollow (Aulus Gellius, X, 15).

The Luperci sacrifice a dog (Plutarch, *Roman Questions*, 68); the Lupercalia begin with the sacrifice of a goat, whose blood is then smeared on the foreheads of the two leading Luperci, while its hide is cut into strips and used by the Luperci as whips (Plutarch, *Romulus*, 21, and so on). In contrast, the *flāmen dialis* must neither touch nor name either dog or goat (Plutarch, *Roman Questions*, 111, where, in the case of the dog, Plutarch himself stresses the contrast between the two behaviors).

The Luperci run through the city naked, in imitation of their prototypes, the companions of Romulus and Remus, who in hot pursuit of cattle thieves did not stop to clothe themselves; whereas the *flāmen dialis* has a complicated style of dress that must never be wholly removed.

The mythic prototypes of the Luperci, Remus and his companions, devour meat still hissing from the flames (*verubus stridentia detrahit exta*, Ovid, *Fastes*, II, 373); whereas the *flāmen dialis* must never touch raw meat (Aulus Gellius, X, 15; Plutarch, *Roman Questions*, 110).

One of the two bands of Luperci bears the name "Fabii" (Ovid, *Fastes*, II, 378-379) or "Fabiani" (common form); whereas the *flāmen dialis* must neither touch nor name the bean, *faba*.

The main activity of the Luperci as they run through the city is to whip the women they encounter, and possibly men as well (Plutarch, *Romulus*, 21, and so on); whereas a condemned man who, being taken away for a flogging, throws himself at the feet of the *flāmen dialis* cannot be whipped that day (Aulus Gellius, X, 15).

With their skin whips the Luperci bring fertility to all the women they encounter, without selection or restriction; their prototypes, Romulus and his companions once carried off the Sabine women who were later also collectively whipped and anonymously made fertile at the first Lupercalia. In contrast, the *flāmen dialis* and the *flāminica* are a model couple, married in accordance with the strictest of all such rituals; they typify the essence of conjugal solidarity and fidelity.

In India, the contrast between the characteristic features of the Gandharva and the interdicts or obligations imposed on the brahmans is no less clear-cut.

The Gandharva are drinkers, whereas the brahmans abstain from drinking. The Gandharva are half-horse, and also tend horses; whereas the brahmans, as we have seen, must cease all religious activity while on horseback. The brahman must never strip him self completely naked, whereas the story of Purūravas, in which he "becomes one of the Gandharva," begins with a lamb-stealing episode in which the Gandharva cause Purūravas to chase after them without taking the time to clothe himself. The Gandharva are so free in their pursuit of sensual pleasure that the summary union of a man and woman is termed "a Gandharva marriage" (as we noted, several texts even say that the Gandharva possesses every woman before her husband does, a claim that we should probably take literally and apply to gandharva-men in masks). In contrast, the brahman must be austere, reserved and passionless; the form of marriage termed "brahman marriage" is one of the most solemn and ritualistic of all.

One particular opposition merits special attention, and even if the Romans, who were not much inclined to either philosophy or art, offer no equivalent, the legends of the centaur Chiron, at once physician, teacher, astronomer and musician do, proving that this is an essential feature: the brahman devotes his life to sacrifice, meditation, and commentaries on the Vedic hymns; he is concerned neither with the arts, human science, nor anything original or in any way related to inspiration or fancy. Indeed, song, dance and music are specifically forbidden to him (Manu, IV, 64). The Gandharva, in contrast, are specialists in these fields. They are such good musicians that their name was very early (or possibly always) synonymous with "earthly musician" (cf. in the epic literature *gāndharva* "music"). Moreover, this characteristic is certainly ancient since in Iran, although the Avesta and the Mazdean texts speak of the *Gandarəva* (*Gandarep…*) only as a monster killed by a hero engaged in virtuous exploits, Firdausi introduces into his poem a certain *Kndrv* (i.e., *Genderev*), who is the steward in charge of the pleasures of the demonic king Dahāk. Further, this *Kndrv* is required by Dahāk's conqueror, Faridūn, to organize festivities in honor of his succession, in an event that includes a great deal of carousing and music.

The opposition, as well as the symmetry, of the concepts denoted in Indo-European by *_bhelgh-men-_ and *_g^{u}he(n)dh-rwo-_ is evident even in the grammatical use made of the words involved. In Latin the inanimate _februum_, the name of the "instrument of violent purifications and fertility rites that the Luperci must hold in their hands while performing their duties," stands in the same relation to the animate masculine "Februus," "patron god of the Lupercalia" (and so to the animate masculine Sanskrit "Gandharva") as, in Indo Iranian, the inanimate Vedic "brāhman" ("sacred formula, incantation, and so on," and, even more precisely, the inanimate Avestic _barəsman_, "sacred bundle held by the officiating priest during sacrifice") do to the animate masculine Sanskrit _brahmān_ (nominative _brahmā_) "sacrificing priest," later "_Brahmā_," "divine creator of the world by his auto-sacrifice." (We know that the Latin nominative _flāmen_ combines an animate value with an inanimate form of the same type as _agmen_, _certāmen_, and so on. The normal animate form would be *_flāmo_.)

Certainly, then, we are dealing with antithetical religious concepts and mechanisms. From the standpoint of method, perhaps it would be best at this point to stress that everything first put forward as a result of a direct comparison between brahman and flamen, then between Gandharva and Lupercus, is now seen to be indirectly reinforced by the fact that the Indian brahman-Gandharva antithesis corresponds exactly with the Roman flamen-Lupercus antithesis. If my "horizontal" comparisons had been artificial, then the artifice would have been revealed by at least some degree of discrepancy in the "vertical" relationships. When it comes to abstract reasoning and constructions, regularity and harmony do not provide the slightest presumption of correctness. But we have not been reasoning in the abstract; rather, we have simply drawn up a register of concrete facts. Material of this sort will not long tolerate the imposition of an order not derived from its own nature and history.

The flamen-Lupercus and brahman-Gandharva antitheses share still other aspects and areas of incidence that I shall touch on only briefly.

III. _Celeritas_ and _gravitas_

The Luperci, the Gandharva and the centaurs are all "swift." All of them, ritually or mythically, are runners in important or famous races;

and although this characteristic is doubtless closely linked with their nature as *equites* or their semi-equine form,[ii] it is also in conformity with a more general mystique. Speed (extreme rapidity, sudden appearances and disappearances, lightning raids, etc.) is that behavior, that "rhythm," most suited to the activity of violent, improvisational, creative societies. In contrast, the ordered public religion that holds sway through out the year, except for that brief period when the masked monsters are unleashed, demands a majestic gait and solemn rhythm. The Romans expressed this in an arresting formula: the bodyguards of Romulus, the first Luperci, are called the *Celeres* (from *celer*, "swift"); and the successor of Romulus, Numa, began his reign with two complementary acts: he dissolved the *Celeres* and organized the triple *flāmonium* (Plutarch, *Numa*, 7). This opposition between the mystique of *celeritas* and the morality of *gravitas* is fundamental, and it takes on its full meaning when one recalls that the dizzying intoxication of speed – among the shamans of Siberia and on our own Grand Prix circuits – is just as much a stimulant, an intoxicant, a means of achieving an illusory transcendence over human limitations, as is alcoholic intoxication, erotic passion or the frenzy stirred by oratory. We know that Mazdaism placed its own particular imprint on this opposition with the notion of the headlong *run* versus the majestic walk: all "ahurian" beings, even when they are heroes doing battle or fighters on behalf of good, are always described simply as "going," "coming," "walking" (roots *i-*, *gam-*); "daêvian" beings alone (demons, monsters, wicked rulers, and so on) "run" (roots *dvar-*, *dram-*).[iii]

---

ii On the importance of the horse in Indo-European societies, see Koppers, *Pferdeopfer und pferdekult der Indogermanen*, Wiener Beitr. z. Kulturgesch. und Linguistik. [Note moved from text. The full reference is Wilhelm Koppers, *Pferdeopfer und pferdekult der Indogermanen*: *Eine ethnologisch-religionswissenschaftliche Studie*, in Wilhelm Koppers ed., *Die Indogermanen- und Germanenfrage: Neue Wege zu ihrer Lösung*, Wiener Beiträge zur Kulturgeschichte und Linguistik, Jahrgang IV (Salzburg-Leipzig: Verlag Anton Pustet, 1936), pp. 279–411.]

iii See H. Güntert, *Über die ahurischen und daēvischen Ausdrücke im Awesta, SB d. Heidelb. Ak d. w., ph. –hist. Klasse*, 1914, 13, sections 14–16, pp. 10–11; cf. Louis H. Gray, *Journ. of the Roy. Asiat. Soc.*, 1927, p. 436. [Note moved from text. The references are to Hermann Güntert, *Über die ahurischen und daēvischen Ausdrücke im Awesta: Eine semasiologische Studie*, Sitzungsberichte der Heidelberger Akademie der Wissenschaften, Philosophisch-Historische Klasse 13 (Heidelberg: Carl

IV. *Iuniores* and *seniores*

It seems that the Luperci and the flamines were also antithetically differentiated as *iuniores* and *seniores*. There are reasons for thinking that this classification by age, although it plays a restricted role in historical Rome, was much more important in early times (cf. my article "Jeunesse, Eternité, Aube" in the *Annales d'histoire économique et sociales*, July 1938, p. 289ff).[5] The Luperci are *iuvenes* (*equestris ordinis iuventus*: Valerius Maximus, II, 2); their founders are the two archetypal *iuvenes* surrounded by youthful companions (*Romulus et frater pastoralisque iuventus*), and as I argued in the article just mentioned (pp. 297-298), both the Gandharva and *Kentauroi* societies, at the time when they functioned within human reality, seemed also to have enjoyed a sort of privileged right over "the maximum vitality, over the *akmé* of life" (Sanskrit *ayus*, Greek αἰών, IE **ayw-*) , in other words, over what constituted the very essence of the Indo-European **yu(w)-en-*, according to the elegant analysis by E. Benveniste (*Bull. de la Soc. de Ling. de Paris*, XXVX III, 1937, pp. 103-112).[6] As for the flamines and the brahmans, although they cannot be congenitally assimilated into the *seniores* (since one can be *captus* as *flāmen dialis* at a very early age, and one is born a brahman), their affinity and their "equivalence" to the *seniores* are nevertheless strongly indicated: they need only practice the morality of their station with the required rigor in order to have the rank of *seniores*. On this point I shall draw on two traditions only; but the agreement between them is significant.

We read in Manu, II, 150-155: "The brahman who gives (spiritual) birth and teaches duty, even if he be a child, is according to law the father of a man of years (*balo 'pi vipro vṛddhasya pitā bhavati dharmataḥ*). Kavi, son of Angiras, while still young (*śiśuh*) taught the sacred knowledge to his paternal uncles (*pitṛn*, literally, "fathers") and addressed them as 'Sons!' (*putraka iti hovāca*). Angered, they demanded of the gods the reason for this. The gods gathered and answered: 'The boy spoke to you correctly, for the ignorant man is a child, he who gives the sacred knowledge is a father…; it is not because he has white hairs that a man is old *(na tena vṛddho bhavati yenasya palitarp śiraḥ*); he who has read the Scripture, even when young, is classed by the gods as an elder (*yo*

Winters Universitätsbuchhandlung, 1914); Louis H. Gray, "The 'Ahurian' and 'Daevian' Vocabularies in the Avesta," *Journal of the Royal Asiatic Society of Great Britain and Ireland* 3, 1927: 427–41.]

vai yuvapy adhiyanas tam devaḥ sthavirarm viduḥ).'" This well-known legend acquires its full meaning when we take into account the fact that it occurs in support of the definition, given in the preceding sloka (149), of the actual name of the brahman or "spiritual father," and that the name is said there to be *guru*, or "heavy." This means that the brahman carries within him the same physical image as that conjured up by the name for the supreme virtue of the Roman *seniores*, which is *gravitas*.

Now, in Livy, XXVII, 8, we read:

> And Publius Licinius, the pontifex maximus, compelled Gaius Valerius Flaccus to be installed as flamen of Jupiter [*flāmen dialis*], although he was unwilling… I should gladly have passed over in silence the reason for installing a flamen perforce, had not his reputation changed from bad to good. Because of his irresponsible and debauched youth, Gaius Flaccus was seized (*captus*) as a flamen by Publius Licinius. As soon as the responsibility of rites and ceremonies took possession of his mind, Gaius reformed his old character so suddenly that no one among all the young men (*iuventute*) of Rome stood higher in the estimation and approval of the leading senators (*primoribus patrum*), neither within their own families nor among strangers. By the unanimity of this good reputation, he acquired a well-founded self-confidence and claimed that he should be admitted to the senate (*ut in senatum introiret*), a right that had long been denied former flamens because of their unworthiness. After, having entered the Senate House the praetor Publius Licinius led him away, he appealed to the tribunes of the plebeians. The flamen insistently claimed the ancient right of his priesthood, saying it had been granted to that office of flamen along with the *toga praetexta* and the *sella curulis* (*vetustum ius sacerdotii repetebat, datum id cum toga praetexta et sella curuli et flamonio esse*). The praetor maintained that right should be based, not on outmoded instances from the annals, but on very recent practice, and that within the memory of their fathers and grandfathers no flamen of Jupiter [*flāmen dialis*] had exercised this right. The tribunes held that obsolescence was due to the indolence of flamens and was justly accounted as their own loss, not a loss to the priestly office. Where upon, without opposition even from the praetor and with the general approval of the senators and of the plebeians, the tribunes led the flamen into the senate, for everyone agreed that the flamen had proven his point by the uprightness of his life rather than by virtue of his priestly privilege (*magis sanctitate vitae quam sacerdotii iure eam rem flaminem obtinuisse*).

This fine text is interesting in several respects. First, for the psychology of the praetor, that great artisan of Roman law, whom we see here attempting to modernize a rule by the legalization, after a lapse of several generations, of a spontaneous innovation. Second, for the opposition it depicts between the *impetus* of the free *iuvenis* and the *gravitas* of the *flāmen*. Last, because it bears witness to the fact that the *flāmen dialis*, in ancient times, was admitted by right into the assembly of that particular set of *seniores* made up of the *senatores*. This last point provides a curious link with the Indian tradition and doctrine dealt with earlier.

V. Creation and conservation

Flamines and Luperci, brahmans and Gandharva, all share equally in the task of securing the life and fecundity of society. But here again it is instructive to note the contrast between the behaviors involved. Not only in the area, dealt with earlier, of their conduct toward women – on one side, individual, sacrosanct marriage and fidelity; on the other, kidnap, sensuality and anonymous fertilization – but in the very purpose and principle of that behavior. One group ensures a continuous fecundity against interruption and accident; the other makes good an accident and reestablishes an interrupted fecundity.

If a celibate *flāmen dialis* is inconceivable, if India "centers" the career of every brahman on his role as husband and head of family, if the *flāminica* and the *brāhmaṇī* are just as holy and important as their husbands, it is all because the presence and collaboration of this feminine element shows that the principal mechanism of fertility is in a healthy state, that all the female forces of nature are functioning fully and harmoniously. In Rome the evidence is particularly clear: should the *flāminica* die, the *flāmen dialis* immediately becomes unfit to perform his functions, and he resigns. The flamen-couple must have children, and those children must also take part in the couple's sacred activity. If the couple do not have children of their own, then they take as *flaminii* the children of another family, both of whose parents are still alive. All these rules signify the potential or actual continuity of the vital flow. The many taboos that oblige the flamen to keep away from funeral pyres, from dead animals, from barren trees, anything that has succumbed to natural decay or failure, are perhaps intended less to protect him from taint than to express the limitations of his activities: he is powerless against that which has already occurred. In other words, although, he can prolong life and fecundity through his sacrifices, he cannot restore them.

That miracle – of restoring fecundity – is on the contrary the great feat performed by the men-animals. In Rome their whipping race commemorated the act by which their legendary prototypes ended the sterility of the women carried off by the first king, Romulus. In India they restored the lost virility of the first sovereign, Varuṇa, with herbs known only to them. The mystique underlying these traditions is not difficult to reconstitute: it is that of the emasculation of Varuṇa's Greek counterpart, Uranos, at once an unbridled, excessive procreator and a tyrannical, intolerable sovereign, who lost his genitals and sovereignty simultaneously. The sterility that strikes the Sabine women because Romulus had the audacity to abduct them from their husbands, the sterility that threatens Rome and the empire at the very moment of its formation, has the same meaning – with a more precise reference to the hubris of Uranos – as the "devigoration" that strikes Varuṇa at the very moment of his consecration as *samrāj* or universal sovereign (cf. my *Ouranós-Vāruṇa*, ch. IV and V). It is no chance coincidence that the restorer of Varuṇa's virility is the (singular) Gandharva (*Atharva Veda*, IV, 4) and that the restorers of the Sabine women's fertility are the Luperci with their *februa*. Excess – the very cause of the accident – also provides the remedy. It is precisely because they are "excessive" that the Gandharva and the Luperci are able to create; whereas the flamines and the brahmans, because they are merely "correct," can only maintain.

I have referred at several points to the fact that the Luperci were instituted by Romulus and that the flamines were instituted (or organized) by Numa. I am thus led to inquire whether the antithesis that underlies the two priesthoods, these two organs of magico-religious sovereignty, is not to be found in the history of the two first kings, the two sovereign-archetypes of Roman history.

It is also noteworthy that the Gandharva are called "Varuṇa's people" (*Śatapatha Brāhmaṇa*, XIII, 4, 3, 7),[7] and in the paragraphs above that deal with the sterility of the women stolen by Romulus and the impotence of Varuṇa (the former cured by the Luperci, the latter by the Gandharva), we can discover an important clue: in terms of his function, does not Romulus embody an archetype of the "terrible" sovereign in Roman history, comparable to the archetypal figure I explored in an earlier work with reference to Varuṇa and the Uranos of the Greek cosmogonies? Further, just as Roman history sets Numa, patron of the major flamines, beside Romulus, leader of the Luperci, so India juxtaposes, closely and antithetically associated in a way that ensures their collaboration, Varuṇa and Mitra: Varuṇa, who has the Gandharva as his people, and Mitra, who is normally associated with the brahman. New perspectives now begin to open up, perspectives that become clearer still when we take into account the "favorite" gods of both Romulus and Numa. In the case of Romulus they are the "terrible" variations of Jupiter; in the case of Numa, *Fides*. And *Fides* is the personification of contractual correctness, as is, beside Varuṇa, the omnipotent magician, the Indo-Iranian *Mitra.

The four chapters that follow are devoted to making an inventory of these new discoveries. Others will then be presented.[8]

CHAPTER III

Romulus and Numa

I. The singular relationship of Romulus and Numa

Romulus and Numa are the two "fathers" of the Roman state. In Plutarch Romulus is compared to Theseus, Numa to Lycurgus. Although these comparisons are instructive, they conceal one important difference: Lycurgus did not succeed Theseus, since each ruled his own city; Numa, on the other hand, did succeed Romulus. Thus, in this instance they both worked on the same material yet modeled it differently.

This relation greatly perplexed the annalists. For even if they knew, generally speaking, that Romulus founded the city in a material sense, whereas Numa was responsible only for its institutions, they still wondered why Rome had to wait (if only during Romulus's lifetime) for the creation of the religious or social institutions that ancient thought and experience found to be so primary and germinal to the existence of the city. Take, for example, the worship of Vesta with its College of Vestals. The logic of the system required that its founder should be Numa, since the Vestals are part of the same whole as, say, the flamines, and since they form an essential part of the "establishment" religion, of the most unchallenged domain of gravitas. Tradition did in effect lay the honor for all that – the priestesses, the form of worship, the sanctuary – at the feet of Numa. But how, on the other hand, could one accept that Rome had been forced, before Numa, to do without the sacred fire, the entire community's source of energy and solidarity, especially when it was so simple and so much in conformity with all known customs to think that

Romulus had brought with him, to his "colony," a spark of the sacred fire from the "mother city," Alba Longa? This was a surprising intellectual dilemma, and some authors, whose reasons are clearly put forth by Dionysius of Halicarnassus (*Roman Antiquities*, II, 65; cf. Plutarch, *Romulus*, 22), did not hesitate to make Romulus the founder of the national hearth even at the risk of dismantling Numa's achievements.[1] Others went further. To them it seemed impossible that Numa should have been the creator even of the *flāmonium*; so he simply "completed" or "reorganized" it.

The annalists were also placed in a delicate situation by the fact that Numa's work emended that of Romulus. And emended it in such a way that in many instances it actually replaced it with its opposite. In short, Numa's work implicitly condemned that of Romulus. Yet Romulus could not be in the wrong. And certainly he was not in the wrong, for the Roman state owed him not only its birth but also certain examples of conduct that, despite being contrary to those of Numa, were nonetheless useful, accepted and sacred. How then to prove that Numa was wise, without stigmatizing as faults, crimes or follies the salutary violence of Romulus? The Roman historians extricated themselves from this dilemma with some skill. They managed to displace the conflict into the realm of abstract notions such as "peace" and "war," so that praise and blame could be avoided (cf. the excellent summary by Livy at the conclusion of Numa's reign [I. 21]: *duo deinceps reges, alius alia via, ille bello, hic pace, civitatem auxerune... tum valida, tum temperata et belli et pacis artibus erat civitas.* "Thus two kings in succession, by different methods, the one by war, the other by peace, aggrandized the state... the state was both strong and well versed in the arts of war and peace"). But, more often, they skirted around these issues carefully, and they accepted the fact that, as in the life of societies and individuals, the most conflicting practices can be harmoniously reconciled – provided that one does not constantly insist on abstract principles.

So much for the ancient writers. As for the moderns, they have subjected the legends of Romulus and Numa to the most detailed scrutiny, and the results of the various critiques are certainly interesting. The literary history of Romulus has been carefully traced, and in the case of Numa it has been established (sometimes with certainty, sometimes not), from which now-lost works Livy or Dionysius or Plutarch borrowed such-and-such a feature. But one must not exaggerate either the scope or the conclusions of this research. It is only very rarely, and generally without absolute certainty, that we are able to transcend literary history and put our finger on the true origin of any detail. To say that Livy took this or that from Valerius Antias does not mean that we know whether Valerius Antias invented it or borrowed it, with a greater or lesser degree of distortion, either from a particular author, genteel tradition or mere rumor. So, when we have taken the whole thing apart and ascertained (as much as possible) the approximate legitimacy of each element, there still remains another line of inquiry and another "point of view," which, together might constitute the essence of the matter: What are the *main trends* within the whole? What are the *lines of force* running through the ideological *field* within which all the details are placed? But let me not search for too modern an image simply to formulate the old and futile problem of not being able to tell "the forest from the trees." And since the trees in this case have found so many observers already, surely a comparatist may be allowed to concentrate his attention on the forest. Certainly it is indisputable that the lives, the works and the very figures of Numa and Romulus, even allowing for some inconclusiveness of detail, were conceived of throughout the entire tradition as strictly antithetical. And it is clear, too, that this antithesis coincides, in many of its manifestations, with the ritual and conceptual antithesis analyzed in the previous chapter.

II. Numa as antithesis of Romulus

Romulus made himself king. He and his brother left Alba because they were possessed by the *regni cupido*, the *avitum malum* (the "ambition of sovereignty," the "hereditary evil") (Livy, I, 6) and could not accept not being rulers there (Plutarch, *Romulus*, 9). Romulus tricked the augurs at Remus's expense, then killed him or had him killed in order to become sole ruler (Plutarch, *Romulus*, 9–10). Later, at the insistence of the Roman people, who were unanimous in their reverence for his wisdom (Plutarch, *Numa*, 5–6), Numa consented to become king, but with repugnance and regret at leaving a quiet life in order "to serve."

Romulus is the typical *iuvenis* and *iunior*. His career as an adventurer begins with his birth. With the *iuvenes* (later given the title *Celeres*) (Plutarch, *Romulus*, 26: ἦσαν δὲ περὶ αὐτὸν ἀεὶ τῶν νέων οἱ καλούμενοι Κέλερες, ἀπὸ τῆς περὶ τὰς ὑπουργίας ὀξύτητος), his constant companions in both peace and war (Livy, I, 15), he governs in such a way as to incur the hostility of the *patres*, of the *senatores* (Plutarch, *Romulus*,

26–28). He would disappear suddenly, either by miracle or as a result of murder, at "the height of his powers," and then appear immediately after ward to one of his friends "fair and stately to the eye as never before" (28–29). On the other hand, Numa is already forty (and his life hitherto had been one of long seclusion) when he was offered the *rēgnum* (Plutarch, *Numa*, 5) on the recommendation of the *senatores* (*ibid.*, 3), after an interregnum during which Rome was governed by the *patres-senatores* (*ibid.*, 2). His first act is to dissolve the *Celeres*, his second to organize the triple *flāmonium* (*ibid.*, 7), or rather to create it (Livy, 1, 20). He lives to be extremely old, past his ninetieth year, and slowly dies of old age, of a "languishing sickness" (*ibid.*, 21). In legend, he came to be the "white" king (Virgil, *Aeneid*, VI, 809); at his obsequies the *senatores* carry the funeral bed on their shoulders (Livy, I, 22); and he remained the standard by which gravitas was measured (Claudian, *Against Rufinis*, I, 114: *sit licet ille Numa gravior…*).[2]

Everything Romulus does is warlike; even his posthumous advice to the Romans is to cultivate the art of war ("*rem militarem colant*") (Livy, I, 16). Numa makes it his task to break the Romans of their warlike habits (Plutarch, *Numa*, 8); peace remains unbroken throughout his reign (*ibid.*, 19, 20). He even offers a friendly alliance to the Fidenates when they raid his lands and on that occasion institutes the *fetiales*, priests whose concern it is to guarantee respect for the forms that prevent or limit violence (Dionysius of Halicarnassus, *Roman Antiquities*, II, 72; cf. Plutarch, *Numa*, 12).

Romulus kills his brother; he is at least suspected of the death of his colleague Tatius (Plutarch, *Romulus*, 23). In the "asylum" that was later to become Rome, he indiscriminately welcomes and protects all fugitives: murderers, defaulting debtors, runaway slaves (*ibid.*, 9). He has the Sabine women carried off (*ibid.*, 14); his violence engenders the no-less violent hostility of the senators who, perhaps, tear him to pieces (*ibid.*, 27). Numa is wholly without passions, even those held in esteem by barbarians, such as violence and ambition (Plutarch, *Numa*, 3). He hesitates before accepting the kingship because, knowing that Romulus was suspected of his colleague's death, he does not want to risk being suspected, in turn, of having killed his predecessor (*ibid.*, 5). His wisdom is contagious: under his rule sedition is unknown, there are no conspiracies, and men live exempt from disturbances and corruption (*ibid.*, 20). His greatest concern is justice, and the reason he wishes to dissuade the Romans from war is because war engenders injustice (Plutarch, *Comparison of Lycurgus and Numa*, 2).

Romulus practices trickery in religion (Plutarch, *Romulus*, 9) and "invents" the god Consus only to use his feast day as an ambush (*ibid.*, 14). Numa's entire life is founded on religion, on religious uprightness; he institutes not only new forms of worship but also the correct outward forms of meditation and piety (Plutarch, *Numa*, 14). He establishes almost all the priestly colleges (*ibid.*, 7–10) and takes upon himself the task of teaching the priests (*ibid.*, 22).

Women and family have almost no place in Romulus's life; he has the Sabine women abducted only to perpetuate the Roman race. Although he himself marries one of them (according to some versions only, for example, Plutarch, *Romulus*, 14), he does not, properly speaking, found a *gens*: either he has no children or else his children have "no future," since they play no part either in person or through their descendants in Roman history. Moreover, it is to Aeneas, not to Romulus, that the emperors were to trace back their title to power. Admittedly he treats the Sabine women honorably when they have procured the consent of their husbands and fathers (*ibid.*, 20), but that does not prevent him, once they proved sterile, from indiscriminately whipping them to make them fertile (Ovid, *Fastes*, II, 425–452, and elsewhere). In truth his whole career, from start to finish, is that of a bachelor, and he establishes a harshly unfair regime of marital repudiation, much to the detriment of married women (Plutarch, *Romulus*, 22). Numa is hardly to be thought of, any more than a *flāmen dialis*, without his wife, Tatia, with whom, until her death thirteen years later, he forms a model couple (Plutarch, *Numa*, 3). Tatia, or a second and no less legitimate wife, gives Numa a daughter, who will become the mother of Ancus, another pious king of Rome, and according to other sources, four sons who are the ancestors of "Rome's most illustrious families" (*ibid.*).

Plutarch has Numa say the following in explaining his reasons for refusing the *rēgnum*, and in so doing he unwittingly gives a very accurate account of the situation (*Numa*, 5): "Men laud Romulus as a child of the gods and tell how he was nurtured in an incredible way and fed in a miraculous manner when he was still an infant. But I am mortal by birth, and I was nourished and trained by men whom you know..." This opposition is indeed an important one, and is similar to the antithesis remarked upon earlier between the Luperci and the flamines and, in India, between Gandharva and brahmans: Luperci and Gandharva, bearers of mysteries, are usually from another world, and are mere transients in this world to which brahmans and flamines rightfully belong. The Romans portrayed Romulus, like the Luperci, in as supernatural a fashion as their rational imaginations allowed, whereas Numa was seen as part of the complete, reassuring humanity of the priesthoods he instituted.[i] Moreover, the Romulus-Numa opposition, under all the headings just listed, coincides even down to its underlying principle with the Luperci-flamines opposition: on one side, the tumult, passion and imperialism of an unbridled *iunior*; on the other, the serenity, correctness and moderation of a priestly *senior*.[ii] This general "intention" of the two legends is clearly more important than the scattering of individual, inevitably varying details through which it is expressed.

Moreover, this opposition of the two founding kings is also strikingly expressed in the contrast between their "favorite" gods.

III. Romulus and Jupiter, Numa and Fides

During his entire life, Romulus founded only two cults. Moreover, they were not cults of Mars, as one might have expected had he been nothing more than a self-made warrior-chief. Rather, they were cults of Jupiter, as is natural to a born sovereign; however, these cults represent two very precise specifications of Jupiter: Jupiter Feretrius and Jupiter Stator. The two legends are linked with the wars that followed the rape of the Sabine women.

Romulus slew Aero, king of Caenina, with his own hand, in single combat, and thus won the battle. In thanks, or else in fulfillment of a vow, he raised a temple to Jupiter Feretrius (the first Roman temple, according to Livy), and there offered King Acro's arms to the gods – the first *spolia opima*. This is a royal cult, a cult in which Jupiter is very much the same Jupiter as that of the old hierarchized triad Jupiter-Mars-Quirinus; in other words, the god of the head of state, the god of the *rēgnum* [cf. Livy, III, 39], who says that *rex* is a name that it is *fas* to apply to Jupiter).[3] Indeed, Roman tradition was to record only two other cases of *spolia opima*, and these offerings were made, in decreasing importance of the triad, to Mars (Cossus, after victory over one of the Veientian kings "in 428 B.C.") and then to Quirinus (Marcellus, after victory over a Gallic chieftain in 222 B.C.: Servius, *Commentary on the*

i Cf. *JMQ III*, p. 110ff. where this point is more clearly brought out by reference to Cicero's *De natura deorum*, III, 2 [note added to second edition].

ii Cf. *Tarpeia*, p. 164 [note added to second edition].

Aeneid, VI, 859).[iii] But this Jupiter, Jupiter Feretrius, is god of the *rex* only in one of the aspects of the *rex* himself; a *rex* fighting in single combat in the name of his whole people, and a *rex* victorious. The words that Livy attributes to Romulus are significant in this respect: *Iupiter Feretri, haec tibi victor Romulus rex rēgia arma fero*...: "Jupiter Feretrius, I, king, Romulus, upon my victory, present to thee these royal arms..." (I, 10; cf. Plutarch, *Romulus*, 16).

Jupiter Stator saved Rome at a moment of grave danger. As a result of the Tarpeian treachery, the Sabines were already in possession of the citadel and on the verge of defeating the Roman army on the plain between the Palatine and the Capitol. The Romans were panic stricken, and Romulus invoked Jupiter: *Deme terrorem Romanis, fugamque faedam siste!* "Dispel the terror of the Romans, and stay their shameful flight!" Courage returned instantly to the Roman forces, who halted their flight, attacked and drove the Sabines back "as far as the place where the House of the King (*rēgia*) and the temple of Vesta now stand." In thanks, Romulus dedicated a temple to the god of their salvation on the very spot where the marvel took place (Plutarch, *Romulus*, 18; Livy, I, 12). And marvel this certainly was: upon invocation of the *rex*, Jupiter instantly and invisibly intervened, took the whole situation into his hands, and reversed the course of the battle. We shall soon have the means to explore the significance of this event; but for now the Roman data are clear enough.

Thus these two specifications of Jupiter coincide in this respect: they both show Jupiter as the divine protector of the *rēgnum*, but specifically in battles, in victories. And the second victory is the result of a supreme being, a sovereign conjuring trick, a piece of public sleight-of-hand against which no human or superhuman power is of any avail, and this overturns the expected, the "correct" order of events. Jupiter Feretrius, Jupiter Stator, both are Jupiter as king, violent and victorious. And Jupiter Stator is in addition a great magician.[iv]

In contrast, all the authors stress Numa's particular devotion to the god Fides. Dionysius of Halicarnassus writes (*Roman Antiquities*, II, 75), "There is no higher or more sacred sentiment than faith (πίστις), either in the affairs of the state or in relations between individuals. Being persuaded of this truth, Numa, the first of mankind in this, founded a shrine

iii Cf. *JMQ I*, p. 189ff. [note added to second edition].

iv Cf. *JMQ I*, p. 78ff. (the magician Jupiter's technique of achieving victory contrasted with that of Mars, the warrior) [note added to second edition].

dedicated to Fides Publica (ἱερὸν Πίστεως δημοσίας) and instituted, in her honor, sacrifices as official as those to other divinities." Plutarch (*Numa*, 16) also says that Numa was the first to build a temple to Fides and that he taught the Romans their greatest oath, the oath of Fides. Livy (I, 21) tells us that Numa established an annual sacrifice to Fides, and that for this event the flamines – clearly the three major flamines – drawn in a single chariot and working together (in other words, symbolizing the cohesion of the social functions represented in early Roman times by the names of Jupiter, Mars and Quirinus), performed the ceremonies with their right hands entirely swathed. This last feature, Livy adds, in agreement with known tradition, signified "that *fides* must be constantly protected, and that anything in which it resides, including the right hand, is sacred" (*significantes fidem tutandam, sedemque eius etiam in dextris sacratam esse*).

IV. *Fides* and *śraddhā*

What the author means here by *fides* is clear. In private as in public life, within the city as well as in relations with outsiders, *fides* is a respect for commitments, a respect for justice (which means that Numa's devotion to Fides is linked to one of the general characteristics by which he was defined earlier in contrast with Romulus). This meaning is generally accepted in all the different contexts where *fides* is discussed: we have just noted Livy's comment about the right hand, and Plutarch makes a significant comparison between the cult of Fides and that of Terminus, which Numa founded, he says, with a similar intention, that of "protecting peace and convicting injustice." "It was he [Numa]," Plutarch tells us, "who set the boundaries of the city's territory, for Romulus was unwilling to acknowledge, by measuring his own, how much he had taken away from others. He knew that a boundary, if observed, fetters lawless power; and if not observed, leads to injustice" (*Numa*, 16; cf. *Roman Questions*, 15). Among the reasons he offers for the establishment of the cult of Fides Publica, Dionysius of Halicarnassus (II, 75) says that Numa had observed that, among contracts in general (τῶν συμβολαίων), those that have been drawn up publicly and before witnesses are protected by the honor of the two parties (ἡ τῶν συνόντων αἰδὼς) and are rarely violated; whereas those, much more numerous, that have been sealed without witnesses have no other guarantee than the good faith of the contractors (τὴν τῶν συμβαλόντων πίστιν). From this Numa concluded that he should give good faith his greatest support and so be made a god of *fides*. Finally, we know that the institution of the *fetiales*, which is generally attributed to Numa (and otherwise to Ancus, his grandson and emulator), was founded to preserve peace through the strict observance of agreements and, when that was not possible, to lend to the declaration of war and to the conclusion of treaties a regulated and ritualistic character. In short, Numa's *fides* is the foundation of Rome's supreme creation, its law.

At the same time, however, it is something very different. Modern writers have often marveled at the way Roman law, from the very outset, appears to have been distinct from religion, the way in which it is constituted, from the first, as a work of reason and reflection, as well as of observation and experiment; in fact, it was truly scientific in its technique. And they are right to marvel. Yet, however precocious this Roman "miracle" might have been – less prestigious perhaps, less multiform, but no less honorable than the Greek miracle – it is impossible to conceive that, in the very earliest times, the future law of the Romans could have been any more separable from their forms of worship and their theology than it is in most semi-civilized societies observable today. The notions on which the early jurists worked, and on which their modern commentators have reflected, can only have been stripped gradually of the magico-religious elements that, in the beginning, constituted the largest, the most certain, the clearest part of their content. This is the case with the substantive *fides*. And on this point comparative linguistics has long since assembled the necessary data.

Antoine Meillet has shown that the word *fides* (root **bheidh-*; Greek πείθω, and so on) serves as a verbal substantive to *credo*; in other words, that it must have replaced an early **crede* (from **kred-dhe-*, with stem legitimately in *-e-*) , by which it seems to have been influenced early on, since it too, without any possible direct justification, has an *-e-* stem.[v] *Fides* and *credo*, in other words, share the same domain: not merely that of law but also that of religion, and additionally, between those two, that of ethics. So when Christianity gave the substantive noun "faith" and the verb "believe" the overtones they still have today, it was at the very least rediscovering and revivifying very ancient usages.

v Antoine Meillet, *Mémoires de la Societé de Linguistique de Paris*, XXII, 1922, pp. 213–214 and p. 215ff. [Note moved from text. These are references to two short articles: "Traitement de *S* suivie de consonne," 211–14; "Lat. Crēdo et Fidēs," 215–18.]

Indeed, among the religious expressions shared by the Indo Iranian, Italic, and Celtic worlds, one of the most striking is that which subsists in the Sanskrit *śrad dadhāmi*, *śraddhā-*, and so on; in the Avestic *zrazdā-*, and so on; in the Latin *crēdo*; in the Old Irish *cretim*, and in the Old Welsh *credaf*. It is also one of the most intensively studied both analytically and comparatively. The Vedic concept of *śraddhā* has been explored by Sylvain Lévi in *La Doctrine du sacrifice dans les Brāhmanas*, 1898, p. 108ff., and its Iranian forms explained by Antoine Meillet in *Mem. de la Soc. de Linguist.*, XVIII, 1913, p. 60ff. The undoubtedly related Celtic words have been dealt with by M. Vendryes in *Revue Celtique*, XLIV, 1927, p. 90ff. While M. Ernout, in *Mélanges Sylvain Lévi*, 1911, p. 85ff. (eliminating the link with Romance forms of "heart") and A. Meillet, in *Mem. de la Soc. de Ling.*, XXII, 1922, (*op. cit.*) have provided the theory of the Latin forms and of the family as a whole.[4]

V. Magic and religion

Sylvain Lévi's work is of particular importance. Using a great number of texts, he has shown that the word *śraddhā*, at first understood rather too hastily as "faith" in the Christian sense of the word, or at least as "trust," in fact denotes something slightly different in the consciousness of the ritual-minded Indians. Correctly understood, it means at most something akin to the trust that a good workman has in his tools and technique. It would be more correct, Lévi says, to place *śraddhā* on the level of magic than on that of religion, and to understand it as denoting the state of mind of a sacrificer who knows how to perform his office correctly, and who also knows that his sacrifice, if performed in accordance with the rules, must produce its effect. Needless to say, such an interpretation is to be viewed within a more general system that, as the ritualistic literature suggests or states in many places, is based on the dogma of the omnipotence of sacrifice. Within this system, sacrifice with its code and its attendants, ultimately emerges, above and beyond the gods, as the sole motive force in this or any other world.

Lévi's *La Doctrine du Sacrifice dans les Brāhmanas* is an admirable book and would still be so if written today – despite the plethora of indexes and catalogues we now have as opposed to the research required in 1896–1897. At that time, the new sociology, in search of clear-cut notions, was striving not only to distinguish between magic and religion but also to define a series of precise levels for each religious phenomenon such as, in this case, sacrifice. The pupil always collaborates with the master, and this was undoubtedly the case with Marcel Mauss and Sylvain Lévi, as the lectures from which Lévi's book emerged were intended to help the young sociologist in his work. And I don't think that I, in my turn, am being disloyal to Mauss if I observe that he speaks not only much more frequently of "magico-religious" facts than of magical facts, on the one hand, and of religious ones on the other, but also that one of his principal concerns is to show the complexity of each phenomenon, and the tendency of each to defy definition and to exist simultaneously on many different levels. Such, certainly is the natural consequence of the article he published in 1899 ("Essai sur la nature et la fonction sociale du sacrifice," *Année Sociologique*, II) and in 1904 ("Origine des pouvoirs magiques dans les sociétés australiennes," 13th *Annuaire de l'École des Hautes Études, Sciences Religieuses*, pp. 1–55).[5] In the human sciences one can, with some precision, define points of view or the directions one's exploration of particular material is to take; but, excluding exceptional cases, the material itself evades simple classification and disconcerts the observer with its metamorphoses. Perhaps we should keep this in mind when evaluating the account that Sylvain Lévi drew up in his day.

Not that the "doctrine of sacrifice" in the *Brāhmaṇa* is in any way different from that which Lévi derived from them: the primacy, the automatism, the blind infallibility of sacrifice that he alleges are indeed established in formulas too clear to dispute. But we ought not to draw conclusions from a very specialized literature, the work of the technicians of sacrifice, and apply them to the whole of contemporary life. And one must not be too quick, even within that literature itself, to regard as a survival, as a mark of "primitive mentality," the more magical than religious form taken on by the relations between man and the mystic forces he sets in motion.

The religion of the Vedic era is rich in individualized gods, most inherited from the Indo-Iranian community, some from the Indo-European community. Possessed of precise personal powers, sometimes the nucleus of proliferating mythological cycles, these gods are not "literary ornaments." They are, both for one another and for man, intelligent, strong, passionate, active partners. And this is hard to reconcile with an absolute automatism of gestures and formulas. We must at least retain as a possibility the hypothesis that the guild of officiants systematically increased the constraining power of sacrifice. Far from being a survival, such a system could have been developed at the expense of the older

Indo-Iranian gods' erstwhile freedom. So, the notion of *śraddhā*, we doubtless should accept that it was already animated by movements of "piety," "devotion," "faith," even at a time when the ritualists were reducing it to nothing more than an almost purely technical attitude within an almost impersonal form of worship. A religious concept is rarely to be defined by a *point*, but more often by an *interval*, by a zone in which variable movements, unstable relationships, are established between two poles. Where does incantation end? Where does prayer begin?

Whatever the nuance of meaning we fasten upon for thc Indian *śraddhā*, however, at whatever level we place this "trust," it is certain that the prehistoric Latin **credes* was capable of expressing analogous values. Numa, in short, is not only the specialized devotee of Fides as "good faith" among men, as a guarantee of human contracts; he also practices a sacrificial *fides*, the same as the *śraddhā*, and one that similarly allows the observer a margin of interpretation between the certainty of the magician and the faith of the priest.

VI. The sacrifices of Manu and of Numa

At this point, we should note the remarkable agreement between the Indian and Roman traditions concerning Numa and Manu, the two fabled legislators and sacrificers: Numa is the true hero of *fides*, just as Manu is the hero of *śraddhā*.

The Indian traditions relating to Manu's *śraddhā* are well known. Sylvain Lévi, in his *Doctrine du Sacrifice* (pp. 115–121), has given an excellent account of them; indeed, this one sentence sums them up well: "Manu has a mania for sacrifice just as the saints of Buddhism have a mania for devotion."[6] The most famous of the stories depicts Manu, enslaved as he is to *śraddhā*, yielding up everything of value he possesses to the two "Asura brahmans," to the demonic sacrificers Tṛṣta and Varūtri. To demand something from him all they need do is say the words, *Mano yaiva vai śraddhā-devo'si* ("Manu, you are a sacrificer, your god is *śraddhā*"). His jars, the sound of which alone could annihilate the Asura; then his bull, whose bellowing replaced the sound of the jars; and, in the end, even his wife, the Manavi, whose speech had acquired that murderous gift – Manu hands them all over, without a moment's hesitation, to be destroyed, sacrificed by the priests who demand them with those words. When Indra, in his turn, wishing at least to save the Manavi, presents himself to Manu in the form of a brahman and announces, using the same formula, that he wishes to make a sacrifice of the two "Asura brahmans," Manu hands them over without any difficulty and, in one variant (*Kāthaka Brāhmaṇa*, II, 30, 1),[7] the two brahmans are actually immolated: Indra beheads them with the water of the sacrifice, and from their blood spring two plants that dry up in the rain. And the god utters the climactic words which in fact justify Manu's conduct: *yatkāma etām ālabdhāḥ, sa te kāmaḥ samṛdhyatām* ("the desire you had in taking your wife to sacrifice her, let that desire be granted you") (*Maitrāyaṇī Saṁhitā*, IV, 8, 1; with many parallel texts).

As for Numa, Plutarch (*Numa*, 15; there is also an allusion to this behavior of Numa's in Plutarch's short treatise, *On the Fortune of the Romans*) summarizes one legend, no doubt residual from a more abundant tradition relating to the king's piety, in which this Roman is truly *śraddhadevaḥ*): "It is said that he had hung his hopes so exclusively upon the divine that, one day when someone came to tell him that the enemy was drawing near, he laughed and said: 'And I do sacrifice.' Αὐτὸν δὲ τὸν Νομᾶν οὕτω φασὶν εἰς τὸ θεῖον ἀνηρτῆσθαι ταῖς ἐλπίσιν, ὥστε καὶ προσαγγελίας αὐτῷ ποτε γενομένης ὡς ἐπέρχονται πολέμιοι, [μειδιᾶσαι] καὶ εἰπεῖν· "Ἐγὼ δὲ θύω." The feeling indicated in that strong expression, εἰς τὸ θεῖον ἀνηρτῆσθαι ταῖς ἐλπίσιν (with the neuter τὸ θεῖον), and the behavior dictated by this primacy accorded to the act of θεῖον, would provide an excellent definition of "the doctrine of sacrifice in the *Brāhmaṇa*": Manu would have acted in exactly the same way.

And the Roman tradition might, in its turn, shed light on Indian custom. If Numa's "faith" operates in this way, in a double domain, one almost mystic, the other wholly legal, it is because in Rome acts of worship and sacrifice are, first and foremost, acts of trade, an execution of contracts of exchange between man and divinity. Their automatic nature – which inspires Numa with his confidence – is less magical than juridical. The acts performed have the constraining force of a pact, at least that implicit kind of pact explored by Marcel Mauss in his *The Gift: Forms and Function of Exchange in Archaic Societies* and which is so well expressed in the traditional formula, *do ut des*: "I give that you may give."[vi] And in fact this notion of a divine "trade" is no less essential

vi [Marcel Mauss], "Essai sur le don, forme archaïque de l'echange," *Année Sociologique*, Nouv. serie, I, 1925, [pp. 30–187], pp. 128–134, 140–152. [Note moved from text. The references are to Chapter III, sections I and II on Roman Law and Hindu Law. The text is reprinted in *Sociologie et anthropologie* (Paris: Presses Universitaires de France, 1950), pp. 143–279,

to the Indian theory of sacrifice (Marcel Mauss has drawn attention to the importance of the formula *dadāmi te, dehi me*, "I give to you, give to me!"). We frequently encounter scenes in which a god evaluates the greater or lesser worth of a proposed offering, or compares the values of two possible victims, and so on. In one famous story, Varuṇa agrees that the young brahman Śunaḥśepa shall take the place of the king's son as the sacrificial victim, "because a brahman is more than a *kṣatriya*." Even the legend summarized above, in which Manu is on the brink of slaying his wife, ends in haggling, with one odd difference: it is Manu who wishes to maintain the assessed initial value, and the god who imposes the "discount." But Manu, deprived of his victim by the merciful intervention of the god, does not intend that his rights be infringed: "Finish my sacrifice," he says to Indra, "let my sacrifice not be set at nought!" And the god generously indemnifies him, in a way: "The desire you had in taking your wife for your victim, let that desire be granted you; *but let that woman be!*" (Sylvain Lévi, *op. cit.*, p. 119).

How can this fail to bring to mind the famous scene in which the pious, ultra-correct Numa bargains with Jupiter to obtain immunity from his thunderbolts, without having to make a human sacrifice – even though, in this case, the roles run more true to form? Here it is the god (a sovereign god, it is true, not a military god, as is Indra) who is exacting, and the king who plays the "bazaar trader," as they would say in the East; who, in other words, argues and barters, who uses his wiles without actually cheating, and yet manages to cheat anyway. At first, Jupiter demands "heads." "Of onions" Numa quickly accedes; "No, of men," the god insists. "I'll give you hair as well, then," the king sidesteps. "No, I want living beings," Jupiter says. "Then I'll throw in some small fish!" Numa concludes. Disarmed, the terrible sovereign of heaven agrees, and immunity from his thunderbolts was obtained from then on at very little cost (Plutarch, *Numa*, 15; Ovid, *Fastes*, III, 339ff.).[8]

Numa's religious "faith" and Manu's *śraddhā* thus share the same domain, rest on the same assurance, are susceptible to the same kinds of transactions. Both combine with the interests of the sacrificer or, rather,

---

here pp. 229–34, 240–50. For the English translation of these passages see *The Gift: Forms and Function of Exchange in Archaic Societies*, trans. W.D. Halls (London: Routledge, 1990), pp. 61–64, 70–77 or *The Gift: Expanded edition*, trans. Jane I. Guyer (Chicago: HAU), 2016, pp. 146–51, 158–69. The original English translation gives the pages 6–16, which makes no sense.]

reconcile his interests, openly and honestly, with those of the god. The important, the irreplaceable thing for the man is to have a true will to sacrifice, and to sacrifice punctiliously whatever has been decided on beforehand by common accord. However, the quantity and quality of the sacrificial material is an affair for negotiation between the parties.

***

It is now time to introduce other elements. All I wished to establish is that, like Romulus and Numa, the two gods peculiar to them, Jupiter Stator (or Feretrius) and Fides stand in an antithetical opposition (whether juridical or religious), to one another. The gods, like the kings, stand opposed as the "Terrible" and the "Ordered," the "Violent" and the "Correct," the "Magician" and the "Jurist," the Lupercus and the flamen. They also stand opposed like Varuṇa and Mitra, with whom there is an even more exact correspondence with the Roman couple – with a masculine form of *Fides* – Jupiter and Dius Fidius.

CHAPTER IV

Jupiter and Fides

I. The dialectical nature of Indian social hierarchy

The Indians' social hierarchy, like the system of ideas that sustains it, is linear in appearance only. In reality it is a sequence, rather Hegelian in character, in which a thesis summons an antithesis then combines with it in a synthesis that becomes in turn a further thesis, thus providing fresh material enabling the process to continue. For example, *brāhmna*, *kṣatriya* and *vaiśya* (priest, warrior and herdsman-cultivator) are not to be numbered "one, two, three." The *brāhmna* is defined at the outset in opposition to the *kṣatriya*; then the two are reconciled and collaborate in a new notion, that of "power" (*ubhe virye*, "the two forces," is the eloquent dual expression in some texts), which is then immediately defined in opposition to *vaiśya* (e.g., Manu, IX, 327), an opposition itself resolved by a synthesis into the *dvija*, "the twice-born," which is then confronted by the appearance of the *śūdra*.

Perhaps it will be possible to pursue the exploration of this classification of the world further at a later stage. I mention it here only to observe it at its source or, rather, at its apparent source, since even the "first echelon" is itself already a synthesis. Perhaps it would be more accurate, at least for very early times (before the rising fortune that expanded the term *Brāhmaṇa* to cover an entire caste), to begin with the *rāj-brahman* couple. Yet even in this historical situation we are able to observe, at a time when brahmanic imperialism is at its height, that the elements and formulation of that synthesis remain perceptible if we consider not the brahmans themselves, but the gods who stand behind them, the gods who govern from on high the great business of the brahmans on earth, which is sacrifice, and who also happen to be the sovereign gods, the cosmic projection of earthly sovereignty: Mitra and Varuṇa.

The coupling is an extremely ancient one. These two gods appear as a couple and in that order, heading the list of Aryan gods called upon to guarantee a Hittite-Mitanian (Hurrite) treaty[1] in the 14th century B.C. (*mi-id-ra-as-sil u-ru-wa-na-as-si-el*: Forrer, *Zeitsch. d. deutsch. morg. Gesell.*, 76, N.F., I, 1922, p. 250ff.).[i] There is also a fairly frequent Avestic formula, Mithra-Ahura, which is generally accepted to be an inheritance from the Indo-Iranian past.[ii] This associates Mithra with an Ahura who is not yet the Ahura-Mazdāh of historical times, but who is linked to the Asura-type figure of the Vedic hymns, Varuṇa. In the *Ṛg Veda*, as in the *Atharva Veda*, Mitra is inseparable from Varuṇa; and, with one exception, all the *Ṛg Veda* hymns dedicated to Mitra are also dedicated to Varuṇa. Moreover, their language makes the couple's interdependence startlingly plain, since it couples the two divinities in various ways by using dual formations: *Mitrā* is "Mitra and Varuṇa," as is, less elliptically, the reduplicated dual form, *Mitrā-Varuṇā* (with single or dual inflection: *Mitrābhyām Varuṇābhyām* or *Mitrā-Varuṇābhyām*), or the simple dual, with two stresses or one, *Mitrá-Váruṇā*, *Mitra-váruṇā*.[iii]

---

i For this list and the functional value of each of the gods that appears on it, see *JMQ III*, pp. 19–55, and my article to appear in the second section of the *Studia Linguistica* of Lund (1948): "Mitra, Varuṇa, Indra, and les Nasatya comme patrons des trois fonctions cosmiques et sociales." [Note added to second edition. *Studia Linguistica* 1 (–3), 1947, 121–29. The full reference is E. Forrer, "Die Inschriften und Sprachen des Hatti-Reiches," *Zeitschrift der Deutschen Morgenlandischen Gesellschaft* 76, 1922: 172–269.]

ii See Benveniste-Renou, *Vṛtra and Vṛθragna*, 1934, p. 46, and J. Duchesne Guillemin, *Ahura-Miθra*, in *Mélanges F. Cumont*, 1936, II, p. 683ff. [Note moved from text. The reference to Duchesne Guillemin is added to the second edition. The full references are to Émile Benveniste and L. Renou, *Vṛtra et Vṛθragna. Étude de mythologie indo-iranienne*, Cahiers de la Société asiatique (Paris: Imprimerie Nationale, 1934); and J. Duchesne-Guillemin, "Ahura-Mithra" in *Mélanges Franz Cumont, Annuaire de l'Institut de philologie et d'histoire orientales et slaves* (Bruxelles, 1936), Vol. II, pp. 683–5.]

iii Cf. Gauthiot, *Du nombre duel, Festschrift V. Thomsen*, 1912, p. 128ff. [Note moved from text. The full reference is Robert Gauthiot, "Du

And, again, the same holds true for this initial couple as for the later couples *Brāhmaṇa-kṣatriya, ubhe vīrye-vaiśya* and *dvija-sūdra*: viewed in relation to the rest of the universe, to the other gods (Indra, say), Mitra and Varuṇa form a unit, seem to occupy the same domain (sovereignty), and are, to some extent, synonymous. This collaboration is made possible, however, only by a congenital opposition: Varuṇa is also to be defined as the contrary of Mitra. The authors of the *Brāhmna* were fully aware of this fundamental fact, and we have only to follow them. We also have only to follow [Abel] Bergaigne, since on this point, as on so many others, his account (*Religion Vedique*, 3 vols., Paris, 1878–1883)[2] is still the most useful. If we cannot now maintain his definitions without some amendments, it is only because sociology has progressed, and because certain notions that seemed simple to him have since been revealed as fairly complex; as, for example, that of "friend."

II. Mitra: Contract and friendship

By interpreting Mitra as "friend" (and a section of the Indian tradition does so) and by linking Varuṇa to the root *var-* ("to cover, to envelop, to bind") and also to *Vṛtra* (the "bad" or "wicked" *Vṛtra*), Bergaigne was led to formulate the opposition of the two gods as being that of "the terrible" and "the friend," while both, as he happily expresses it, are "sovereigns."

Varuṇa is assuredly "the terrible"; as a result of his magic, of his *māyā* as an *asura*, thanks to which, omnipresent as he is, he has the power of immediate prehension and action everywhere and over everything, and thanks to which he also creates and modifies forms and makes the "laws of nature" as well as their "exceptions." In my own analysis, in which I compare him with the no less terrible, tyrannical and unbridled Uranos, I had many opportunities to illustrate this characteristic of the god. In particular, he has an unfortunate affinity with human sacrifice, both ritually and mythically.

As for Mitra, the word "friend" is clearly insufficient. Yet it is less so today than it appeared in 1907, when Antoine Meillet, in a classic article, put forward his definition of "the Indo-Iranian god Mitra" as the "contract" personified (*Journal Asiatique*, 10th series, vol. X, pp.

---

nombre duel," *Festschrift Vilhelm Thomsen* (Leipzig: Otto Harrassowitz, 1912), pp. 127–33.]

143–159).[3] Those few pages are a milestone in the history of our field, since for the first time linguistics and sociology worked together with assurance. But since 1907 the theory of the contract has progressed in its turn with the result that the notions of legal contract and emotional friendship, which seemed scarcely reconcilable to Meillet, now appear as no more than two reductions, two divergent and more clearly defined meanings, both fairly recent, derived and now detached from an earlier "complex" that in fact, has left its vestiges still very much alive not only in India and Iran but even in our own civilizations, as is evidenced by such proverbs as "gifts foster friendship."

Meillet's interpretation was disputed by mythologists faithful to the naturalism of Max Müller, and also by philologists with mistaken notions as to the limits of their jurisdiction. Nonetheless, it is unavoidable as far as Iran is concerned, as a reading of the *Yast* of *Mithra* with an open mind will make clear. As for India, it would be a waste of time attempting to dispute the fact that *mitra* in the *Ṛg Veda* appears to be something quite different from "contract," and that the meaning of "friend" is dominant throughout. But the difference is illusory. It exists only insofar as one conceives of friendship as something modern and romantic, and of the contract as something Latin and, as it were, notarial. One has only to recall the research undertaken in France and elsewhere in response to the discovery of that very widespread phenomenon now termed, using a noun taken from the American Indians of British Columbia, the *potlatch*; one has only to re-read Davy's *La Foi jurée, étude sociologique du problème du contrat, la formation du lien contractuel* (Paris, 1922),[4] and Mauss's book *The Gift*; whereupon the two semantic poles between which India and Iran seem to have stretched the prehistoric **mitra-* begin to seem much less far apart. It becomes apparent that this word, formed with an instrumental suffix or an agent-suffix on the root **mei-* ("to exchange"), this word to which we find so many others related throughout the Indo-European territory – words with nuances of meaning as diverse as Sanskrit *mayate* ("he exchanges"), Latin *mūnus* ("gift, service performed, obligation, duty") and *commūnis*, Old Slavonic *mêna* ("change, exchange, contract") and *mirū* ("peace, cosmos"), and so on – this word **mitra-* must have originally denoted the means or the agent of operations of the *potlatch* type – in other words, of "obligatory exchanges of gifts." Evolving from customs in general, and doubtless as a result of contact with very early civilizations which possessed codes, the meaning of the word naturally narrowed to the more precise one of "contract," as occurred in Iran. On the other hand, however, the state the potlatch inevitably creates between its participants, of peace, of order, of collaboration, with alternating rights and duties, is indeed a beginning of "friendship," particularly among the semi-civilized, where a simple absence of relations is already equivalent to hostility: India merely developed this germ of meaning in terms of human feelings, without losing sight of its ancient economic and social origins.

As epigraph to his text on the gift, Mauss quotes several stanzas from the *Hâvamâl*,[5] an Eddic poem that describes, in the form of maxims, some of the important motivating forces underlying early Scandinavian societies. Readers will readily appreciate how close and interdependent the notions of "regularized exchanges" and "friendship" are in this text:

> 39. I have never found a man so generous and so hospitable that he would not receive a present nor a man so liberal with his possessions that to receive in return was displeasing to him…
> 41. Friends should please one another with weapons and garments; everyone knows it for himself, that those who give one another gifts are friends for longest (*vidhrgefendr erusk lengst vinir*), if things turn out well.
> 42. One should be a friend to one's friend and give back gift for gift (*vin sînum skalmadhr vinr vesa, ok gjalda gjöf vidh gjöf*); one should earn laughter for laughter and trickery for lying.
> 44. You know it yourself, that if you have a friend in whom you trust, and if you wish a long-standing friendship, you must mingle your soul with his, exchange gifts and visit him often… (*veiztu, ef thû yin âtt thanns thû vel truit, ok vildu of hânum gôtt geta, gedhi skaltu vidh thann blanda ok gjöfum skipta, fara at finna opt*).
> 46. Gifts given should be like those received…[6]

One ought really to explore in greater depth, throughout the Germanic world, the notions expressed in these lines by the verbs *trûa* ("to trust in, to believe")[7] and *gjalda* ("to pay back, to expiate"). I shall limit myself here, however, to pointing out that the Scandinavian noun for "friend," *vinr* (Swedish *vän*; cf. Old High German *wini*), not only is related to the Irish noun for "family," *fine*, which is defined by precise and varied degrees of interdependent responsibility (hence the Old Irish *an-fine*, for "enemy," is formed as the Old Icelandic *ô-vinr*, which has the same meaning), but is doubtless also related to the first element of Latin, *vindex* (formed as *iudex* is on *ius*), which expresses essentially a legal notion, the *vindex* being, in fact, "the bailbond provided by the defendant, who replaces it with his person before the court and declares himself ready to submit to the consequences of the legal process" (Ernout and Meillet, *Dictionnaire etymologique latin*).[8] Thus, to judge from the noun that denotes him, the Swedish "friend" (and we know to what peaks of poetry, what depths of delicacy, friendship can attain in that favored land), the *vän*, emerged over the centuries from an economic complex in which self-interest and personal "investment" played a role still present in early medieval Scandinavia, given the evidence accorded us by the *Hâvamâl*, and also, no doubt, from a legal complex in which the "vendetta" must have played an important part, since the related Irish and Latin words place it in the foreground. Similarly, again, Irish *cairde* (literally, "friendship," cf. Latin *carus*, etc.) denotes any treaty concluded between two clans, from a simple armistice to the most far-reaching agreements (see the extensive treatment of this in Thurneysen's commentary on the *False Judgements of Caratnia*, section 17, *Zeitsch. f celtische Philologie*, XV, 1925, p. 326ff.).[9] *Mutatis mutandis*, the relations between Sanskrit *mitraḥ* ("friend," and also, in post-Vedic, *mitram*, in the neuter, "friend, ally") and Avestic *mithra*, "contract," must be of the same sort.

I shall explore in more detail some of the juridical functions of the Indo-Iranian **Mitra*. Here it is sufficient to have pointed them out. But it should also be noted immediately that they constitute only one part of Mitra's activity as a whole; and that activity, as the earliest Indian ritualists were still aware, was defined at all points by reference, by opposition, to Varuṇa.

III. Mitra, antithesis of Varuṇa[iv]

Noting in his *Doctrine du Sacrifice*... (p. 153) a passage from the *Śatapatha Brāhmaṇa* (IV, 1, 4, 1) in which Mitra and Varuṇa are contrasted as intelligence and will, then as decision and act, and also another passage from the same *Brāhmaṇa* (II, 4, 4, 18) in which the contrast between them is likened to that between the waning and the waxing moon, Sylvain Lévi observes: "The disparity between these interpretations

iv I am delighted to be in agreement here, in essence and in many details, with Mr. A. K. [Ananda Kentish] Coomaraswamy, in his fine book, *Spiritual Authority and Temporal Power in the Indian Theory of Government* (American Oriental Soc[iety]., New Haven, 1942) [note added to second edition].

proves that they are the product of imagination." Yes, if one sticks to the letter of the texts; no if one takes into account their spirit. Leaving aside the moon, the other two formulas link up with many others,[v] and this collection of "coupled notions" provides an excellent definition of two different ways of regarding and directing the world. When it is said, for example, that Mitra is the day and Varuṇa the night; that Mitra is the right and Varuṇa the left (in accordance with the view of the right as the *strong* or *just* side); that Mitra takes (in order to reward) "that which has been well sacrificed" and Varuṇa takes (in order to chastise) "that which is badly sacrificed"; that this world is Mitra and the other world Varuṇa; that to Mitra belongs, for example, all that breaks of itself and to Varuṇa that which is cut with an axe; to Mitra the unchurned butter,[10] to Varuṇa the churned butter; to Mitra that which is cooked with steam and to Varuṇa that which is roasted over flame; to Mitra milk, to Varuṇa soma, the intoxicating drink; that Mitra is the essence of the brahmans and Varuṇa the essence of the *rājanya* or *kṣatriya* – all these twinned expressions define homologous points on the two levels we have learned to recognize through Numa and Romulus. Mitra is the sovereign under his reasoning aspect, luminous, ordered, calm, benevolent, priestly; Varuṇa is the sovereign under his attacking aspect, dark, inspired, violent, terrible, warlike. Some of these expressions have been subjected to much commentary, in particular those that assimilated "this world" to Mitra and "the other world" to Varuṇa, and are easily understood in this context. We have already seen (see above pp. 52–53/22–23) that Numa and Romulus, like the flamen and the Lupercus and the religious systems they institute or express (one perpetual and public, the other fleeting and mysterious), and like the brahman and the Gandharva, too, also stand in opposition to one another as the purely "earthly" does to the "supernatural," as this world does to the other. "Romulus was born of the gods and I am a mere man," Numa says when justifying his hesitation at accepting the *rēgnum*; and the Gandharva normally live in a mysterious world of their own, beyond the darkness into which, according to one of the hymns of the *Ṛg-Veda*, Indra smote the (singular) Gandharva for the greater good of the brahman. Let us not forget that Varuṇa is said elsewhere to have the Gandharva as his people, and that in his legend the Gandharva intervene at a tragic moment (see above, p. 45/17) to restore

---

v Which we must take care not to dissociate – as has been done recently – and to make use of separately, outside the system that gives them their meaning [note added to second edition].

his failed virility with a magic herb, just as the first Luperci, wielding their goatskin whips, put an end to the sterility of the women Romulus had abducted.

Mitra as brahman, Varuṇa as king of the Gandharva: we could hardly have wished for a more suggestive formula.

IV. Jupiter and Dius Fidius

There are reasons for thinking that the "order of the gods" and the "order of the flamines," which in Rome record the ancient Indo-European tripartite division of social functions, is no more linear than the brahmanic hierarchy. In the triad of gods, Jupiter and Mars are homogeneous, but Quirinus is not. Whereas Jupiter and Mars are strongly characterized and autonomous, Quirinus alone poses problems: sometimes seen as akin to Mars (from whom he nevertheless remains essentially distinct), sometimes to Romulus (which draws him rather into the ambit of Jupiter), he appears more as "hero" than "god." Whereas *Iupiter (*dyeu-)* and Mars (*Mauort-*: Sanskrit *Marut-aḥ*, name of the warrior-god of Indra's warrior band) have certain or probable Indo-European etymologies, *Quirinus* can be explained only in accordance with an Italic origin (cf. *curia*, *quirites*);[11] and the same is true of Vofionus, who occupies the place of the Roman Quirinus, after a well-established Jupiter and Mars, in the corresponding triad of the Umbrians.[vi] When a triad with feminine preponderance came to replace the older masculine triad, the sovereign Jupiter and Juno, goddess of the *iuniores*, emerged quite clearly as a "couple" in our sense of the word (and not merely in imitation of Zeus and Hera), contrasting with a third term, *Minerva*, the goddess of workers. Lastly, if we consider the three major flamines, the Quirinalis, like his god, cuts a poor figure beside the Dialis and the Martialis, who are moreover linked (to judge by a number of inevitably lacunary indications) by a strict "statute" of similar interdicts. In short, given the uncertainties and dilutions only to be expected from the fact that this double *ordo* had lost almost all interest for the late Republic, it seems that vestiges still remained from a time when the composition of these triads of gods and

vi On Vofionus as the exact synonym of *Quirinus*, see Benveniste, *Rev. de l'Hist. des Rel.,* CXXIX, 1945, p. 8ff. [Note added to second edition. Émile Benveniste, "Symbolisme social dans les cultes gréco-italiques," *Revue de l'Histoire des religions* 129, 1945: 5–16.]

priests was a matter not of simple enumeration but of deduction by successively constructed couples.[12]

At the summit of the hierarchy there stands one "couple" whose existence is well attested, not only by the fact that the *flāmen dialis* appears, both by his activity and by the legend of his institution, as the *rex*'s double, but by the very complexity of the theological province to which the word *dialis* refers. In historical times, *flāmen dialis* and *flāmen Iovis* were accepted as being equivalent terms. But Festus (in his *De significatione verborum*), when describing the *ordo sacerdotum*, glosses *flāmen dialis* with *universi mundi sacerdos, qui appellatur dium*. And this substantive, *dium*, provides us with an opportune reminder that there survived a divinity alongside Jupiter, certainly a very ancient one, who in the historical era seems no longer to be anything more than an "aspect" of Jupiter: Dius Fidius. And Dius Fidius, moreover, enshrines *fides* within his very name.

Not that it is of any great importance here whether, fundamentally, Dius Fidius was an "aspect" of Jupiter or whether he had once been an autonomous divinity later absorbed by Jupiter, since these are mere historical contingencies or, possibly, a simple question of vocabulary. What does count is the articulation of the divine concepts. And the fact is that Dius Fidius, whether alongside Jupiter or as a mere aspect of Jupiter, certainly stands in opposition to certain other "aspects" of the same god.

V. Dius Fidius, the antithesis of Jupiter Summanus

Lightning, when there are no nice distinctions to be made, generally belongs to Jupiter. But when such distinctions become necessary, daytime lightning is called *fulgur dium* and is understood to come from Dius Fidius (alias *Semo Sancus*) or from Jupiter (when his name is understood according to the strict etymological value expressed by the root **deiw-*); nocturnal lightning is termed *fulgur submanum* (or *summanum*) and is understood to come from a god who is called either *Iupiter Summanus* or simply *Summanus*, and for whom the question of his relations with Jupiter ("aspect" or "absorption") poses itself in the same terms, and has the same lack of importance, as in the case of Dius Fidius.

Weinstock's article on Summanus in the Pauly-Wissowa *Encyclopédie* (1932) sets forth all the documentary evidence very clearly; but its conclusions are distorted, in my view, by unwarranted deduction and also by a mistaken assumption.[13] The unwarranted deduction bears upon the "Etruscan" origin of the god, for which Weinstock, opposing Thulin, finds what he takes to be his proof in Pliny's *Natural History*, II, 53 (*Tuscorum litterae novem deos emittere fulmina existimant, eaque esse undecim generum; Iovem enim trina iaculari. Romani duo tantum ex iis servavere, diurna attribuentes Iovi, nocturna Summano*: "The Tuscan writers hold the view that there are nine gods who send thunderbolts, and that these are of eleven kinds; because Jupiter hurls three varieties only, two of these deities have been retained by the Romans, who attribute thunderbolts in daytime to Jupiter and those in the night to Summanus").[14] However, we can not conclude from this text, as Weinstock does, that Summanus was "captured" from the Etruscans by the Romans. The comparison between the two systems is typological, and the word *servavere* no more signifies a borrowing in the case of Summanus than in the case of Jupiter, to whom he stands in opposition. Pliny is simply recording the fact that the Roman system does not coincide with the Etruscan system, which, he presumably regards as the more advanced, the more scientific, the more in conformity with reality, and, also, the older; and that, whereas the Etruscans were able to distinguish as many as eleven different kinds of lightning, the Romans have "retained," which is to say "recognize," only a meager distinction between "day lightning" and "night lightning." As for Weinstock's mistaken assumption, this concerns the logical impossibility he experiences in accepting the traditional explanation of the name Summanus (from *sub* and *mane*) and, consequently, its Latin derivation. The transition from "*morgens*" or "*gegen, um, kurz vor Morgen*" to "*nachts*" seems inconceivable to him. "It would be strange," he writes, "if we were forced to look for the word *mane* ("morning") in the name of a god of the night." But we must always be wary of things that seem, to our modern minds, logically impossible or strange. It so happens that another Indo-European language, Armenian, denotes night – the whole of the night, and without any possibility of dispute – by the periphrasis "until dawn" (*c'ayg*, i.e., *c'*- "until," and *ayg*, "dawn")[vii] and, in parallel, the day – the whole day, and even in modern speech, from "noon" – by the periphrasis "until evening" (*c'erek*, i.e., *c'* "until," and *erek* "evening"). The use of "Summanus" to

vii Could this throw light on the enigmatic Irish *adaig (*ad-aig*?) for "night"? But where does the final phoneme come from? [Note added to second edition.]

denote the nocturnal lightning-hurler is no more astonishing, and there is no reason to suspect its latinity.

VI. Day and night

Jupiter as Dius Fidius and Jupiter as Summanus, or, at some earlier time, an autonomous, heavenly divinity Dius Fidius and an autonomous, heavenly divinity Summanus, may thus be distinguished as the owner of the day and the owner of the night. We have already seen – and J. Muir's *Original Sanskrit Texts* (V, 1870, p. 58ff.)[15] had already highlighted this before Bergaigne – that such is also the naturalist form taken by the opposition of Mitra and Varuṇa: "the day is of Mitra, such is the tradition… and also the night is of Varuṇa" (*Maitram vai ahar iti śruteḥ... śrūyāte ca vāruṇi rātrir iti*) Sāyana says in his commentary on *Ṛg Veda*, I, 89, 3, borrowing the terms of the *Taittirīya Brāhmaṇa* (I, 7, 10, 1). The *Taittirīya Saṁhitā* (VI, 4, 8) states the same fact in cosmogonic terms: "This world had neither day nor night, it was (in this respect) nondistinguished; the gods said to the couple Mitra-Varuṇa (note the dual form *mitravaruṇau*) 'Make a separation!'… Mitra produced the day, Varuṇa the night" (*Mitro'har ajanayad Varuṇo rātrim*). Upon these formal statements by the ritualists, Bergaigne (*Religion védique*, III, p. 117) based his reflections which, because of their lucidity, merit lengthy consideration and which, moreover, ought to be extended to all the antithetical features of these two gods:[viii] "I propose to show that the distinction made here was already present in the minds of the Vedic poets, albeit without possessing any absolute nature for them. Mitra and Varuṇa, linked to form a couple, are both of them gods of the day and gods of the night, and Varuṇa, even alone, retains a luminous side. But he also has a dark side, and when compared with Mitra it is indisputably this dark side that stands out in contrast to the predominantly luminous nature of his companion." Bergaigne then justifies this broad statement with a well-ordered list of texts, supported (p. 122n.) by a quotation from a hymn in the magical Veda (*Atharva-Veda*, IX, 3, 18) addressed

viii These admirable pages should be read in their entirety. I have attempted to develop other suggestions from them in *JMQ III*, p. 107ff. [note added to second edition].

to the *śālā* the hut constructed for sacrifice: "Closed by Varuṇa," it says, "be opened by Mitra!"[ix]

The relations between Jupiter and Dius Fidius are the same. Taken together, their functions coalesce: the oath belongs to Dius Fidius, but also to Jupiter. Similarly, all lightning belongs to Jupiter, though it would be ridiculous to maintain that the Romans essentially sense the night sky in Jupiter. But the standpoint changes when they consider the autonomy of Dius Fidius: from the Jupiter complex there emerges a "nocturnal" power, a Summanus, which enables Dius to define himself, in conformity with his etymology, as "diurnal."

At the sacrificial stake, Mitra, god of day, receives white victims, whereas Varuṇa, god of night, receives black ones (*Taittirīya-Saṁhitā*, II, 1, 7ff., cf. V, 6, 21; *Maitrāyaṇī Saṁhitā*, II, 5, 7) – an eminently natural symbolism.[16] And this symbolism is also found in Rome, where, as we know from an inscription (*Corpus inscr. lat.* VI, 1, 574), the Arvales sacrificed *Summano patri verbeces atros*.[17] Weinstock, in the *Encyclopédie* article cited earlier, sees this as proof that Summanus has nothing to do with Jupiter. "Jupiter never receives black victims," he says, "whereas such victims appear regularly in the worship of the chthonian gods." This, it seems to me, is not a valid argument. In the single case in which Jupiter is specifically described as "nocturnal" or *summanus*, in contrast to the "diurnal" Dius Fidius, it is natural that his victims, like those of Varuṇa (in his role as "nocturnal" divinity) should be black. It is of no consequence that he does not receive black victims in any other function. Or, rather, one cannot conclude from that circumstance anything other than a close link between the color black and the god's nocturnal specification.

We may also note in passing that this opposition of Varuṇa and Mitra, of the violent sovereign god and the just sovereign god, as "night sky" and "day sky," seems to occur also in the case of the two Greek figures, Uranos and Zeus. Zeus is, beyond dispute, the sunlit sky. As for

ix Cf. also *Atharva-Veda*, XIII, 3 (addressed to the sun), stanza 13: "This Agni becomes Varuṇa in the evening; in the morning, rising, he becomes Mitra…" For arguments against an inverse interpretation (Mitra as originally nocturnal) in India and Iran, cf. my arguments in *Rev. de l'Hist. des Rel.*, CXXIII (1941), p. 212ff. [Note added to second edition. The reference is to a review article by Dumézil, "H. S. Nyberg, *Die Religionen des alten Iran…* [and] Geo Windengren, *Hochgottglaube im alten Iran…*," *Revue de l'Histoire des religions* 123, 1941, pp. 206–14.]

Uranos, let us not forget how Hesiod introduces the scene of his castration (*Theogony*, lines 173ff.):[18]

> Thus spoke Kronos and giant Gaia
> rejoiced greatly in her heart
> and took and hid him in a secret ambush
> and put into his hands
> the sickle, edged like teeth, and told him
> all her treachery.
> And huge Uranos came on,
> bringing night with him… (ἦλθε δὲ νύκτ' ἐπάγων μέγας Οὐρανός).

As if that terrible god was not capable of consistency, could not act, could not become accessible, except by night; as if he could not even appear without bringing on the night.

VII. Dius Fidius and Fides

That Dius Fidius was the guarantor of good faith and the recorder of oaths is clear from his name, and, moreover, is attested by much evidence. And the nocturnal Jupiter, to whom he stands in opposition, certainly participates in the magical, disturbing nature of the night. So we have been led back to the opposition – doubtless not merely analogous but in fact identical to this one – of the two "favorite" gods of the grave Numa and the violent Romulus: that of Fides and Jupiter in his terrible aspect (Feretrius or Stator).

Needless to say, in the case of oaths as in that of lightning, Dius Fidius is not in conflict with Jupiter, with "the other Jupiters." We must not forget that these oppositions define complementaries, not incompatibles, and that, viewed in relation to the rest of the world, gods and men alike, this group of divine figures or divine aspects presents a common front. Consequently, although many texts, as well as the expression *me Dius Fidius* and much well-known ritual evidence, prove that the oath is properly the realm of Dius Fidius, the tradition as a whole nonetheless places the oath under the protection of Jupiter or, rather, under that of the deity I would like to term "Jupiter in general." Similarly, in India, even though it is Mitra who carries contractual correctness within his actual name, this does not prevent Varuṇa from occasionally being a god of oaths. It is true that this apparent confusion, in Rome and India alike, might have overlaid an earlier and stricter division of functions. Just as, in the relations between men and gods, Mitra takes "that which is well sacrificed" (that which, therefore, poses no question, since the ordinary mechanism of sacrifice suffices to guarantee its fruit), and Varuṇa "that which is badly sacrificed" (so as to punish the clumsy or ill-intentioned sacrificer), so, in the relations between men, Varuṇa the binder and Jupiter the avenger might have been involved at first with the oath as "avengers," whereas Mitra and Dius Fidius were "recorders" of the oath, or seen as the "drafters" of its terms. This, indeed, is what seems to emerge from the climactic formula of the *fetialis*, when the pact is concluded, in Livy, I, 24: Jupiter is invited to strike down the Romans if they are the first to break the conditions agreed to by both sides (*tu, illo die, populum Romanum sic ferito, et ego hunc porcum hic hodie feriam; tantoque magis ferito, quanto magis potes pollesque*: "on that day do thou, o Jupiter, so strike the Roman people as I shall here, this day, strike this swine; and do thou strike them so much the more, as thou art more able and more powerful").

Whatever the exact truth, however, these balances are unstable, and here again I raise the question of how the perspective can change according to whether one regards the divine couple from an internal viewpoint – each component then seen as defined by its opposition to the other – or from an external one, in which case the attributes specific to each component form a sum total, are combined in opposition to the rest of the universe and, if needs be, even concentrated entirely onto one of the two components, so as to form the complete figure of sovereignty.

VIII. Mitra, Numa and blood sacrifices

Numa is the "correct" sacrificer par excellence, the man of *fides*. Yet he meets his obligations with the least possible cost. Not only does he use cunning to substitute onions, hair and little fish for the human victim demanded by the terrible aspect of Jupiter, he also, Plutarch says, avoids making sacrifices that involve blood, limiting himself to offerings of flour, libations and "the least costly gifts" (*Numa*, 8). In particular, when he institutes the worship of Terminus, he refrains from sacrificing living beings because "enlightened by reason, he understood that the god of boundaries was a guardian of the peace and witness of just dealing, and should therefore be clear from slaughter" (*ibid.*, 16). This is one of the "scruples" that link the Numa of Roman legend with the Pythagorean sect. But we must be wary of supposing that it was artificially transferred from Pythagoras to Numa by moralistic historians, since it is a perfectly fitting characteristic for a typical king-priest hostile to all violence. By abstaining from the shedding of blood, Numa is simply embodying the extreme of his type.[x]

In India, on the divine level, a repugnance of the same kind is attributed to Mitra himself (*Śatapatha Brāhmaṇa*, IV, 1, 4, 8). The text in question is concerned with explaining a detail of the double offering termed *MaitrāVaruṇagraha*, in which milk (for Mitra) is mingled with soma (for Varuṇa): "Soma was Vṛtra; when the gods killed him they said to Mitra: 'Kill him, you also!' He would not, and said: 'I am the friend (*mitra*) of all things…' 'We will exclude you from the sacrifice, then!' Then he said: 'I, too, kill him!' The animals drew away from Mitra, saying: 'He who was a friend, he has become an enemy (*amitra*)…' " So Mitra is opposed, by his nature at least, to blood sacrifice. He is hostile to all violence, even when it is sacred, because he is "friend" – and we need only restore the word's broad meaning in Indo-Iranian prehistory – that is, he is on the side of order, of agreement, of the peaceful settling of difficulties. But Vedic India could not condemn a form of sacrifice that its rituals demanded and that its brahmans, as much as the Roman flamines, practiced constantly. Consequently, Mitra "yielded," rather as the Romans, "after Numa," offering animal victims to the god of boundaries (Plutarch, *Numa*, 16). How could men, how could the gods, live without compromise, without concessions to the conventions?

On the human level, however, the Indian Manu, whose similarity to Numa we began to sketch earlier, and who is the hero of punctiliousness and good faith, of *satyam* and *śraddhā*, does not, to my knowledge, manifest any such repugnance to the shedding of blood. As we have seen, he was prepared to sacrifice his own wife. And yet we must remember that it was on the occasion of this cruel sacrifice, albeit certainly not by Manu's wish, that Indra lastingly, definitively, replaced the efficacy of the human victim with "the merit of intention." We should also bear in mind that extremely anodine oblation which plays an all-important role, sometimes in its own form and sometimes personified as a goddess, in both Manu's sacrificial and legislative activities. I refer, of course, to

x Needless to say, this does not preclude other Latin texts from speaking of *more Numae* in relation to animal sacrifices (*Juvenal*, VIII, 156). [Note added to second edition. The reference is to the *Satires*.]

the *iḍā*, the offering he makes for the first time when the great flood, by "carrying away all creatures," has deprived him of the material for any other form of sacrifice. The *iḍā* consisted solely of water, clarified butter, whey, cream and curds; yet it was by the exclusive and repeated use of this powerful but bloodless offering that he repopulated an entire universe utterly laid waste.

Thus, it is not impossible that, from the very earliest times, one of the two magico-religious "systems" that served to explain and also to govern the universe (Mitra, Manu; Fides-Terminus, Numa) had oriented men's minds toward non-bloody forms of worship, while the other "system" (Varuṇa, Jupiter) had required the sacrifice of living beings, of animals or, occasionally, men. (It would not be too difficult, it seems to me, to reconcile these reflections with those of Jean Przyluski, *Revue de l'Histoire des Religions*, XCVI, 1927, p. 347ff.).[19]

CHAPTER V

Ahura and Mithra

I. *Iḍā* and *Egeria*

For Manu, however, *Iḍā* (or *Iḷā*) is something far more than just an idyllic and powerful offering.

In the first place, it is the equivalent of *śraddhā*, as Sylvain Lévi has rightly stressed (*Doctrine du Sacrifice*..., p. 115): "The ideal type of the *śraddhādeva* in the *Brāhmaṇa* is precisely the ancestor of the human race, the model sacrificer, Manu. The bond that links Manu to *śraddhā* is so close and so strong that the memory of it has been perpetuated throughout the literature: the *Bhāgavata Purāṇa* refers to *śraddhā* as Manu's wife. The *Brāhmaṇa* translate this same idea into a different form: the feminine personage they associate with the Manu legend is *Iḍā*. *Iḍā*, in the language of the ritual, is a solemn offering that consists of four milk byproducts...; but the offering is so simple, and its effect so miraculous, that it deserves to be regarded as the perfect symbol of trust. The *iḍā* is *śraddhā*" (*Śatapatha Brāhmaṇa*, XI, 2, 7, 20: *śraddhā*; the text adds that he who "knows well that *iḍā* is *śraddhā* [*sa yo ha vai śraddhāeḍeti veda*] is assured of every success").

This trait is important. It establishes a link between bloodless offering and Manu's *śraddhā* as close as that which we found, in Rome, between Numa's devotion and the innocence of his offerings: confirmation of what was stated at the end of the previous chapter. But there is more.

Iḍā is transmuted into a sort of demigoddess, and this supernatural being appears to Manu in the desolation that follows the deluge. "Through her" (by which we should understand, in this context, "by following her advice in the matter of sacrifice") he procreated that posterity which is "the posterity of Manu" (*Śatapatha Brāhmaṇa*, I, 8, 1, 10: *tayemāṃ prajātiṃ prajatim prajajñe yeyam Manoh prajātiḥ* – a unique piece of evidence, since we know that the flood story is not found elsewhere in the *Brāhmaṇa*). The text then adds: "Every blessing he called down through her was realized fully and entirely" (*ibid.*, *yām v enayā kāṃcāśisham āśāsta sāsmai sarvā samārdhyata*). In another story, which has several variations, *Iḍā* spies on the Asura (regarded as demonic) to see how they prepare their ritual fire, then on the technique used by the gods, and notes the failure of the first and the success of the second. Then "she said to Manu: I shall set up the fire for you in such a way that you will have abundance in your posterity and in your cattle, both male and female, and you will be made strong in this world, and you will conquer the world of heaven" (*Taittiriya Brāhmaṇa*, I, 1, 4, 7), and she then gives him detailed instructions as to the rites to be performed.[1]

Iḍā is, in short, Manu's inspiration, his teacher, his Egeria. And that last word, used here in its everyday meaning, nevertheless points us toward the analogy between the tradition surrounding *Iḍā*, the demigoddess whose advice made the greatness of Manu, and the well-known tradition of Egeria, the demigoddess to whose counsels Numa owed the largest part of his wisdom, his knowledge, and his successes: a new and important point of contact between the two legislators. After he had lost his wife, Tatia, Numa preferred to live alone in the countryside, walking in the groves and meadows sacred to the gods. "It was said that if he thus fled from men, it was neither from melancholy nor grief. He had tasted the joy of a more august companionship and had been honored with a celestial marriage. The goddess (δαίμονι) Egeria loved him; and it was communion with her that gave him a life of blessedness and a wisdom more than human" (εὐδαίμων ἀνὴρ καὶ τὰ θεῖα πεπνυμένος γέγονεν: Plutarch, *Numa*, 4).

II. Manu, Numa and Manius

And now we are touching on a divinity and a type of legend that must have been common among the Latins, since they are met with not only in Rome but also in Aricia. In fact, there is a nymph called Egeria who resides, as a secondary divinity, in the famous wood of Diana, where the *rex nemorensis* succumbed so frequently to his fate before encountering

Frazer and immortality. And this Arician Egeria seems to be inseparable from a legendary personage who bears the same name and who is, in fact, the actual founder of the cult of Diana, the "dictator of the Latin league," Manius Egerius. This Manius was, above all, famous for his descendants: there sprang so many Manii from him that this became the basis of a proverb which, to tell the truth, even the Romans were no longer certain they fully understood. In the *De significatione verborum* of Festus-Paulus, under Manius, we find: *Manius Egeri(us?)... nemorensem Dianae consecravit, a quo multi et clari viri orti sunt et per multos annos fuerunt* ("he consecrated the grove of Diana; from him many famous men sprang and lived many years"), and under *proverbium: multi Manii Ariciae* ("the many Manii of Aricia") (cf. Otto, *Sprichworter der Römer*, p. 208ff.).[2] One more certain element in this lacunary dossier is that pregnant women offered a sacrifice to "the nymph Egeria" in order to secure an easy delivery (Festus-Paulus, p. 67); so Egeria was as much a mid-wife as Manius Egerius was a procreator.

We do not know from what source Roman legend derived the name "Numa." Unexplained though its origin is, however, we should not be too hasty to say that it was Etruscan. Typologically, Numa is a Roman counterpart of the Indian Manu, the first man and the first king, who peopled the world with "the posterity of Manu" (*Manoh prajātih*), which is to say, with men. Numa, like Manu, is the sacrificer and legislator par excellence, the hero of "trust," the founder of cults; and he is "inspired" by Egeria just as Manu is by *Iḍā*. Given all that, one is tempted to pay particular attention to Manius Egerius of Aricia, a political organizer, the founder of a cult, and, moreover, the ancestor of the proverbial multitude of the Manii. Might we not have here, in the pseudo-historical guise favored by Roman legend, not only the typological equivalent of Manu but even his phonetic near-equivalent? In fact, there is no reason to dissociate this Manius and these Manii from the *manes*, meaning "souls of the dead," or consequently from *Mania*, "mother or grandmother of dead souls" (Festus-Paulus, p. 115); from the *Maniae*, plural of Mania, denoting the manes, in the language of nurses, as larvae used to frighten the children in their care and, by extension, people of an unprepossessing appearance; or, lastly, from the *maniae* or *maniolae*, which are cakes in the shape of men (Festus[-Paulus], *ibid.*). Now, this entire series is evidence that the Latins were familiar with the stem *Mani-*, denoting, either on its own or through its derivatives, "dead men." And it so happens that Manius, the simple masculine form of the *Mania*, who is described as "*manium* (or *maniarum*) *avia materve*," is in fact the father and ancestor of innumerable Manii. More fortunate than the *manes* or *Maniae* of Rome, were these Manii of Aricia literally "men" in general, living men not yet passed into the state of manes? It is possible; and the difference would be slight. We know – from the Indo-Iranian Yama, if not from Manu himself – how closely contiguous or, more precisely, how continuous the notions of "first man" (first king, father of the human race) and "first dead man" (and thus king of the dead) were in practice.

The question remains open to know whether one can phonetically link this Latin **mani-* "(dead) man" and the **manu-* which, apart from the Sanskrit *Manu* (both the name and the common noun for "man"), has given, in particular, the Germanic *Mannus* (*-nn-* from **-nw-* regularly), mythical ancestor of the Germans (Tacitus), the Gothic *manna* "man" (genitive *mans*; stem **manw-*), and the Slavonic *monži* "man" (from **mangi-*, from accusative,**manwi(n)*: A. Vaillant, *Revue des Etudes Slaves*, 1939, pp. 75–77),[3] and of which we also have representatives in Phrygia (Μάνης) and possibly in Armenia. (I am thinking of that legendary Saint Mané grotto into which Gregory the Illuminator withdraws and vanishes. Perhaps, in pagan times, it was a pathway to the other world, inhabited by a spirit of that other world?) It is only the differing quantities of the *-a-* in Latin **māni* and Indo-European **mānu-* that present a difficulty, since the ending can be taken as just one more example of the well-known hesitations between stems in *-i-* and stems in *-u-* (cf. Cuny, *Revue de Philologie*, 1927, pp. 1–24).[4] This link has already been proposed (see the state of the question in F. Muller Jzn, *Altitalisches Wörterbuch*, 1926, p. 254);[5] but I do not propose to attach any more importance to it than it warrants, so that critics kind enough to take an interest in my work will not, I hope, regard this as a major structural element in my thesis.

III. Solar dynasty and lunar dynasty: *Iḷā*

If the two heavenly sovereigns, Mitra and Varuṇa, stand opposed not only as law and violence, not just as "brahman" par excellence and "leader of the Gandharva," but also as day and night, then it can come as no surprise to find on earth, in Indian epic "history," two dynasties of which one traces its ancestry back to the king-legislator Manu, and the other to the king-Gandharva Purūravas; one of which is called the "sun dynasty" (Manu being regarded as a descendant of the sun) and the other the "moon dynasty" (Purūravas being the grandson of the moon). These are the *sūryavamśah* on the one hand, and the *candravamśah* or *somavamśah* on the other.

I recounted earlier the circumstances in which Purūravas was "initiated" into the world of the Gandharva, or "became one of the Gandharva." Thereafter, his life remained consonant with that beginning, and although it formed the basis for a variety of narratives, all of them have the same general sense (cf. Muir, *Original Sanskrit Texts*, I, 1868, p. 306ff.);[6] supernatural powers, familiarity with animals and monsters, violent acts against the brahmans. In the first book of the *Mahābhārata* (I, 75, 19ff.), for example, we find Purūravas reigning over thirteen ocean islands, surrounded by nonhuman beings, whereas he himself was a man of great fame (*amānusḥair vrtaḥ sarvair mānuṣaḥ san mahāyaśaḥ*). Then, intoxicated by his strength (*viryonmattah*), Purūravas entered into conflict with the brahmans and carried off their jewels despite their cries. Sanatkumāra came down from the world of Brahmā and addressed a warning to him, which he did not heed. Then, cursed by the angered *ṛṣi*, this greedy king, who had become drunk with his own strength and thus lost all sense (*balamadad naṛtasamjno narādhipaḥ*), perished. This tradition and others like it are interesting because they clarify the "morality of the Gandharva" in those times and social environments within which the terrestrial Gandharva operated. It is very similar to that of the first Luperci, Romulus and his uncouth companions, brigands, men of violence, reckless of rules and remonstrances alike, leading in this world the life of a feral world elsewhere. And Purūravas eventually perished as a result of his own excesses, cursed by the *ṛṣi*, by the Wise Men, as Roman Romulus was by the *senatores* he had not been afraid to defy. Nevertheless, Purūravas was far from being a "bad" or "wicked" king. Although the epics depict his behavior as excessive, and naturally take the side of the brahmans against him, he is no more condemned totally and outright than was Romulus, who had murdered his own brother and set himself against the Elders. Purūravas is in fact admired. One text even calls him *nṛdevaḥ* "the man-god" (*Harivarmśa*, 8811).[7]

The lunar dynasty, descended from Purūravas, proved worthy of its ancestor. Although Purūravas's own son, Ayus, is not remarkable except for his name ("vitality"), Ayus's son and successor Nahuṣa (whose name conceals a Semitic name for the snake: Sylvain Lévi, *Mémorial*..., pp. 316–318),[8] is also destroyed by hubris, albeit only after a brilliant and just reign. So great was his prestige, in fact, that the gods at first summoned him to replace the vanished Indra at their head, and granted him the terrible gift of the "evil eye." Drunk with these unheard-of honors, however, the king harnessed the most venerable of his wise men to an aerial chariot and went riding through the sky, until, cursed by one of the wise men whom he had kicked, he fell to earth, struck by lightning, and was changed into a snake.

The solar dynasty is descended from Manu through his son Iksvāku. Although none of the princes who compose it reproduces the exceptionally priestly and exemplarily wise character of Manu, none, on the other hand, presents any "gandharvic" symptom. For our present purpose, in other words, Manu remains the only characterized element of the family.

The two dynasties are not entirely distinct. To be precise, it is the king-priest Manu's own daughter Iḷā, who, having gone to reside with the moon god and having known the son of that god (the warlike Budha), gives birth to the first Gandharva-king, Purūravas, "Aila" Purūravas. This daughter, Iḷā, is a figure with whom we are already acquainted. In the early ritualistic literature, in the archaic form of Iḍā or Iḷā, she is in fact Manu's "daughter" and Egeria, as well as the personification of his oblation. In the epic literature – doubtless inheriting features from extra-priestly traditions (although Purūravas is already qualified as Aila in *Ṛg Veda*, X, 95, 18) – she has a different character and cuts a rather different figure.[i] One constant tradition has it that after journeying to visit the moon god, she was obliged to change sex several times; some texts assert that she thereafter continued to change sex every month. According to the *Linga Purāṇa* (I, 65, 19), she was even transformed into a *Kimpuruṣa*, which is to say into a monster, half-horse and half-man, a variety, already, of Gandharva. Thus, through Iḷā, Manu's daughter, a direct line of communication is established between the sun dynasty and the moon dynasty, between the "wise" and the "tumultuous," between the king priest and the race of Gandharva-kings.

IV. Roman kings: The pious line and the warlike line; *Ilia*

We have no means of interpreting this curious tradition, but it is interesting to rediscover it in Rome. The analogy is very striking, even down to its details, if we follow a number of exegists in their opinion

i Cf. Johannes Hertel, "Die Geburt des Purūravas", *Wiener Zeitschrift für die Kunde des Morgenlandes*, XXV, 1911: 153–186 [note moved from text].

that Numitor, the "good" king of Alba and grandfather of Romulus, is a doublet of Numa.

The list of Rome's first kings contrasts and alternates war-loving, terrible kings with pious, peace-loving kings:[ii] the former are Romulus and Tullus Hostilius, who was a descendant of one of Romulus's principal lieutenants; the latter are Numa and his grandson, Ancus Marcius. Tullus Hostilius, Numa's successor, met a fate even more tragic than that of Romulus, and quite as tragic as that of Nahuṣa, even though his reign had earned the qualification *egregium*. He mocked his predecessor's finest institutions, above all his piety to the gods, which he (Tullus) presumptuously (καθυβρίσας) accused of making men cowardly and effeminate. In this way he directed the minds of the Romans toward war. "But this imprudent temerity did not last long: seized by a grave and mysterious illness, which troubled his reason, he fell into a superstition that was far removed from the piety of Numa… and he died by a stroke of lightning" (Plutarch, *Numa*, 22).[iii] On the other hand, Ancus Marcius, the son of Numa's daughter and *gloriae avitae memor*, was primarily concerned to restore, in all their rigor and purity, the religious customs that Tullus had flouted (Livy, I, 32). Thus the Romulus-Numa opposition continued after them. In Ancus's case we can speak quite literally of "dynasty," and in that of Tullus there is at least moral "filiation," since he is descended from one of Romulus's most typical henchmen. Moreover, these two lines stand in the same typological relationship to one another as the first representatives of the moon dynasty and the ancestor of the sun dynasty in India.

Now, we know how Romulus came to be born: the true daughter of the wise Numitor, a Vestal, had been impregnated by a god, by Mars, and the blood of that warlike god, mingled with the human blood of Numitor, produced the future king-Lupercus, the child who was to be suckled by the she-wolf and formed by a childhood in the wilderness. And that daughter of Numitor, "functionally" symmetrical to the Indian Iḷā, daughter of Manu, is called Ilia.

V. Mithra and Ahura-Mazdāh, Mihrjān and Naurōz

In Iran, where the facts are more confused, and where one senses the purposeful hand of the reformers even in the earliest texts, I shall leave it to

ii See *Tarpeia*, p. 196ff. [note added to second edition].

iii Cf. *Horace et les Curiaces*, p. 79ff. [note added to second edition].

the specialists to prospect in their own territory. The Uppsala school, inspired by Mr. H. Nyberg, is already addressing itself, with happy results, to this question of the sovereign god (G. Widengren, *Hochgottglaube im alten Iran, Uppsala Univ. Aarsskrift*, 1938, VI).[9] I shall therefore limit myself to a few observations made in the light of the Indian and Roman material we have been examining.[iv]

It is certainly important, from a historical point of view, to record the ups and downs of Mithra's career; to note, for example, that he is absent from the *Gāthās* and to determine how he found his way back into the other parts of the Avesta. But the details of such misfortunes tell the comparatist very little, since his task is to search through the documents, of whatever kind, from any era and any source, for vestiges of the early state of the Indo-Iranian couple *Mitra-*Varuṇa, already present in the Mitani list of gods and so well preserved in India.[v] I have already referred, in this context, to the customary Avestic formula *Mithra-Ahura*, which, associating Mithra as it does with a "supreme Ahura" on an equal footing, is certainly anterior to Mazdaism proper. Is Ahura-Mazdāh the

---

iv Cf. *JMQ III*, ch. 2 and 3; L. Gerschel has also pointed out to me a significant linking of "Zeus" and "Helios" in Xenophon, *Cyropaedia*, VIII, 3, 11ff.; and 7, 3. [Note added to second edition. Dumézil's reference is to Henrik Samuel Nyberg, who worked on Indian and Iranian materials, and was a teacher of both Geo Windengren and Stig Wikander. See: https://iranicaonline.org/articles/nyberg-henrik-samuel.]

v A curious lapse has led to these lines being taken as an admission that I am attempting to set up a jealously "comparative" method, in opposition to the "historical method" (R. Pettazzoni, *Studi et materiali di Storia delle Religioni*, XIX–XX, 1943–46, *Rivista bibliografica*, p. 7ff.). A close re-reading, however, will confirm that they simply draw a legitimate distinction between two problems, that of Mithra's history and that of the vestiges that subsist, within that history, from his prehistory. "Comparatist" in this context is merely a shorthand method to denote the scholar who is trying to reconstitute, like I am in this book, by means of comparisons, fragments of the religion of the Indo-Iranians or the Indo-Europeans. The same observation applies to the other passage in this book (see the section on Dius Fidius above: "Not that it is of any great importance, etc…" [p. 87/49]) which Signor Pettazzoni also uses, with no greater justification, for the same purpose. [Note added to second edition. Dumézil's reference is to Raffaele Pettazzioni's review of several of his books (*Mitra-Varuna*, *JMQ I*, *II* and *III*, *Horace et les Curiaces*, and *Servius et la fortune*) in *Studi et materiali di Storia delle Religioni* XIX–XX, 1943–46, 217–20. The reference to p. 7ff. seems to be a mistake.]

heir of this "pre-eminent Ahura" and, consequently, homologous with Varuṇa, the great Vedic Asura? This hypothesis, long accepted without argument, has subsequently been hotly disputed – wrongly, in my belief. On this point I regret being in disagreement with a mythologist of such standing as H. Lommel, but, since all my research has fully confirmed the validity of the description "sovereign" as applied to the Asura Varuṇa by Bergaigne, it seems to me more than probable that the rise of Ahura-Mazdāh derives precisely from the fact that he was an extension of the sovereign god of the premazdeans.[10] The work of the Iranian reformers would then have consisted in a successful attempt to improve the morals of this ancient sorcerer, on the one hand, and, on the other, to isolate him in a position far above all other divine entities (cf. my *Ouranós-Vāruṇa*, pp. 101–102).[vi]

One consideration concerning Mithra strengthens this opinion still further. It is a fact that a religion's great annual festivals are less easily reformed than its dogmas. It is therefore probable that, like Christianity in other times and other places, Mazdaism was simply "sanctifying" the previous state of affairs when it balanced its year on two great festivals separated by the maximum interval (spring equinox to autumn equinox) and clearly antithetical in their meaning and their myths. And those festivals are placed under two invocations, one of Ahura-Mazdāh, the other of Mithra.

On the cosmic level, Naurōz, the Persian New Year and feast of Ahura-Mazdāh, celebrated "on the day Ohrmazd" of the first month, commemorates creation. The feast of Mithra (*Mithrakāna*, *Mihragān*, *Mihrjān…*), celebrated on "the day Mihr" in "the month Mihr," prefigures the end of the world. Why is this? Albiruni replies (*The Chronology of Ancient Nations*, trans. C.E. Sachau, 1879, p. 208):[11] "Because, at Mihrjān, that which believes attains its perfection and has no more matter left to believe more, and because the animals cease to couple; at Naurōz it is the exact opposite." In this opposition between immobilized perfection and creative force, there is no difficulty in recognizing the theological adaptation of an old law-magic, conservation-fecundity opposition that we have seen expressed in India by the couple Mitra Varuṇa and in Rome – even apart from the opposite and complementary activities of flamines and Luperci – by Numa "perfecting" the "creation" of Romulus. There is an even more precise correspondence, however: this division of seasonal roles (the beginning of winter, the beginning

vi *JMQ III*, p. 86ff. [note added to second edition].

of summer) between Ahura-Mazdāh and Mithra, in accordance with the "faculty of growth" and the "arrest of growth" that they express, clearly rests on the same symbolism as the assimilation of Mitra to the waning moon and Varuṇa to the waxing moon, which has sometimes been rather overhastily attributed to the "fancy [*fantaisie*]" of brahman authors.

In epic terms, Naurōz was instituted by Yim (Yama), a king whose carnivalesque features leap to the eye, and who is specifically thought of as the father of the monster Gandarep (Gandarəva), just as the Vedic Yama is said to be the son of the Gandharva. Mihrjān, on the contrary, was instituted by Faridūn (Thraetaonoa), a law-abiding hero, who re-established justice and morality after the tyrannical masquerade of the monster Aždahāk (Azhi-Dahāka), for whom Kndrv (again Gandarəva) acted as steward of royal entertainment. Here, once again, we find the distinction so clearly made in India between a "moon dynasty" and a "sun dynasty," between Gandharva kings (Purūravas, Nahuṣa) and the legislator king (Manu).

This comparison is reinforced even further by the fact that Yim's acting out of his triumph, commemorated annually during Naurōz, coincides exactly with that of Nahuṣa (see p. 104/53): he harnesses *devs* to an aerial chariot and has himself carried at tremendous speed through the sky; and men, "praising God for having raised their king to such a degree of greatness and power," institute this annual feast (Al Tha'ālibī, *Histoire des Rois de Perses*, trans. Zotenberg, p. 13).[12] The scene commemorated by Mihrjān, on the contrary, is one of calm and serenity: Faridūn, having driven out Aždahāk, seats himself upon the throne, surrounded "near and far" by his vassals, and gives an audience to his people. "His physiognomy was illumined, from his mouth fell gracious words, the reflection of his divine majesty shone within him," and his subjects founded the feast of Mihrjān "to express that they had recovered through his justice the life that they had lost...." Here we recognize a set of oppositions only too familiar by now: *celeritas* and *gravitas*, violent triumph and ordered organization, powerful king and just king.

These systems of antithetical representations, linked by a deeply rooted tradition to the two complementary feasts of Ahura-Mazdāh and Mithra – at the two equinoxes – seem to me to confirm that, before reform, the couple Mithra-Ahura had the same meaning, the same double orientation, the same balance, as the Vedic couple Mitra Varuṇa, and that, consequently, the Ahurah Mazdāh of the Avesta is to be linked, typologically and genetically, with the Vedic Varuṇa.

CHAPTER VI

Nexum and *Mutuum*

I. Romulus as binder

Varuṇa is the "binder." Whoever respects *satyam* and *śraddhā* (in other words, the various forms of correct behavior) is protected by Mitra, but whoever sins against them is immediately bound, in the most literal sense of the word, by Varuṇa. I have pointed out elsewhere that the Greek Uranos is also a "binder," even though his "binding" lacks any moral value.[i] Uranos does not enter into combat any more than Varuṇa does. Like Varuṇa, he seizes whomsoever he wishes, and he "binds" him (see below, pp. 202/131–2). Once in his grasp, there is no possibility of

i I have never claimed that there was no other binding god in Greece than Uranos; or denied that Zeus, in other mythic groupings, was also occasionally a binder, and so on (cf. Ch. Picard, *Revue Archéologique*, 1942–43, p. 122, n. 1). I am simply saying that, in the dynastic history of the Uranides –which is a constructed narrative, and one of the rare pieces of Greek mythology that seems to me to call directly, genetically, for Indo-European comparison – the opposition, the differential definition of the two modes of combative action is clear-cut: Uranos binds, with immediate and infallible seizure; Zeus wages a hard-fought war. See below, p. 202/131–2. [Note added to second edition. The full reference is to Ch. Picard, "Une peinture de vase lemnienne, archaïque, d'après l'hymne de Démodocos odyss. VIII, 256 sqq," *Revue Archeologique* 20, 1942–43: 97–124, 122, n. 1; which criticises Dumézil's *Mythes et dieux des Germains: Essai d'interprétation comparative* (Paris: Ernst Leroux, 1939), p. 22.]

resistance. The rituals and the fabulous "history" of the Romans retain, in the expected places, vestiges of these same representations.

The *flāmen dialis* is an "unbinder": any man in chains who takes refuge with him is immediately set free, and his chains thrown from the house, not through the window but from the roof (Aulus Gellius, X, 15: *vinclum, si aedes eius introierit, solui necessum est et vincula par impluvium in tegulas subduci atque inde foras in viam demitti*; cf. Plutarch, *Roman Questions*, 111). Moreover, if a man condemned to be beaten with rods falls in supplication at his feet, then it is forbidden to beat him that day (*ibid*., *si quis ad verberandum ducatur, si ad pedes eius supplex procubuerit, eo die verberari piaculum est*). These two interdependent privileges make the *flāmen dialis* the exact opposite of a cog in the machinery of "terrible kingship," and of Romulus (or other kings of his type, such as Tullus Hostilius or Tarquin, to whom the institution of the *lictores* is sometimes attributed). Always accompanying Romulus, according to Plutarch (*Romulus*, 26), were "men with staves, keeping off the populace, and they were girt with thongs with which to bind at once those he ordered to be bound" (ἐβάδιζον δὲ πρόσθεν ἕτεροι βακτηρίαις ἀνείργοντες τὸν ὄχλον, ὑπεζωσμένοι δ' ἱμάντας ὥστε συνδεῖν εὐθὺς οὓς προστάξειε). This, Plutarch says, is the origin of the *lictores*, whose name derives from *ligare* (cf. *Roman Questions*, 67). And there is no reason to reject this link sensed by the ancients between *lictor* and *ligare*: *lictor* could well be formed on a radical verb **ligere*, for which no evidence has survived, which would stand in the same relation to *ligare* as *dicere* to *dicare* (cf. Ernout-Meillet, *Dictionnaire étymologique latin*).[1] Romulus, then, in direct contrast to the *flāmen dialis*, was a binder and also a flogger, since his escort carries both kinds of weapon and since the lictors of the historical era carried the *virga* in addition to their *fasces*. This group of representations would seem to merit closer scrutiny: indeed, it does seem, both in the Romulus legend and in the rituals derived from it, that *lictores*, Celeres and Luperci are all closely related notions. In particular, the equipment of the first lictors is also that of the historical Luperci, who were belted with leather straps and used them as whips.

Since the essential nature of the *flāmen dialis* is, in the highest degree, anti-binding, it becomes easy to understand why the *flāmen dialis* should be a very heavily clothed man who must never wear any kind of knot, either in his hair, his belt or anywhere about him (*nodum in apice neque in cinctu neque in alia parte ullum habet*, Aulus Gellius, X, 15), whereas the Luperci are naked men "girt" with straps; and why the

Luperces, as *equites*, necessarily wear a ring (see p. 43/16), whereas the *flāmen dialis* only has the right to "mock rings," that are broken and hollow (*annulo uti, nisi pervio cassoque, fas non est* (Aulus Gellius, X, 15).

An analogous interplay of representations occurs, put to rather more subtle use, in India. In the *Śatapatha Brāhmaṇa* (III, 2, 4, 18) we read, for example, that if one speaks the formula "May Mitra fasten you by the foot" at the moment a sacrificial cow is fastened, it is for the following reason: "The rope assuredly belongs to Varuṇa. If the cow were bound (without any special formula) with a rope, then she would become the thing of Varuṇa. If she were not fastened at all, on the other hand, she would not be controllable. But that which is Mitra's is not Varuṇa's...." The trick is clear enough: as long as the necessary bond is put on the cow by a god other than the special divinity of binding, the risk of automatic confiscation is avoided. And if that office is entrusted to Mitra, Varuṇa's complement in the order of things, that is enough to avoid the danger of any counter offensive, any attempt on Varuṇa's part to claim a share of the sacrifice. Such ruses are customary in India (cf. in my *Flamen-brahman*, pp. 62–63, the "brahmanic" ruse adopted with regard to the Roman rule that requires the *flāminica* to be a woman, *univira*, one who has had no other husband before the *flāmen*).

II. Mitra, Varuṇa and debts

It is natural that the punctiliousness over which the Mitra-Varuṇa couple presides should be religious in nature. But the very name "Mitra," as well as the value of personified "contract" that the Avestic Mithra clearly possesses, attests that even in prehistory this god's activity extended beyond the realm of ritual and sacrifice. In addition, the *Ṛg Veda* hymns, as Meillet points out, contain more than vestiges of the specifically juridical values attributed to Mitra and also, interdependently with him, to Varuṇa. In particular, these two gods have a link with debts. They are termed – along with the Āditya as a whole – *cayamānā ṛṇāni* (*Ṛg Veda*, II, 27, 4), "those who collect, gather in, exact repayment of, debts." And it has been observed that the activity proper to Mitra is expressed by an obscure verb that lawyers have finally managed to elucidate: the causative of the root *yat-*. With reference to a textual variant in Manu (VIII, 158) and to the word *vairayātana* (cf. later *vairaniryātana* with the meaning "revenge, vengeance"), which originally meant "settlement, payment (*yātana*) for hostility or, rather, of a man's price (*vaira-*),"

J. Jolly[ii] has suggested that this causative *yātay-* should be translated as "to see that something is paid back" (in accordance with a custom or a contract; cf. Old Scand. *gjalda*, etc.), which is more or less what Meillet has done in his article in the 1907 *Journal Asiatique*.[2] There, Mitra is qualified (*Ṛg Veda*, III, 59, 5; VIII, 102, 12) as *yātayaj-janaḥ*), "who sees that men are paid back." This epithet also appears (*ibid*., V, 72, 2) applied to Mitra and to Varuṇa in a context dominated by the words *vrata* ("law") and *dharman* ("rule") (*vratena stho dhruvakṣemā dharmaṇā yātayaj-jąnā*: "with the law you are firmly established, with the rule you are those who make men fulfill their commitments," Meillet translates). I am not sufficiently informed about the regulations governing debts at the time of the Vedic hymns to comment on these terms. However, we are assured that insolvent debtors were "bound" by the same token as those lax in sacrifice, and doubtless in a more material sense.[iii] As the ritualistic literature repeats to satiety, bonds belong to Varuṇa. Once more, then, we glimpse a collaboration between Mitra and Varuṇa, the former presiding benevolently over correctly executed exchanges, the latter "binding" any defaulters. And various texts do suggest, with differing nuances, a functional division of this kind: Mr Filliozat has brought to my attention, for example, *Kathaka*, XXVII, 4 (ed. L. v. Schroeder, 1909, p. 142, 1, 9–13): *imāḥ prajā mitreṇa śantā varuṇena vidhṛtaḥ* "the creatures were calmed by Mitra, *held in check* by Varuṇa."[iv]

ii J. Jolly, *Beiträge zurindischen Rechtsgeschichte, Zeitsch. d. deutsch. morgenl. Gesellschaft*, XLIV; 1890, pp. 339-340 [Note moved from text. Full reference is J. Jolly, "Beiträge zur indischen Rechtsgeschichte," *Zeitschrift der Deutschen Morgenländischen Gesellschaft* 44 (2), 1890, 339–62.]

iii Pischel and Geldner, *Vedische Studien*, I, p. 288. [Note moved from text. Full reference is Richard Pischel and Karl F. Geldner, *Vedische Studien* (Stuttgart: Verlag von W. Kohlhammer, 1889), Vol. I, p. 288.]

iv On the magico-legal symbolism of the "bond," see most recently H. Decugis *Les étapes du droit*, 2nd ed., 1946, I, ch. VI, "Le pouvoir juridique des mots et l'origine du *nexum* romain," p. 139ff. (p. 143: the binding gods; p. 157: the power of knots; p. 162: the *nexum*, etc.). [This note and the preceding sentence were added to the second edition. References are to Henri Decugis, *Les Étapes du droit des origines à nos jours*, two volumes (Paris: Recueil Sirey, 1946), pp. 139–78; *Kāṭhakam: die Saṃhitā der Kaṭha-Çākhā*, ed. Leopold von Schroeder, three volumes (Wiesbaden: F. Steiner Verlag, 1900–10).]

III. The *nexum* and the *mutuum*[v]

It is impossible not to be reminded here of one of the earliest fragments of Roman law, one that has come down to us as scarcely more than a memory and moreover stripped of any religious element. Although Jupiter and Fides were probably involved in these transactions at one time, this had been forgotten before the earliest documents; nor is it surprising that the material takes the form it does in a land that had successfully separated its law from its religion as early as prehistoric times.[3]

I am referring to the very earliest system of debt, dominated by two words *nexum* and *mutuum*. The first is derived from the conjugation of the verb *necto-nexus*, "I bind-bound" (remodeled on *plecto-plexus*, from the root **nedh-*, "to bind," which is also that of *nodus*, "knot," Sanskrit *naddha-*, "fastened," Irish *naidim*, "I bind": Meillet-Ernout, *Dictionnaire étymologique latin*).[4] The second is formed on the very same root, **mei-*, "make exchanges (of the potlatch type)" that also gave us *Mitra*; and the form *mutuus* must be early, since Indo-Iranian (Sanskrit *mithuna*, Avestic *mithvara*, *mithvana* "pair"; Sanskrit *maithuna*, "union, coitus, marriage") and Balto-Slavonic (Old Slavonic *mitusi*, "alternatively," Lettish *miêtus*, "exchange") also have derivatives in *-t-u-* from this root. *Mutuum* is, literally, (*aes*) *mutuum*, "the money borrowed," and also "borrowing." *Nexum* is the state of the nexus, of the insolvent debtor who was, very literally, bound and subjugated by the creditor. Latin is the only Indo-European language in which the vocabulary of debt is constituted by such clear-cut terms. And it is doubtless no mere chance that we are able to recognize here, in two coupled, abstract words, a strict equivalent of the exchange-god Mitra (with the same root) and the binder-god Varuṇa (with the same image).

It has often been pointed out, with regard to the *nexum*, that it is the most ancient form of relation between the man who gives (or lends?) and the man who receives; and stress has often been laid on its mechanical, inhuman character, which contrasts so strongly with the casuistic direction taken by later law, and reminds us rather of the rigor and the automatic nature of magic transactions. Perhaps we are not quite so far from the sacred as I assumed a moment ago, and when Livy terms this system *ingens vinculum fidei* – using two words that are semantic

v I hold to the contents of this section, even though it provides easy prey for specialists in Roman law. May it at least give them food for thought! [Note added to second edition.]

neighbors of *nexum* and *mutuum* – perhaps he is conjuring up, behind the human legal procedure and as its foundation, the ancient Fides coupled with some divine and terrible "lictor."

Legal historians, however, do not agree on the relation between the two terms. For some, *nexum* and *mutuum* denote two successive phases in the development of a single mechanism. For others, they denote two distinct mechanisms contemporary with one another but opposed in their mode and point of application. I shall take care to offer no opinion either way. It will be sufficient if I observe that in both hypotheses, even in the first (and it is, naturally, on the first that I lay stress here, since it is the only one that could make for difficulties), we are dealing with two "coupled" notions that are interdependent in the second case and parallel in the first.

It is accepted in the first hypothesis that the *mutuum* is not a new mechanism that replaced an earlier one, called *nexum*. Rather, it is seen as a later name given to a system first called *nexum*; and it is generally accepted that *mutuum* was substituted for *nexum* simultaneously with the first attenuation of that cruel mechanism, and at a time – another progressive step – when the mechanism was extended from the *ius civile* to the *ius gentium*. All this is possible. But, even if this evolution is accepted, we may merely be dealing with one of those illusory factual details that abounds in the "early days" of all forms of Roman history, whether political, religious or legal.

It is undoubtedly the case that it is by extension alone that *mutuum* could have become the *nomen* of the legal act, of the contract, for which *nexum* already provided a perfectly adequate *nomen*. For, as we have seen, *mutuum* is the *res* borrowed; it is the material of the act and not the act itself. Thus I am quite disposed to accept, if the texts indicate such a conclusion, that *mutuum* replaced *nexum* at a time when the terrible aspects of the act had been eliminated or greatly softened (very early, it seems, since the process was in any case complete by the fourth century B.C.). But that would not entitle us to ignore the fact that there must always have been, even during those times when the *nexum* was at its strictest, a "material" involved in the contractual act, and that this material must in fact have been called *mutuum*, since the word is Indo-European, archaic in form, and denotes "the thing exchanged," not metaphorically but directly by its very root. Thus the coupled notions *nexum-mutuum*, whatever their subsequent history, originally will have denoted the two components of the mechanism – a mechanism that will then have been successively denoted by first one, and then the other of the two terms, according to whether it was the "violent" or, later on, the "juridical" element proper that was dominant. To this observation I shall add one more. Historians often argue as though the beginnings of Roman law were an absolute beginning. Yet before the *aes mutuum*, even before the *aes* itself, there surely must have been contracts (at least constraining gifts, exchanges, potlatches, all those things expressed by the root **mei-*, likewise, those earlier juridico religious acts must have involved some material element. It is not by chance that *pecunia* is derived from *pecus*. When the pastoral Indo-Europeans invaded Latium, the *mutuum*, "the thing given with – obligatory – duty to reciprocate" (later: "the thing lent"), normally must have been an animal or animals. At this point, I would like to draw attention to the epithet applied in the Avesta to *Mithra*: *vourugaoyaoitis* (cf. Vedic *gavyuti*, which seems to denote a certain acreage of pasture), and also to verse 86 of the *Yast* of *Mithra* in which, in a list of human beings likely to invoke that god and summon him to their aid (leaders of countries, provinces, etc.), there suddenly appears from among all the nonhuman creatures, a lone cow which is "imprisoned" and presumably stolen: "Who, she asks, will take us back to the byre?"[vi] In other words, however archaic such procedures as that carried out *per aes et libram* might now seem in relation to later Roman civilization, it is likely that they originally appeared as innovations in relation to such early pastoral traditions.

The authors who accept the second hypothesis relating to *nexum* and *mutuum*, either sociologists or writers influenced by sociology, do not hesitate to restore a magical or quasi-magical value to the *nexum*.[vii] They

vi On the relations between the cow and both Mithra and Vohu Manah, cf. *JMQ III*, pp. 101, 133–134. [Note added to second edition. As a later note makes clear, Dumézil used the text in *Zend-Avesta*, trans. James Darmesteter, three volumes (Oxford: OUP, 1884–87); reprinted (Delhi: Motilal Banarsidass, 1965), Vol. II, pp. 119–58, here p. 141.]

vii Popescu-Spineni, *Die Unzulässigkeit des Nexum als Kontrakt*, Iaşi, 1931, cf. *Zeitsch. der Savigny-Stiftung*, 1933, p. 527ff.; H. Lévy-Bruhl, *Nexum et mancipatio*, in *Quelques problemes…*, 1934, p. 139ff.; Pierre Noailles, Nexum, in *Rev. histor. du droit français et étranger*, 1940–1941, p. 205ff.; Raymond Monier, *Manuel élémentaire de droit romain*, II (3rd ed.), les Obligations, 1944, p. 13ff., cf. Marcel Mauss, "Essai sur le don", p. 129 ff.., and the work of Huvelin mentioned on Mauss's p. 129 n. 2. [Note moved from text. The references to Noailles and Monier are added to the second edition. The first edition has a reference to Huvelin-Monier, *Traité élémentaire du droit romain* II, *Les Obligations*, 1927, pp. 45 et suiv., i.e.

sometimes go so far as to dispute that the *nexum* is in fact a true contract, but in any case regard it as a radically different type of commitment from that of the *mutuum*; and different, as I indicated, not merely in its form but also in its area of application. According to this view, the operation of the *nexum* presupposes the coexistence of men both free and of very different levels (as regards both wealth and status), whereas the *mutuum* is seen as functioning between equals (between "friends," Monier says on p. 21).[5] By means of the *nexum*, a *humilis* would bind himself to a *potens* and would accept bond-service of some kind, because no more-balanced form of exchange is conceivable between them.[6] By means of the *mutuum*, one *aequalis* would render some service to another, either without payment or with the understanding of a – theoretically free – return. If we accept this hypothesis, then we are led to conceive of two early types of contractual law – according to whether economic relations are being established between classes or within a single social class – both equally far removed, but in opposite directions, from traditional law, and defining it in advance by that very gap between them: a terrible law and a flexible law, a magic law and a trusting law. This would imply a particular Roman utilization, with the

---

Paul Huvelin, ed. and updated by Raymond Monier, *Cours élémentaire de droit romain*, two volumes (Paris: Receuil Sirey, 1927–29), Vol. II. The other references are to Ilia Popescu-Spineni, *Die Unzulässigkeit des Nexum als Kontrakt* (Iaşi: Presa Buna, 1931) ; M. Kaser, "I. Popescu-Spineni, *Die Unzulässigkeit des Nexum als Kontrakt,*" *Zeitschrift der Savigny-Stiftung* 1933, 527–31; Henri Lévy-Bruhl, "Nexum et mancipation," in *Quelques problemes du très ancien droit Romain (Essai de Solutions Sociologiques)* (Paris: Les Éditions Domat-Montchresien, 1934), pp. 139–51; Pierre Noailles, "Nexum," *Revue historique du Droit français et étranger* 19, 1940–41, 205–74; Raymond Monier, *Manuel élémentaire de droit romain,* Volume II : *Les Obligations* (Paris: Éditions Domat-Montchrestien, 1944), p. 13ff. (probably pp. 13–26) The Mauss references are to the original article. See *Sociologie et anthropologie*, pp. 229–34, 229, n. 3, *The Gift*, Routledge ed. pp. 61–64, 169, n. 5; Hau ed. pp. 146–51, 146, n. 5. The Huvelin references given by Mauss are to "Nexum ou Nexus," in Charles Victor Daremberg and Edmund Saglio, eds., *Dictionnaire des Antiquités grecques et romaines d'après les textes et les monuments* (Paris: Librairie Hachette et Cie, 1919), Vol. 4 Part 1, pp. 77–83; "Magie et droit individuel," *Année Sociologique* 10, 1905–06, 1–47; and a series of reviews in *Année Sociologique* 7, 472–75; 9, 407–14; 11, 432–43; 12, 482–87.]

division occurring between *two possible types of social relation*, of the dualist system that occurs in Vedic India with no (apparent) distinction in its social application, but with a division between the two possible attitudes of the debtor (Mitra protecting the good debtor who repays, Varuṇa seizing the bad debtor). But perhaps this interpretation of the Roman facts is too simple, since it does in fact appear that it was the bad debtor only – himself, and doubtless also his wife and his children *in manu* – who was *nexus*. In other words, the *nexum*, the "binding," the subjugation, happened only after a default on repayment had occurred, and we remain uncertain about the state that followed the making of the commitment and preceded defalcation.

That, at least is what seems to emerge from the accounts of historians, for it is naturally to the historical or pseudo-historical traditions that we must turn in order to gain some idea of how this archaic mechanism functioned. For example, we need to re-read Livy's account of the abolition of the *nexum* (VIII, 28): in the last quarter of the fourth century B.C., a libidinous creditor wished to abuse a handsome youth who, as a result of debts contracted by the boy's father, was in his household as a *nexus*. The young man resisted, and the master, having run out of threats, had him stripped naked and whipped. The victim ran out of the house and aroused the people in his defense. The consuls convoked the senate, and a law was voted on the spot. "On that day," Livy tells us, "through the criminal act and abuse of a single man, the awesome bond of *fides* (*ingens vinculum fidei*) was vanquished. By order of the senate, the consuls announced to the people that no man, unless as the result of a merited sentence and while awaiting punishment, should thenceforward be held in shackles or bonds, and that in the future it should be the property and not the body of the debtor that should be answerable for money borrowed (*pecuniae creditae*). Thus it was that the 'bound' (*nexi*) were 'unbound' (*soluti*). And measures were taken to see that they should not be bound in future (*cautumque in posterum ne necterentur*)."

IV. Indra against the bonds of Varuṇa

For our purposes, another passage from Livy (II, 23–24) is even more important. It belongs to that group of epic narratives describing the wars of the early Republic against its neighbors. In a different way, but for the same reason, these stories are as much charged with "mythology" as the traditional accounts of the city's kings, in the sense that they illustrate and justify, if not actual festivals and cults, at least those law-abiding forms of behavior and those moral constants of the historical era to which the Romans adhered at least as firmly as to their religion. But in order to evaluate this document correctly, we first need to return to the India of the brahmans.

There, with the exception of the allusions to debt mentioned a little earlier, the material we have to deal with is of a magico-religious nature, or what one might venture to term "ritual law," that is, the rules that regulate exchanges between sacrificers and gods. As we have seen, the guarantors of this law are Mitra and Varuṇa, and the clumsy or fraudulent sacrificer runs the risk of being "bound" promptly by Varuṇa, just as, in ancient Rome, the defaulting debtor automatically became nexus in the household of his creditor. But the *Brāhmaṇa* recount several stories in which a sacrificer escapes from this gloomy situation thanks to an unexpected intervention. These incidents merit investigation.

I have already cited the first: it is the story of Manu, slave to *śraddhā*, preparing to sacrifice his wife on the demand of two demonic priests. The fatal mechanism is set in motion, inevitable and blind: if Manu does not go through with it to the end, if he succumbs for an instant to his humanity, then he transgresses the law of sacrifice and falls prey to the bonds of Varuṇa. In fact, he doesn't waver: he is going to go through with it. And then another god steps in, one who is neither Mitra nor Varuṇa, a god who feels pity and who decides, having taken the initiative and the responsibility of slicing through this terrible dilemma, that the sacrifice shall not in fact take place and that Manu shall still secure the benefit of it. That god is Indra.

The second story to place on file is that of Śunaḥśepa, which is also important in other respects. A king has been "seized" by Varuṇa and stricken with dropsy because he did not keep his cruel promise to sacrifice his own son to the god. Varuṇa eventually consents to a substitution; but, whatever happens, he wants a human victim equal or superior to the prince. And that is how the young brahman Śunaḥśepa, duly bought and bound to the stake, comes to await his death in accordance with the ritual of *rājasāya* (royal consecration), especially revealed by Varuṇa on this occasion. In order to escape his death, Śunaḥśepa prays to various gods; first to Prajāpati, who passes him on to Agni, who passes him on to Savitṛ, who sends him back to Varuṇa: "It is by the king Varuṇa that you are bound," he tells the young man, "go to him!" Varuṇa listens to him, but, as is the way with great specialists imprisoned by their own technique, the god apparently can do nothing to help the person he has bound. The young man addresses himself once more to Agni, who sends him to the Viśve Devah, who in their turn send him to Indra, who sends him to the Aśvin, who tell him to pray to Dawn. And the miracle occurs: stanza by stanza, as he prays, Varuṇa's "bonds" which hold the king fall away; his dropsy disappears; and there is no further need of a victim. In this story the "savior gods" are numerous, and Indra's role is not as clear-cut as in the previous one; though at least he is well placed beside those beneficent and noncombatant divinities the Aśvin. And doubtless his intervention was more decisive still in the less "priestly" forms of the story, since later writings were to contrast the ancient ritual of royal consecration instituted by Varuṇa (*rajasuya*), stained from the first by human blood (as the Śunaḥśepa story presupposes and several details confirm), with that which has no human victim, instituted by Indra (*aś-vamedha*). I am thinking here, in particular, of Chapter 83 of Book VII of the *Ramayana*, in which Rāma, preparing to celebrate *rajasuya*, is dissuaded by his brother. "How could you carry out such a sacrifice, O Prince," the latter asks him, "one in which we see the extermination, here on earth, of the royal line? And those heroes, O King, who have achieved their heroism here on earth, it will be destruction for them, all of them, below, and a cause for universal anger" (*sa tvam evaṃpvidham yajnam arhitāsi kathaṃ nṛpa pṛthivyaṃ rājavaṃpsanaṃ vinaśo yatra dṛśyate? pṛthivyaṃ ye ca puruṣā rājan pauruṣam agatāḥ sarveṣam bhāvita tatra samkṣayah sarvakopajaḥ*, slokas 13–14). The implications here are clear: the classic ritual of *rajasuya* simulated – and thus once required in reality – the killing of the *rājanya*, nobles who are related to the king. Happily, however, Rama yields to his brother's argument and unhesitatingly renounces "the greatest of all the sacrifices, the *rajasuya* (*rajasuyat krattutamāt nivartayāmi*)," because "an act detrimental to the world ought not be performed by wise men (*Lokapīḍakararṃ karma na kartavyaṃ vicakṣaṇaiḥ*)." In its place he celebrates the no less effica-cious, no less glorious *aśvamedha*, that very *aśvamedha*, respectful of human life, originally instituted by Indra.

V. The morality of the sovereign and the morality of the hero

An attempt to explore fully the import of these interventions by Indra would explode the entire framework of this present work. Indra, the war-rior-god, first among his brothers the Marut, leader of a band of heroes, is set here in opposition to Varuṇa the magician, king of the Gandharva. We are no longer in the realm of mythology proper to the sovereign-priest, but rather at that point of high drama where it mingles violently with the mythology of the military leader. We are passing from one "social function" and – since this is India – from one "social class" to another, and consequently from one morality, one law, one *Weltanschauung* to another. Sociological research on the Marut, the Indo-Iranian "society of warriors," has been set in motion by Stig Wikander (*Der arische Männerbund*, Lund-Upsal, 1938) and is to be pursued.[7] For the moment, however, the evidence is not clearest in the Indo-Iranian world, but in the Germanic world, and it is not by chance that Wikander's work is inspired by Otto Höfler's *Kultische Geheimbünde der Germanen* (Frankfurt-am-main, 1934).[8] I have also sketched in a number of links between the two domains in Chapters VI and VII of *Mythes et dieux des Germains*.[viii] What emerges from the evidence as a whole (even as early as Tacitus, *Germania*, 31) is that the economic morality of such warrior groupings, as well as their sexual morality and conduct in general, both in peace and in war, had nothing in common with principles regulating the rest of society. "None of them," Tacitus tells us (*Germania*, 31), describing the "military society" of the *Chatti*, "has house, or land, or any business; wherever they present themselves they are entertained, wasteful of the substance of others, indifferent to personal possessions..." (*nulli domus aut ager aut aliqua cura; prout ad quemque venere, aluntur, prodigi alieni, contemptores sui...*). It is not difficult to perceive from this how distant such societies were from Mitra and Varuṇa – from all "punctiliousness," from all mechanisms of the *nexum* and even the *mutuum* types, from any system of property, debts, loans. And it becomes easier to understand how one of the most forceful texts that Wikander has found in the Avesta – directed against the *mairya-*, in whom he rightly recognizes the members of an Iranian Männerbund and not mere "bandits" (as Darmesteter translates the term, *Zend-Avesta*, II, p. 445)[9] – presents such groups as the archetypal *mithrō-drug-*, those, in other words, "who violate contracts" on the human level and those "who lie to Mithra" on the divine level. This text, which actually occurs at the beginning of the great *Yast* of Mithra (*Yast*, X, 2), is the fossilized evidence, as it were, of very early conflicts between the moralities and religions of society's first two "functions" and "classes."

viii *Mythes et dieux des Germains*, Paris, Leroux, 1939. See, in particular, p. 93n., pp. 97, 102ff.; and Chapter X, "Census iners..." [note moved from text].

It should come as no surprise that the god of these "societies of men," even though they are "terrible" in so many respects, figures in Indian fable – in opposition to the binder-magician – as a merciful god, as the god who unfetters Varuṇa's (legally) bound victims; for the warrior and the sorcerer alike or, on another level, the soldier and the policeman, make inroads when necessary on the life and liberty of their fellow man, but each operates in accordance with procedures that the other finds repugnant. And the warrior especially, because of his position either on the fringe of or even above the code, regards himself as having the right to clemency; the right to break, among other things, the mandates of "strict justice"; the right, in short, to introduce into the terrible determinism of human relations that miracle: humanity. To the old principle that can be formulated as *ius nullum nisi summum*, he at least dares to substitute something that already resembles the principle that we still revere while often ignoring it in practice: *summum ius summa iniuria.* Having studied the same phenomenon in the Chinese domain, Marcel Granet has accustomed us, in lectures and books alike, to watch for, to weigh the significance of what one might term the "advent of the warrior."[10] Throughout the world this revolution signals one of the great moments, constitutes one of the great openings of societies to progress. The Indian traditions we have been dealing with here belong to this general category, as does, I believe, the inspiring legend recounted in Livy, II, 23–24, which does not, naturally enough, take place between men and gods (as in India), and in which it is no longer religious and liturgical debts that are at stake but legal and pecuniary debts. It is a story of creditors, debtors and soldiers.

VI. Military oath versus *nexum*

War against the Volscii is imminent, and Rome is torn apart by hatreds engendered by its laws governing debt. "We are fighting abroad for freedom and empire," the indignant *nexi* cry, "and in Rome itself we are seized and oppressed (*captos et oppressos esse*) by our fellow citizens!" The city rumbles with unrest, and then an incident occurs that precipitates the storm. An old man in rags, pale, exhausted, wild-eyed, hair and beard in disarray, hurls himself into the forum. He is recognized as a former centurion. He displays his chest, covered with wounds earned in many battles and he gives voice to his misfortunes. He has been forced into debt since the enemy laid waste his land. Swollen by the interest rates levied upon them, those debts have stripped him, successively, of the field handed down to him by his father and his grandfather, of all his goods and of his freedom itself (*velut tahem pervenisse ad corpus*). He has been removed from his home by his creditor, and placed not merely into bond-service but thrust into a veritable prison, into a place of execution (*non in servitium, sed in ergastulum et carnificinam*). Finally, he shows his back, bloody from recent blows. A riot breaks out. Those who are currently *nexi*, as well as those who have been in the past (*nexu vincti solutique*), rush from all sides to the scene, invoking the *fides Quiritium*. The senators are besieged and threatened; they would be massacred but for the consuls who intervene. The people refuse to be pacified until a consul, learning that a formidable Volscian army is on the march, imposes the following decision upon the senate: "No man must detain a Roman citizen, either in chains or in prison, so as to hinder him from enrolling his name before the consuls (*nominis edendi apud consules potestas*). And nobody may either seize or sell the goods of any soldier while he is in camp." Upon this, all the *nexi* there enroll for service (*qui aderant nexi profiteri extemplo nomina*), and the others, learning that their creditors no longer have the right to hold them captive (*retinendi ius creditori non esse*), run to the forum to take the military oath (*ut sacramento dicerent*). Livy adds that these *nexi* formed a considerable military body, the very corps that eclipsed all others in the ensuing war, both in its courage and its deeds (*magna ea manus fuit*; *neque aliorum magis in Volsco bello virtus atque opera enituit*).

Historians are free to think that what they have here is pure history; in other words, a real, accidental event, recorded and embellished by "tradition." I think that it is epic in nature, which is to say – in the sense made clear earlier – it is Roman mythology. Not that the two conceptions are mutually exclusive, of course, since myth is often no more than the transposition into a typical and unique narrative (presented as a fable, or lent verisimilitude according to the taste of the narrator) of a regular mechanism or behavior of a particular society. It is not impossible that, in very early Roman times, a mechanism existed that enabled victims of the *nexum* to free themselves, on a more or less regular basis – not "in return for *virtus*" but rather "in order to display *virtus*"; not "by redeeming themselves" through their exploits but by truly canceling their past, by beginning a new kind of life. Livy (or the annalists who preceded him) would then have been simply summing up in a single event, presented as fortuitous, old traditions relating to this obsolete custom. But, in any case, that could be no more than a hypothesis. The only factual datum is the epic story, which is enough for those exploring Roman sociology. It expresses, in classical costume, the opposition between the automatic and blind law of the jurist and the flexible counter-law of the warrior. In opposition to a capitalist morality based upon magico-religious sovereignty, it erects a heroic mystique that has as its justification the shifting, unpredictable task of the *milites*. For the mechanism geared to function *per aes et libram*, it substitutes an entirely heterogeneous commitment – the *sacramentum*, made man to man, in front of the commander-in-chief. Once stripped of the "legionary" form that it has acquired in Livy, this band of former *nexi*, which distinguishes itself by courage and deeds (*virtute* and *opera*) in the legendary war that Rome saw as the origin of its empire, is doubtless one of the rare pieces of evidence we have relating to the very earliest Italian *Männerbünde*.[ix]

ix Cf. *Horace et les Curiaces*, p. 85ff.; V. Basanoff, *Annuaire de École des Hautes Études, Section des sciences religieuses*, 1945–47, p. 133, and *Le conflit entre «pater» et «eques» chez Tite Live* (explication of the myth of the transvectio equitum), *Annuaire…* 1947–48, p. 3ff. And M. P. Arnold has just published a book entitled *Mavors*. [Note added to second edition. The references are to Vsevolod Basanoff, "XII – Religions de Rome," *École pratique des hautes études, Section des sciences religieuses: Annuaires 1945–1946 and 1946–1947*, 132–34; "Le Conflit entre 'pater' et 'eques' chez Tite Live (esquisse d'une recherche)", *École pratique des hautes études, Section des sciences religieuses. Annuaire 1947–1948*, 1946, 3–23. It is not clear that Arnold's book on *Mavors*, the old Latin name for the God Mars, was actually published. Paul Arnold was a friend of Dumézil, and published an article entitled "Le Mythe du Mars," *Cahiers du Sud*, 37 (299), 1950: 93–108. There is a discussion of the old name on pp. 103–104, and several references to Dumézil throughout.]

CHAPTER VII

*Wôdhanaz and *Tîwaz

I. Collaboration between antithetical sovereign gods

Before confronting the systems already investigated with the homologous systems found among other peoples speaking Indo-European languages, I shall set out clearly the constants and variables encountered so far.

Thus far, both in Rome and among the Indo-Iranians, we have brought together various pairings or "couples" – of notions, of human or divine personages, of ritual, political or legal activities, of naturalist symbols – that are everywhere apprehended as antithetical. This characteristic could develop, theoretically, in two directions. To say "antithetical" is to say either "opposed" or "complementary"; the antithesis could be expressed either by conflict or by collaboration. In practice, however, we have nowhere encountered conflict, but rather, in all areas and in a variety of forms, collaboration.

There is no trace of conflict, either mythic or ritual, between Mitra and Varuṇa, or rather, to give them their dual form, within Mitrāvaruṇā. Neither is there conflict between Mithra and Ahura-Mazdāh, even though a jealously "Mazdean" Iran had every reason to isolate its great god and abase before him everything that was not of him. The *Gathās* make no mention of Mithra, and do not make him into a *daēva*. Then, as soon as he reappears and everywhere that he reappears, he is the "almost equal" and distinguished collaborator of Ahura-Mazdāh.

In Rome, it does not matter at all that Numa's views are diametrically opposed to those of Romulus: "history" still takes the greatest pains to avoid even the shadow of a conflict between them. They meet neither in time nor space, even though their lives slightly overlapped. Typologically, Numa, even when reforming or actually annulling his predecessor's work, is thought of as "completing" or "perfecting" it, not abolishing it. The work of Romulus subsists after Numa, and throughout its long existence Rome will be able to call upon both its fathers equally. Ritually, the Luperci and the *flāmen dialis* (and no doubt the flamines in general) are certainly opposites in every way as regards their behavior, yet the opposition remains morphological: on the one day of the year when the Luperci get wild they do not find their "foils" standing in their way. On the contrary, on the morning of the Lupercalia, the *flāmen dialis*, his wife, the *rex*, and the *pontifices* appear to accord the wild magicians both an investiture and a free hand (see above p. 31 n. 1/7 n. v).[1]

Whenever such a couple – or one of its two components, thereby explicitly or implicitly involving the other – finds itself engaged in a conflict, its adversary is always external, heterogeneous, as in the conflict we have just observed between Indra and Varuṇa, or that between the *sacramentum* and the *nexum*.

In particular, neither in Rome nor in India nor Iran do our couples appear in certain mythic and ritual episodes to which their antithetical structure might be thought to make them specifically suited. I am referring to the various narratives and scenarios of "temporary kingship" ("false king," "carnival king," etc.). Such stories are encountered in India, with the overweening Nahuṣa thrusting himself between the fall and restoration of Indra; in Iran, with the monstrous tyrant Aždahāk seizing power between the fall of Yim and the advent of Faridūn; and in Rome, in the legends that serve as myth for the annual *regifugium*, with Tarquinius Superbus taking power between Servius Tullius and the consulate. In every case, we are dealing with a "bad" or "wicked" king, a temporary usurper, framed between two legitimate, "good" reigns. Also in every case, as can easily be verified, at least one of the two legitimate rulers, either the one before usurpation or the one after, and sometimes both (Indra-Indra; Faridūn; the consul Brutus[2]) is or are of the *military*, a combatant. These two features radically distinguish such stories from those in which our couples appear. First, both components of the Varuṇa-Mitra couple, as well as of the Romulus-Numa couple, are equally legitimate, equally necessary, equally worthy of imitation, and equally "good" in the broad sense of the word. (In particular, as we have seen, "terrible" kings, even when they come to a bad end, are not "bad" kings.) Second, although Roman positivism has tended to reduce Romulus to a strictly warrior-type, all four are something quite different from "military leaders"; Varuṇa and Mitra, Romulus and Numa are all kings in their essence, one pair by virtue of their creative violence, the other by virtue of their organizing wisdom.[i]

II. The priority of the terrible sovereign

Within these couples, when they are constituted by human or divine personages, it has been possible to observe a kind of supremacy of one of the two components – and always the same one. This supremacy is difficult to formulate, and of no great consequence; it is usually external and quantitative rather than qualitative; but it is a fact too constant to be passed over in silence.

Mitra is a very pale figure among the Indians of Vedic times, even though – possibly merely for reasons of rhythm – he figures first in the ordinary term for the couple (Mitrāvaruṇā or, simply, Mitrā, in the dual; cf. Avestic Mithra-Ahura). He has only a single hymn that is specifically his in the *Ṛg Veda*; everywhere else he appears within the surroundings of Varuṇa, who is, on the contrary, very strongly characterized and has a great many hymns to himself. Varuṇa very often represents the couple entirely on his own (guaranteeing justice, annexing the day as well as the night to himself), whereas such an expansion would be exceptional, if it could be found, on the part of Mitra. When a reformed Iran isolated a single sovereign god and set him over the entire universe, it was Ahura, not Mithra, who benefited from this promotion. In Rome, on the divine level, it was Jupiter who captured Dius Fidius, and who became, when there is no call for fine distinctions, the god of both day-lightning and night-lightning, as well as the god of the oath, of Fides itself. On the human level, Romulus is the true founder of Rome, while Numa, historically, is only the second, his second.

Reasonably convincing explanations can be put forth for this particular form of relation. Since these personages fall into the categories, among others, of magician-creator and jurist-organizer, it is quite obvious that they are bound to "succeed" one another, at the beginning of a

i On another type of kingship, acquired by merit, see *Servius et la fortune*, p. 137ff., p. 196ff. [note added to second edition].

world or at least a state, cosmogonically or historically, in accordance with an inevitable order Ahura-Mazdāh creates, Romulus founds, but Mithra and Numa cannot organize and regulate until that has been done. Moreover, since our earliest Indian documentary evidence consists of texts relating to sacrifice, to the magico-religious life, and not juridical or economic texts, it is natural that of the two sovereigns it should be Varuṇa, not Mitra, who is predominant. These considerations, one must admit, are certainly rational enough; but in our field of study it is necessary to be wary of "proofs by reason." Let us simply say, for the time being, that the couples expressing the Roman and Indo-Iranian conceptions of sovereignty present themselves with a *de facto* hierarchy that does not exclude a *de jure* equality. A further element, to be introduced shortly, will enable us to clarify this situation somewhat, if not to interpret it (see p. 158/100).

III. Mithra armed

Having listed these agreements, we must now take note of a difference, one that is all the more interesting because it leaves Vedic India isolated in the face of Rome and Iran; the Avestic Mithra also presents himself as an armed god, a combatant. His entire *Yast* depicts him as embattled, and he is closely associated with Vrthragna, the spirit of offensive victory. In Vedic India, on the contrary, Indra, and Indra alone, is the god who strikes like the thunderbolt, while Mitra never engages in combat in any form; and, again, it was Indra who was linked so early and so closely with Vṛtrahan that he absorbed him, and became for the cycles of the ages "Indra-Vṛtrahan." One detail expresses this difference in a very tangible way. The Indo-Iranians already possessed a name for and a precise representation of the divine weapon: the Sanskrit *vajra*, the Avestic *vazra* (whence by borrowing, in the Finno-Ugric languages, come the Finnish *vasara* and Lapp *vaecer* for "hammer," and the Mordvin *vizir* for "axe": Setälä, *Finn.-ugr Forschungen*, VIII, 1908, pp. 79–80).[3] And M.B. Geiger (*Sitzb. d. Ak. d. Wiss.*, Wien, 1916, 176, 7, p. 74ff.)[4] has pointed out coincidences in the Indian and Iranian descriptions of these two weapons which in fact seem to guarantee a prehistoric figuration and even prehistoric formulas. Now, the *vajra* (Donnerkeil, thunderbolt-weapon) is exclusive to Indra, while the *vazra* is exclusively the "club" of Mithra.

It is probable that this Iranian state of things is the result of an evolution. In the first place, it must fall within the intentions of the Zoroastrian reformers who extended their moral system even to the field of war, as well as to the particular form of relations there between warrior power and the royal administration.[5] Whereas in ancient India, a land of many small kingdoms, the fighter Vṛtrahan (or, more precisely, Indra-Vṛtrahan) became highly developed and quickly pushed Mitra and Varuṇa, along with the Āditya as a whole, into the background (of the whole of post-Vedic religion). In imperial Iran, on the contrary, Vrthragna remained the genie, the "officer" of a precise function – offensive victory – while the essential role of state religion became fixed on the truly sovereign entities: AhuraMazdāh, with his council of abstract powers, and also Mithra. And it is Mithra, in those sections of the Avesta where he is accepted, who has annexed the various traits of the warrior-god, without going quite so far, nevertheless, as to absorb Vrthragna. Whatever the details of these developments, that at least is their probable direction.

However, it is also possible that the Iranian Mithra, a fighter armed with the *vazra*, simply developed a power already inherent in the Indo-Iranian; **Mitra*, one that the Vedic Mitra let fall into disuse. Although, in Rome, neither Numa, Fides nor Dius Fidius is in any degree a fighter, Dius Fidius, in his role as jurist, a thunderbolt god, is nevertheless armed with the *fulmen* he employs to "sanction" the *faedera*, as his other name (Semo Sancus) seems to indicate, and as Virgil tells us when he transfers the term to the Jupiter complex (*Aeneid*, XII, 200). It is the thunderbolt of a notary, not that of a captain – a legal impress rather than a weapon of war, but a thunderbolt all the same. It is also worth noting that the terrible Jupiter, the other component of the Roman sovereign couple, is also – in essence and in a warlike context – a god of lightning. It is he (as Elicius) who presents the good and peace-loving Numa with the awesome problem of how to ward off his lightning – the problem, that is, of human sacrifice. And Mars, the Roman god of the *milites*, whose cosmic domain is in fact the lower atmosphere and the earth's surface – Mars, the god of battle, is not a wielder of the thunderbolt.[ii] In that respect, too, Rome is in conflict with India and in agreement with Iran, whose victorious genie Vrthragna is also not armed with lightning. India, on the contrary, is in agreement here with the Germanic world, where the god of the second of the three cosmic and social functions, the fighter-champion, is called

ii *JMQ I*, p. 95 [note added to second edition].

Thor, which is to say **Thunraz* or "Thunder," and is armed with a hammer that is also a thunderbolt.

IV. Uranos and Zeus

One might think that the perspectives opened up by this book regarding the early Indo-European conception of sovereignty ought to enable me to complete the short book I devoted to *Ouranós-Vāruṇa* in 1934, in which Mitra was neglected. In fact, however, they merely shed further light on the peculiarity of the Greek myths, and the impossibility of reducing them to the Indo-European systems.[iii]

Uranos does not form a couple with any other god. Beside this terrible king, this binder with his irresistible powers of seizure (see below pp. 202/131–32), this chaotic creator, we find no ordered, lawgiving, organizing sovereign on his "mythic level." It is true that such a sovereign does appear later in the story – Zeus. But he does not come as one part of a couple to balance Uranos, not even in the same way as Numa balances Romulus; instead, he comes to abolish his predecessor's mode of activity forever, to begin a new phase in the world's life – one in which the powerful whim of Uranos will no longer have a place, either as driving force, model or object of worship. So in what measure are this Zeus and this Uranos – the one the luminous sky and the other the night sky, the one a warrior with his thunderbolt and the other a "seizing and binding" magician, the one δικαιος (even though Prometheus would disagree) and the other chaotic, the one merely superhuman and the other monstrous[6] – in what measure are they heirs, within a quite different theological framework, of the ancient, balanced couple whose Indo-European antiquity is so amply underwritten by the Roman and Indo-Iranian evidence? In his defeat Uranos was hurled into the dark reaches of fabulous times, and thus, as it were, beyond us whereas Zeus lives on with us, among us. Is this difference of "framework" equivalent in some way to what the Indians mean when they say that "Mitra is this world, Varuṇa is the other world"? It would not be the first time that relations in space had evolved and had been reformulated into relations in time.

We are assured, however, that Zeus and the living religious concepts of Greece in their entirety are essentially formed of a substance that

iii Cf. [p. 113/67] n. 1, Chapter VI [note added to second edition].

is Aegean and not Indo-European. What to me seemed to have come from the Indo-European fund can no longer be regarded as more than fable, matter for literature alone, not for worship. Here Uranos, there the centaurs; but no, those "everyday" monsters, embodied in processions, are not the centaurs, only satyrs and silens; and Uranos is now nothing more than the figurehead of an "academic" cosmogony. We must not therefore search for any simple relation between the fossil Uranos and the living Zeus. Above all, we must not suppose too hastily that Zeus could have acquired, like Mithra in Iran, a warlike appearance and a lawyer's soul. The object of my present investigation no longer has any existence in Greece, since no form of Greek mythology or society is any longer articulated by the Indo-European schema of the "three social functions (or classes)" that were preserved in India, in Iran and in very early Rome, and that are still recognizable in the Celtic and Germanic worlds.[iv] Zeus does indeed preside over a divine hierarchy, but of a different type, probably Aegean, in which Poseidon and the waters of the sea, Pluto and the underworld, are the other components. It is true that in every area of Greece war and agriculture have their patron figures; but nowhere beneath the magic sovereign do they form that triad, of which the three flamines, Jupiter, Mars and Quirinus, riding in the same chariot to sacrifice to Fides Publica, are still such clear-cut evidence. Perhaps a time will come when we will be able to make a probable distinction regarding, not only the relations of Uranos and Zeus, but also those of Uranos and Oceanos and of both with Kronos, between the Aegean data and the shreds of Indo-European material that have successfully survived around the names of the personages (which are either certainly or probably Indo-European). But for the present I shall pass by the temples of Greece without entering – deserved punishment, perhaps, for having explored them without sufficient prudence in my earliest forays.

There will be occasion, moreover, to extend the inquiry beyond the Uranides later. One of my students, Lucien Gerschel, is now investigating the problem of how far the oppositions defined in this book can be linked to the opposition, so dear to Nietzsche and so perfectly real, between Apollo and Dionysos.[7]

---

iv See some reservations relating to this negation in *JMQ I*, p. 252ff., and in *Tarpeia*, p. 221ff. [note added to second edition].

V. *Wôdhanaz and *Tîwaz

In a recent work (*Mythes et dieux des Germains*, 1939, ch. 1: "Mythologie indo-européenne et mythologie germanique"), I began the task of comparing the earliest forms of religious representation in the Indo-European North with the system that emerges from a comparison of East and West, that is, from the Indo-Iranian, Italic and Celtic data.[8] At that time I commented on the way the absence of a large priestly body, analogous to the brahmans, the magi, the Druids or the pontifical college (flamines and pontiffs), in combination with the ideal of a classless society (which had struck Caesar so forcibly among the peoples beyond the Rhine), had softened the system without actually dismantling it. We can still recognize, in various formulas, in divine groupings, in the general division of the mythology, that great triple division of cosmic and social functions: magical sovereignty (and heavenly administration of the universe), warrior power (and administration of the lower atmosphere), peaceful fecundity (and administration of the earth, the underworld and the sea). The Scandinavian triad is defined in precisely this way: Odhinn, the sovereign magician; Thor, the champion-thunderer; Freyr (or Njodhr), lubricious and peaceful producer. Possibly, these are the triad already recorded by a disconcerted Caesar in excessively naturalist terms: Sol, Vulcanus, Luna; in other words, we may assume, *Tîwaz or *Wôdhanaz, *Thunraz, *Nerthuz (*De Bello Gallico*, VI, 21; cf. my *Mythes et dieux*..., p. 12); and also the triad discernible in Tacitus (*Germania*, 2), behind the religious groups descended from the mythical sons of Mannus, Erminones, Istraeones (a better reading than Istuaevones), Inguaeones (*Ermenaz: cf. Old Scand. *jörmunr*, appellation of Odhinn; *Istraz: adjective in **-raz* from IE **-ro-*, a frequent formation in the names of powerful fighting gods: Indra, Rudra, *Thunraz himself; *Inguaz: cf. Old Scand. Yngvi, appellation of Freyr; see J. de Vries, *Altgermanische Religionsgeschichte*, I, 1935, pp. 212–216).[9]

But among the Germanic peoples, as in Rome and in the Indo-Iranian world, the first function, sovereignty, is not presided over by a single god. In Scandinavia, beside Odhinn there is Ullr (Norway, north and central Sweden) or Tyr (Denmark, Scania). On the continent, alongside *Wôdhanaz there is *Tîwaz or *Tiuz (German: Wotan and Ziu). When Tacitus (*Germania*, 9) names the three great gods of the German tribes as Mercurius, Mars and Hercules, we should recognize them as the couple *Wôdhanaz-*Tîwaz, the two gods of sovereignty, plus the champion *Thunraz (J. de Vries, *Altgerm. Religionsgesch.*, I, pp. 166–179).[10] The patron of agriculture, whoever he was, is omitted, probably because of the contempt in which he was held, at least in theory, as noted by Caesar earlier (*agriculturae non student*, etc.; *De Bello Gallico*, VI, 22). Tacitus goes on to say that the god he has called Mercurius requires human victims on a particular day, whereas Mars and Hercules require only animal sacrifices: an excellent criterion that defines one of the two sovereigns as "terrible" in contrast both to the other sovereign and to the warrior god; and this fits nicely with the Indian and Roman sets of data dealt with in preceding chapters (pp. 95ff/54ff and 125ff/76ff).

In Chapter 2 of *Mythes et dieux des Germains*, I examined the narratives of Saxo Grammaticus, which, opposing as they do Othinus and Ollerus (that is, Odhinn and Ullr) or Othinus and Mithothyn (that is, Odhinn and *mjötudh-inn*, "the judge-leader" or, less probably, "the anti-Odhinn"), enable us to define each of the components of these couples in relation to the other. Let me stress first, however, that contrary to what we have constantly found in Rome, Iran and India, the mythological theme of the "bad, temporary king" is fused with the mythological theme of the "two antithetical types of sovereign": Ollerus and Mithothyn are both usurpers who occupy the sovereign's place only during Othinus's absences (either obligatory or voluntary) from power. Here, I shall leave the "Othinus-Ollerus" form of the antithesis to one side. It does in fact open up a very important line of research, but one that we cannot pursue here, since Ullr seems to be opposed to Odhinn, his other specifications apart, as the patron of very specific techniques (he is the "inventor" of the skate, the ski, etc.), in contrast to Odhinn's all-powerful magic – an artisan god as opposed to a shaman god. And it will not suffice, in this context, merely to liken him to the Irish Lug *samildânach*, "the god of all trades," the artisan god to whom the king-god in a well known mythological story ("The Second Battle of Moytura [*Mag Tured*]", *Revue Celtique*, XII, 1891, section 74),[11] voluntarily gives up his throne for thirteen days, since it is the entire question of "craft religions" that would have to be investigated throughout the entire Indo-European world, which, in turn, would entail a consideration of the concordance, and sometimes the union, of the concepts of jurist and artisan, law and recipe, legal practice and technical craft. For the moment, then, let me simply repeat that, from their names alone, Ullr (also called Ullinn, a form well attested by Norwegian toponymy: Magnus Olsen, *Hedenske Kultminder i norske Stedsnavne*, I, Oslo, 1915, p. 104ff.)[12] and Odhinn (derived from *ödhr*, which, moreover, exists as the name of a god) coincide very closely indeed with the opposition we have been exploring in earlier chapters: Ullr, a Scandinavian form of the Gothic *wulthus*, "δόξα," expresses "majestic glory,"[v] while *ôdhr*, the Scandinavian form of German *Wut* and Gothic *woths* "δαιμονιζόμενος" denotes all the material and moral forms of frenetic agitation (J. de Vries, *Folklore Fellows Communications*, 94, Helsinki, 1931, p. 31: "rapid and wild motions of sea, fire, storm" and also "drunkenness, excitation, poetic frenzy"; as an adjective, *ôdhr* is to be translated either as "terrible, furious [raging, furious, terrible]" or as "quick, swift"); and I can only refer readers to what was said earlier, with reference to homologous beings, about the mystique of *celeritas*.[13] De Vries, whose vegetation theory for Odhinn I do not entirely accept, nevertheless gives very good definitions of the etymology of the two gods: Ullin-Ullr is "a divine person whose activity consists in a cosmic brilliance";[14] Odhinn is the possessor of the multiform *ôdhr*, of that night favoring *Wut* that also animates, on the continent, those wild rides in the supernatural hunt, *das wütende Heer*, of which Wöde or Wöden is sometimes still the leader, just as the terrible *Harti* warriors, with their black shields and painted bodies, chose the darkest nights for combat and gave themselves the appearance of a *feralis exercitus* (Tacitus, *Germania*, 43; cf. the *ein-herjar*, that is **aina-hariya-*, dead warriors who form Odhinn's court in the other world). It is gratifying to find the same symbolic opposition coloring these two northern figures of sovereignty, the same contrast between light and darkness we have already observed, in varying forms, in India (Mitra, day: Varuṇa, night) and in Rome (Jupiter, "Summanus": Dius Fidius, "diurnus"). In the *Wôdhanaz-*Tîwaz form of the couple, the same nuance is again attested by the etymology of the second name: *Tîwaz is IE **deiwo-*, Sanskrit *devah*, Latin *deus* – in other words, a god whose essence contains the light of heaven.

However, it is in his role as jurist that the adversary of Othinus will prove of particular interest to us here.

---

v It is also the Latin *vultus*. Cf. also Illyrian personal names in *Voltu* (*Voltuparis*, *Volt(u)-reg-*): Kretschmer, "Die vorgriechischen Sprach- und Volksschichten," *Glotta*, XXX (1943), p. 144, n. 1. On *ullr*, see now I. Lindquist, *Sparlösa stenen*, Lund, 1940, p. 52ff., 179ff. [Note added to second edition. The full references are P. Kretschmer, "Die vorgriechischen Sprach- und Volksschichten (Fortsetzung von Gl. XXVIII 231–278", *Glotta* 30, 1943: 84–218; Ivar Lindquist, *Religioiösa Runtexter II: Sparlösa-stenen: ett svenskt runmonument från Karl den Stores tid upptäckt 1937; ett tydningsförslag*, Lund: Gleerup, 1940.]

CHAPTER VIII

"Communiter" and "Discreta Cuique"

I. *Tîwaz: War and the law[i]

In my research Jan de Vries has aided me greatly with his passages devoted to the Germanic god Romanized as Mars. This god must certainly be *Tîwaz, homonym of the Scandinavian Tyr (*Altgerm. Religionsgesch.*, I, pp. 170-175). *Tîwaz undoubtedly had an essential connection with military activity, since both the local population and Romans sensed his resemblance to Mars. Yet one could and should say the same for the majority of the Germanic gods. Julius Caesar was very emphatic that the only activities in which the continental Germanic tribes deigned to take an interest were war and preparation for war; nothing else counted. And I, too, have noted this "military inclination" in the entire mythology, beginning with Odhinn himself (*Mythes et dieux...*, p. 145ff.). However, to content ourselves with affixing such a summary label is scarcely permissible.

What are the relations of *Tîwaz-Mars to war? To begin with, relations that are not exclusive, as he has other activities. In several inscriptions he is qualified as Thincsus, which means, despite interminable arguments on the matter, that he is, without a doubt, protector of the *thing* (German *Ding*) – in other words, of the people when assembled in a body to arrive at judgments and to make decisions. But even apart

i Cf. Rudolf Holsti's thought-provoking book, *The Relation of War to the Origin of* [the] *State*, Helsingfors, 1913. [Note added to second edition. Helsinki: Suomalaisen Tiedeakatemian Toimituksia.]

from this important civil function, *Tîwaz-Mars remains a jurist in war itself. And here let me quote de Vries:

> Thus the god Mars Thincsus was closely connected with the people's assembly, with the *Ding*, the same thing can be seen in Denmark, where *Tislund*, in Zealand, was a place of assembly. *Tîwaz was therefore both a protector in battle and a protector of the assembly. In general, his character as a god of war has been brought too much into the foreground, and his significance for Germanic law insufficiently recognized... These two conceptions (god of battles, god of law) are not contradictory. War is not, in fact, the bloody hand-to-hand combat of battle; it is a *decision*, arrived at by combat between two parties, and governed by precise rules in law. One has only to read in the works of historians how the Germans were already fixing the time and the place of their encounters with the Romans to realize that for them a battle was an action to be carried out in accordance with fixed legal rules. Expressions such as *Schwertding*, or Old Scandinavian *vâpnadômr*, are not poetic figures, but correspond precisely to ancient practice. The symbolic gestures linked with combat are incontestable proofs of this: the declaration of war among the Latins by the *hasta ferrata aut praeusta sanguinea* is directly comparable to the ceremony in which the northern Germans hurled a spear at an opposing army. And that spear bears the same essential significance as the one planted at the center of the *Ding*: if the Scandinavian Tyr bore a spear, as J. Grimm has already pointed out, it was less as a weapon than as a sign of juridical power (cf. H. Meyer, *Heerfahne und Rolandsbild, Nachr. d. Gesellsch. f. Wiss., Ph.-bist. Klasse*, Göttingen, 1930, p. 460ff.). From these facts considered as a whole, it becomes evident that, in every respect, the name Mars Thincsus is a very fitting one for this god of law. Naturally, the Romans were unable to perceive him as any thing more than a god of war because their first contacts with the German tribes were all in terms of war.[ii]

ii De Vries, *Altgermanische Religionsgeschichte*, 173–175. [Note moved from text. Dumézil partially expands one of de Vries's references. The full reference is Herbert Meyer, "Die Oriflamme und das französische Nationalgefühl," *Nachrichten von der Gesellschaft der Wissenschaften zu Göttingen, Philologische-Historische Kalsse*, 1930, pp. 95–135. De Vries also references his own "Studien over Germaansche Mythologie IV. De Goden der West-Germanner," TNTL (*Tijdschrift voor Nederlandse Taal- en Letterkunde*) 51, 1392: 277–304.]

That is an excellent summary which makes plain that the sociological mythology of our day is no more satisfied with summary definitions such as "military god," "agricultural god," than with those other definitions that were once regarded as exhaustive, such as "sun god," "storm spirit" or "vegetation spirit." There are many ways of being a war god, and *Tîwaz is a clear example of one very poorly defined by such labels as "warrior god" or "god of battle." The legitimate patron of battle (defined as an exchange of blows) is *Thunraz, the champion (cf. *Mythes et dieux...*, ch. VII), the model of physical force, the divinity whose name the Romans translated as Hercules. *Tîwaz is something quite different: the jurist of war and, at the same time, a kind of diplomat, rather like those *fetiales* supposedly created by the peace-loving legislator Numa (or by his grandson and imitator Ancus) in order to reduce or curb violence. As for *Wôdhanaz, he is not a fighter either – any more than the binder Varuṇa is; even in battle, he remains the magician.[iii] Patron of the band of men-beasts, the *Berserkir* or the *Ulfhedhnir*, the "bear-coats" or "wolf-skins" (as Varuṇa is of the half-man, half-horse Gandharva, as Romulus is of the feral band of Luperci), *Wôdhanaz communicates his own gifts to them: the power of metamorphosis, *furor* (*ôdhr*!), invulnerability, certainty of aim and, above all, a paralysing power by which the enemy is immobilized, blinded, deafened, disarmed and brought to its knees before it has even begun to fight. In one famous story (*Saga des Völsungar*, XI, end), we see him rise up in the very heart of the battle, one-eyed, fate-bearing, brandishing a spear that he does not use to fight with but against which the sword of the chief, whose death he has decreed, is shattered; and, abruptly, the tide of battle turns: those about to conquer weaken, then fall as one, and are conquered. It is precisely the technique of Jupiter Stator, of that terrible sovereign homologous with Odhinn – a technique of an omnipotent wizard, not that of a fighting warrior. Moreover, according to Ranisch (*Eddalieder*, Göschen Collection, no. 171, p. 111 n.),[1] the early Scandinavians called this paralyzing fear, this military panic, *herfjöturr*, "army bond" or "army shackle." It will come as no surprise to the reader to find the image of the "bond" appearing at this point; and I shall take advantage of this opportunity to take sides in the argument relating to an apposite passage in Tacitus (*Germania*, 39; cf. J. de Vries, *Altgerm. Religionsgesch.*, I,

iii Cf. *Tarpeia*, p. 274ff. [note added to second edition].

pp. 180–181).[iv] Among the Semnones, the *regnator omnium deus* has a sacred wood, and not only are human sacrifices made there, but no one may set foot within it *nisi vinculo ligatus*, "unless bound with a shackle" – precisely, says Tacitus, to indicate that the place belongs to that *regnator* to whom everything and everyone else owes obedience, *cetera subiecta atque parentia*. In which case, it certainly can not be the jurist sovereign who is involved, but rather the terrible sovereign, not *Tîwaz but *Wödhanaz. This whole present comparative inquiry confirms the indication of such an identification already provided by the link between Odhinn and the *Fjöturlundr*, the "sacred wood of the Bond," in *Helgakvidha Hundingsbana* II (prose before strophe 38), and renders null and void the frail arguments to the contrary with which all the writers in the field seem to have been satisfied hitherto, with the exceptions of K. Zeuss, A. Baumstark, G. Neckel, B. Kummer and Jan de Vries.[v]

II. Saxo, I, 7 and Caesar, VI, 22

But let us return to times of peace. The legend that opposes Othinus and Mithothyn (Saxo Grammaticus, I, 7) raises a difficulty of great importance. Let me begin by summarizing the story. His kingly dignity having been sullied by the misconduct of his wife, Othinus goes into voluntary exile. In his absence, a magician, Mithothyn, usurps his place and introduces an essential change into the mode of worship: "He

---

iv L[eopold]. von Schroeder, *Arische Religion*, [Leipzig: H. Haessel, two volumes] I, 1916, p. 487 n. 1, has already linked this Germanic *regnator omnium deus* with Varuṇa, lord of bonds, but, paradoxically, making *Tiwaz the beneficiary [note added to second edition].

v Cf. the original but rather unlikely solution offered by Mr R. Pettazzoni in the *Atti della Accad. dei Lincei* (mor., hist., and philol. sc.), CCCXLIII, 1946, (Rome, 1947), p. 379ff. (expanding a thesis first propounded in an article in *Studi e Materiali di storia delle Religioni*, XIX–XX, 1943–46): it would seem that the problem doesn't in fact exist [note added to second edition. The full references are Raffaele Pettazzoni, "Regnator omnium deus", *Atti dell'Accademia Nazionale dei Lincei: Classe di Science morali, storiche e filogische* CCXLIII, 1946: 379–86; "Regnator Omnium Deus," *Studi e Materiali di storia delle Religioni*, XIX–XX, 1943–46: 142–56; trans. as "Regnator Omnium Deus", *Essays on the History of Religions*, trans. H.J. Rose, Leiden: E.J. Brill, 1967, pp. 136–50.]

asserted that the anger and resentment of the gods could not be appeased by conjoined and mingled sacrifices; he therefore forbade them to offer up their prayers collectively, establishing separate libations for each of the gods" (*Hic deorum iram aut numinum violationem* confusis permixtisque sacrificiis *expiari negabat; ideoque eis vota communiter nuncupari prohibebat,* discreta superum cuique libamenta constituens). But Othinus abruptly reappears, and the usurper flees and meets a wretched end, where upon the legitimate king reestablishes the previous order, "obliging all those who had borne the titles of celestial honors in his absence to lay them down, as not rightfully theirs" (*Cunctos qui per absentiam suam caelestium honorum titulos gesserant tanquam alienos* deponere coegit).

Thus the usurper, the one of the pair who is the "bad" king, fleeting as opposed to durable, is not the "inspired madman"; he is the "distributor," he is not the god of tumult (*Odhinn-ôdhr*); he is the judge-leader (*mjôtudhinn*), in other words, a personage of the *Tîwaz type. A scandal, no less! If we transfer this legend, undoubtedly an ancient myth, into human reality, we are forced to envisage a society whose entire life consists of one vast Lupercalia interrupted by a single brief period every year in which life is regulated by law; in other words, the exact opposite of what we found in Rome, for example, and recognized as being in conformity with reason.

Once again, however, let us be wary of reason. And first of all, let us take care not to confuse the representations a society creates from its own mechanisms with the actual functioning of those mechanisms in reality. It is quite true that mythologies project into the "Great World" the machinery of this one; but the "Great World" can tolerate anything; there, there is no need for the compromises, for the hypocrisies that, in this low world of ours, enable the majority of societies to live without too great a strain, proclaiming an ideal while betraying it at every moment. That is true in our modern world, and it was true among the ancient Germans. Saxo's legend, or rather the ancient myth to which it bears witness, does not prove that the users or consumers of that myth lived a life that ran diametrically counter to our own good sense; but perhaps it does prove that it would have been their ideal to lead such a life, and that they pretended to live it. A passage from Caesar's *De Bello Gallico* (VI, 22) enables us to be rather more positive in this matter, since in this case it does not define a myth, but a feature of early Germanic economic ethics that is again "excessive," that again corresponds to an ideal rather than to practice, and of which the underlying principle is the same as that which triumphs in the passage from Saxo.

"No man," Caesar tells us, writing of the German tribes, "has any fixed quantity of land, or sites that belong specifically to him. Each year the magistrates and chiefs parcel out the land among the *gentes* and among groups of kinfolk living communally, in such quantities and in such places as they deem fitting. The following year they oblige them to move elsewhere" (neque quisquam agri modum certum aut fines habet proprios; *sed magistratus ac principes in annos singulos gentibus cognationibusque hominum qui una coierunt quantum et quo loco visum est agri distribuunt, atque* anno post alio transire cogunt). And Caesar then records as many as five justifications for this system, all of them, he assures us, provided by those involved (*eius rei multas afferunt causas*). Moreover, all five justifications are admirable ones, and for our purposes have the advantage of providing proof that there actually is an economic mystique involved here, an ideal of purity and justice that could thus be maintained and loudly proclaimed as an ideal even at a time when practice was already perceptibly diverging from it; for I accept entirely, along with the legal historians, that even at the time of Caesar and Tacitus (a parallel but obscure passage in *Germania*, 26), there already existed among the Germans *festes und geregeltes Grundeigentum* (J. Grimm, *Deutsche Rechtsaltertümer*, II, 1899, p. 7 n.).[2] Thus these five *causas* (or "reasons") lie in the moral domain: Caesar tells us that the Germans feared that prolonged habituation to agriculture would cause them to lose the taste for war; to yield to peasant greed, with the injustices that brings in its wake; to become demanding in the matter of comfort; to see factions and discords arising among them caused by love of wealth; and, lastly – a positive argument – that their communizing system was well suited to satisfying and containing the people, "since each member... can see that his resources are equal to those of the most powerful" (*ut animi aequitate plebem contineant, quum suas quisque opes cum potentissimis aequari videat*).

III. Totalitarian and distributive economies

I have emphasized in these two texts, that from Saxo and that from Caesar, the terms that correspond. In Saxo, Mithothyn's error is to condemn "the good system," that is, the *confusa permixtaque sacrificia*, the offerings made to all members of divine society *communiter*, and to institute *discreta superum cuique libamenta*. But when Othinus returns, as representative of "the good system," he forthwith strips these pseudo-proprietors of their titles, forces them to lay those usurped honors down (*tanquam alienos deponere coegit*), and, though the text does not explicitly say so, clearly reestablishes the old system. In Caesar, "the good system" consists in preventing any person from establishing any true ownership, *neque quiquam agri modum certum aut fines habet proprios*. Once a year, of necessity (because the land must be cultivated), temporary distribution (*distribuunt*) of the land is made among the members of society; but, also once a year, the leaders force those pseudo-proprietors to abandon the lands consigned to them (*alio transire cogunt*). In the one instance, divine society alone is involved, and the only properties in question are the benefits, the sacrifices, conferred by worship; in the other, human society is involved, and the properties are areas of land. But the principle is the same: the same consecration of a communizing system, the same repugnance for permanent enclosure and appropriation.

There is no means of establishing, or, indeed, any necessity to think, that the prehistoric myth from which the Scandinavian legend derived was in fact the very myth that corresponded to an annual practice ensuring that collective wealth, temporarily divided and owned, was recalled and merged once more into that ideal "unity." But it is more than probable that the annual mechanism described by Caesar, even though much attenuated and almost obsolete, was backed up by mythical representations. Moreover, those representations could not have been very different from Saxo's narrative, and, since a function of the sovereigns was involved (Caesar writes: *magistratus ac principes distribuunt... cogunt*), the two gods symbolizing the two rival structures must have been, as in Saxo's story, the two sovereign gods: the jurist-god and the inspired-god, *Tîwaz and *Wôdhanaz. The condemnation of the "stable and liberal economy" presided over by *Tîwaz was a preparation for the glorification of the "shifting and totalitarian economy" presided over by *Wôdhanaz.

This text of Saxo's therefore obliges us to introduce a new and all-important consideration into the theory of sovereignty: that of the *economic* system within which, along with the two sovereign gods, the coupled concepts, rituals and moralities they represent are seen to function. This fact has not become evident before because India, Iran and Rome have all presented us with societies that are equivalent in this respect, since all have systems of divided, stable and hereditary property. In their case, the wealth of each person, or at least of each autonomous group (of the *gens*, for example), is fundamental and sacred. And all types of relations, even those between man and god and god and man, are conceived of in accordance with one and the same model: the ceding of property with precisely specified compensation. The ideal of such societies is a division of wealth kept as strict and as clear as possible, with a view to peaceful enjoyment of it. A day of undefined violence, like that erupting in the Lupercalia, can be no more than an exception during the year, as feared as it is necessary. The everyday, permanent morality is that of the flamines.

In contrast, the ideal of the early Germanic societies, as recorded by Caesar, is a "confusionism," a permanent social melting-pot, a "unanimism" upholding a heroic and anti-capitalist ethic. Each year, during a single and doubtless brief meeting, this confusionism is given its full realization as the wealth temporarily distributed the previous year is returned to the community. That wealth is then immediately redistributed for the next period; nonetheless, this distribution is apprehended as an evil, a lesser evil, that the Germans would have liked to avoid. Their mystique of *aequitas*, as Caesar terms it (an equality secured by the negation of property so as to maintain a warlike *Stimmung*), must cause them to regard that annual day or group of days as an exception as regrettable as it is necessary, devoted as it is to organizing a system in violation of their ideal that, however uncertain and temporary, constitutes a minimum of ownership and a risk or an onset of appropriation.

The opposition is thus total. And yet perhaps India, Iran and Rome do bear in their very mythology the mark of a prehistoric system comparable to that of the Germans. We know how very conservative myths, and the legends in which they survive, can sometimes be. For instance, the passage from Saxo we are dealing with now is remarkable not only as regards its "morality," but also as regards the contradiction that exists, as far back as we can reach in history, between that morality and Scandinavian practice. If there is one area of the Germanic world in which hereditary property and family wealth acquired "sacred" value and functions very early on, that area is Scandinavia (cf. Magnus Olsen, *Ättegaard og Helligdom*, Oslo, 1926).[3] That being so, are we not justified in perceiving an archaism of the same kind in the anomaly I indicated earlier without attempting to explain it? To wit, in Rome as in India, the predominant god of the divine sovereign couple is not the ordered, just god (Dius Fidius, Mitra), but on the contrary the terrible, magician god (Jupiter, Varuṇa), even though the fundamental religion is, in practice, that of the flamines and the brahmans, not that of the Luperci and the Gandharva?

At all events, the information on the Germanic world provided by these passages from Caesar and Saxo enables us to gauge, in one precisely defined context, the irreparable loss for the comparatist created by the almost total disappearance of the Slavonic mythologies; for a few names of gods with brief definitions cannot, in effect, be called a mythology. Yet forms of collective ownership with periodic redistribution of wealth are known to have existed among the Slavs even into the historic era. Their mythology of sovereignty must have been modeled on these practices; and it would have been all the more interesting to have known what precise form it took, for the human depositories of sovereignty among the Slavs appear to have been more than commonly unstable. But all that is irremediably lost.

IV. Nuada and Bress

I said earlier that Saxo's text dealing with the "temporary usurpations" of Mithothyn and Ollerus show that the Germans, unlike the Indo-Iranians and the Romans, fused into a single schema the two mythical themes of the two "good" sovereign gods as antithetical couple and of the "bad" temporary sovereign. This gives us good reason to look at related mythologies with a view to establishing whether this second theme does not, on occasion, have an economic value there too. At first sight this appears not to be the case: the tyranny of Nahuṣa, of Aždahāk, of Tarquinius Superbus, is characterized by excessive *pride* and by serious *sexual* malefactions, demands or violent acts, rather than by economic misdemeanors. Nahuṣa demands the wife of the god-king Indra, whom he "re-places"; Aždahāk sexually possesses the two sisters of King Yim, whom he has dethroned, and Faridūn liberates them (this feature is already Avestic); Tarquin is doomed because, under his rule, under the "cover" of his kingship, he commits the greatest sexual crime in Roman fable, the rape of Lucretia. In all this, there is no economic element whatsoever, unless we take into account the links recorded by tradition between Tarquinius and forced labor (Livy, I, 56).

The economic element is, on the contrary, in the very forefront of an Irish myth that should probably be placed in this context – less for its coupled sovereign gods than for the temporary usurper it presents – and which is all the more interesting for simultaneously being – according to whichever point of view one takes – both the homologue and an inversion of the Germanic myth.

The Irish, and the sedentary Celts in general, of the period after the great migrations, are of the Roman and Indo-Iranian type with respect to property. The "confusionism" of Othinus is utterly alien to individualists, attached to wealth, and even more so to the external marks of wealth. They look on any development of central power, any control, any risk or first symptom of statism, with repugnance; and this is no doubt what is being expressed in the myth of the temporary eclipse of "Nuada of the Silver Hand," a legendary king of the Tuatha De Danann – that is, even earlier, of the gods – and himself a god whose antiquity is confirmed by the fact that he also appears in a Welsh Mabinogi under the name "Lludd of the Silver Hand" (Llud for *Nud by assonant assimilation to the initial consonant of *llaw*, "hand") and, above all, by the fact that he appears under the name Nodens, Nodons, very early in several Latin inscriptions from Great Britain. Having lost a hand, Nuada becomes unfit to reign by virtue of an ancient law common to many peoples, until such time as the physician-god and the bronzesmith-god have made him a silver replacement hand, which takes seven years. His temporary replacement is the tyrannical Bress, a chief of the Fomorians, which is to say, a being of another race that simultaneously is kin to and in fundamental conflict with the Tuatha De Danann – just as, for example, the Asura are with the Deva in India. Now, the tyranny of Bress is purely economic.[vi] Greedy, and equally miserly, he demands, for the first time in history, taxes, and exorbitant taxes at that. He also introduces forced labor and declares war on private property. The ruses he employs are still famous. For example, he lays claim to the milk from all hairless, dun-colored cows. At first this bizarre specification sounds reassuring, but then he orders a great fire of ferns to be lit, and all the cows in Munster driven through it, so that their hair is singed off and their hides browned (*Dindsenchas* de Rennes, *Revue Celtique* XV, 1894, p. 439).[4] None of this wealth he extorts is used in any act of generosity, and he is eventually cursed or – which comes to the same thing – mocked by a *file*, by a poet, for his avarice. The Tuatha De Danann then oblige him to abdicate, granting him a reprieve only on one condition. You must guarantee us, under surety, they tell him, the enjoyment of all the products on which you lay your hand, houses and lands, and gold and silver and cows and victuals; and also exemption from tax (*cêis*, borrowed from Latin *census*) and fines until the end of

vi Cf. *Servius et la fortune*, p. 230ff. [note added to second edition].

your reign. Bress is forced to accept these conditions, but immediately goes to complain, or rather confess, to his father, asking him for help. "It is my own injustice and pride," he says, "and nothing else that have removed me [from the throne] (*nim-tucc acht m'anfhir ocus m'anuabhar fesin*). I took from my subjects their treasures and their jewels, and even their victuals; and until now no one had taxed or fined them." To this admission his father very properly replies: "It was ill done: it would have been better (to have) their (good) wishes then to reign over them; better their (good) prayers than their curses..." ("The Second Battle of Moytura", ed. W. Stokes, *Revue Celtique*, XII, sections 25, 40, 45, 46).[5]

And, indeed, that is the great question, for all leaders under all skies. But one also needs to determine whether, in order to have the people's good wishes and blessings, the leader should be the active embodiment of a communizing, greedy, fiscal, dispossessing but equalizing state (which in consequence, as Caesar says of the Germans' system, *animi aequitate plebem contineat, quum suas quisquis opes cum potentissimis aequari videat*), or whether, on the contrary, he should be the figurehead of an aristocratic federation or the president of a bourgeois association, an impotent and liberal leader whose sole duty – can he but perform it – is to protect each individual against the envy of others and to guarantee him, with the minimum of taxation for public services, inviolable enjoyment of his personal wealth. It is clear that the Irish composers of this legend made the opposite choice to that of the continental German tribes observed by Caesar or of the prehistoric Scandinavians responsible for the story in Saxo. Bress and Othinus are both for state control and against private appropriation; Nuada and Mithothyn are both for personal ownership and against communism. It is just that the roles of "hero" and "villain" have been reversed: in Ireland the wicked usurper is the nationalizing Bress; in Scandinavia he is the privatizing Mithothyn.

CHAPTER IX

The One-Eyed God and the One-Handed God[1]

I. Odhinn's eye

Odhinn and Tyr are not just the Scandinavian heirs of the magician sovereign and the jurist sovereign. They are also the one-eyed god and the one-handed god. Their disabilities form a couple, as do their functions; and this parallelism suggests that we ought perhaps to investigate whether there is in fact any interdependence, at least on a symbolic level, between the disabilities and the functions.

Although Odhinn's one-eyed state is a constant, Jan de Vries (*Altgerm. Religionsgesch.*, II, p. 192ff.) is correct in saying that the circumstances of his mutilation are not clear. The meaning of it, however, is not inaccessible. From strophes 28 and 29 of the *Völuspâ* we know that Odhinn's lost eye is "in the spring of the Mîmir." "I know," the witch says, "I know, Odhinn, where your eye is sunk; I know that Odhinn's eye lies at the bottom of the famous spring of Mîmir (*veit hon Odhins auga foigit î enum maera Mîmis brunni*); Mîmir drinks hydromel every morning on the pledge of the Father of warriors" (*drekr mjödh Mîmir morgon hverjan af vedhi Valfödhur*).[2] Clearly, there is an allusion here to a story that has no other trace in the Eddic poems; but we do know who Mîmir is (J. de Vries, *op. cit.*, p. 361ff.). The name occurs in three forms denoting the possessor of three objects – the head of Mîmr, the tree of Mîmi and (just quoted) the spring of Mîmir. In all three cases, moreover, this personage is linked with the power of Odhinn. The best known of these three traditions is the one concerning the head of Mîmr, which possesses knowledge of the runes and teaches it to Odhinn. Snorri (*Ynglingasaga*, 4, at the end of his account of the war between the Ases and the Vanes) records a tradition relating to the way this head came to Odhinn's aid, and the invaluable revelations it made to him about "the hidden things."[3] The tradition might have been embellished, but it would be incautious to reject it *in toto*. Similarly, it would be hypercritical to dismiss as pure auctorial imagination the commentary that Snorri offers on strophe 29 of the *Völuspâ* (*Gylfaginning*, 15): at the foot of one of the roots of the world-tree Mîmameidhr, there lies the spring of Mîmir (*Mîmisbrunr*), in which knowledge and intelligence lie hidden; "the master of this spring is Mîmir, who is full of knowledge, because he drinks from it daily; once Alfödhr (Odhinn) came and asked for a sip of the spring, but he was not given permission until he had thrown one of his eyes into it as a pledge."[4]

Thus Mîmr-Mîmir, one way or another, is Odhinn's instructor, his professor of runes; and the loss of a bodily eye was the means by which the magician-god acquired in exchange a spirit eye, the power of second sight, and all the supernatural powers that its possession brings. As Roger Caillois has pointed out, the case of Tiresias is somewhat similar, in that he too received his powers of clairvoyance at the same time he became blind. In the case of the Scandinavian god, however, even the outward mark of this profitable exchange benefits him. It is the proof of his powers, so that when the unknown one-eyed figure appears in battles, for example, then the moment of destiny is at hand, and those involved are left in no doubt of the fact. Thus, for Odhinn, mutilation and function are indeed interdependent: the mutilation was a payment, the resulting disfigurement an enabling certificate, empowering the god to perform his magician's function.[5]

II. Tyr's hand

The case of Tyr is comparable in part. A tale in Snorri, with which the philologists have wreaked no small havoc, but which I (along with Jan de Vries, it would appear) persist in regarding as based on early material, recounts at length how Tyr came to lose his hand (*Gylfaginning*, 35; cf. *Lokasenna*, stanzas 38 and 39).[6] This tale tells of the binding, before he grows to full size, of the wolf Fenrir, who, according to prophecy, is fated to become the scourge of the gods.

The young wolf has already broken out of two strong chains without the slightest difficulty. Odhinn, becoming apprehensive, then turns to the Black Elves, who are ironworkers,[7] and has them make a magic leash that looks no stronger than a silken thread. The gods invite the wolf, as though in play, to let itself be fastened and then to break the thread. The wolf suspects that this apparently harmless device has been fabricated with guile and trickery (*gört medh list ok vêl*), but the gods pursue their aim with flattery, then temptation: "If you do not succeed in breaking the leash, that will be proof that the gods have nothing to fear from you, and we will release you." The wolf still hesitates: "If you succeed in binding me so fast that I can not free myself, then you will laugh in my face!" In the end, in order not to lose face, he accepts, but on one condition: "Let one of you place his hand in my mouth as a pledge that there will be no trickery!" (*thâ leggi einn hverr ydharr hönd sîna î munn mér at vedhi, at thetta sê falslaust gört*). "Not one of the gods wished to pledge his hand, until Tyr held out his right [hand] and placed it in the wolf's mouth" (*ok vildi engi sîna hönd framselja, fyrr enn Tyr lêt framm haegri hönd sîna ok leggr î munn ûfinum*). Of course, the wolf is unable to free itself. The harder it tries, the stronger the magic leash becomes. "The Ases laughed then, all save Tyr, who left his hand behind there" (*thâ hlôgu allir nema Tyr, hann lêt hönd sîna*). Thanks to this combination of the magic bond invented by Odhinn and the heroic pledge provided by Tyr, the gods are saved, and the wolf will remain leashed until the end of the world – at which time, I might add, he will wreak his revenge.

It is a serious mark of the legend's authenticity, it is scarcely necessary for me to stress, that Tyr's action is precisely of the kind appropriate to a jurist-god. An entrapping pact must be concluded with the enemy, one that entails a pledge forfeit in advance, and Tyr, alone among all the Ases, offers that pledge. The enemy is foolish enough to accept the contractual risk of an exchange in which the mere mutilation of one god is offered as compensation for utter defeat. Tyr, the heroic legal expert, seizes his opportunity. And with his sacrifice, he not only procures the salvation of the gods but also regularizes it: he renders legal that which, without him, would have been pure fraud.

I drew attention in the previous chapter to the fact that the **Tîwaz* (or Mars-Thincsus) of the continental Germans was the god who presided over the law of war, the god of war viewed as a matter of jurisprudence. The extent of that domain needs to be measured: even in earliest times, since law was already involved, the great thing must have been to keep up appearances, to act in the best interests of one's people without putting oneself in the wrong "internationally." How far is one committed when one makes a commitment? How is one to draw the enemy into one of those treaties that is as good as an ambush? How does one respect the letter of the law and yet betray the spirit of one's oath? How can one make the adversary appear to be in the wrong when he is plainly in the right? All these questions in Rome required the skill of the *fetiales* and, among the Germans, the counsel of *Tîwaz.

III. The one-eyed and the one-handed

Thus Tyr's disfigurement, like Odhinn's, is directly related to his divine function and permanent mode of action. It is possible that, in its earliest form, the myth from which Snorri's story derives had as its object the *justification* of Tyr's already-recognized juridical nature. In that case, there would be strict symmetry between the two gods, the one being the Magician because he has dared to lose his eye, the other being the Jurist because he has dared to pledge his hand. They would have become what they are in the same way that specialists were prepared for their tasks in China – a comparison much loved by Marcel Granet – by adaptive mutilation. However, even in its attested state, the tradition already gives us enough without that hypothesis. Perhaps it was not *in order* to become the divine lawyer that Tyr lost his right hand, but it was at the very least *because* he was the lawyer that he, alone among the gods, was the one who did in fact lose his hand.

In sum, alongside **Thunraz-Thôrr* (who wins wars without resorting to finesse, by infighting, by relying on his strength alone), the two sovereign gods represent two superior techniques. **Wôdhanaz-Odhinn* terrifies the enemy, petrifies him with the glamor of his magic, while **Tîwaz-Tyr* circumvents and disarms him with the ruses of the law. We do not know who, on the earthly level, the "men of Tyr," the guardsmen of the Germanic armies, actually were, but we have already seen who "Odhinn's men" were: the *berserkir*, the beast-warriors, invulnerable and wild, of whom Odhinn himself is the prototype, since we read of him (*Ynglingasaga*, 6): "He could make his enemies blind and deaf, or like stones with fear, and their weapons could no more cut than sticks..." Such are the various but equally efficient – one might almost say "equally elegant" – privileges of the one-eyed god and the one-handed god.

The symbolism here is probably very ancient, since Roman epic literature has preserved an invaluable variant, linked not to two "sovereigns" (the Republican orientation of these stories would not permit that), but to two "saviors of the state." I am thinking of the two famous episodes that together constitute the greater part of the Republic's first war: that of Horatius the Cyclops and that of Mucius the Left-handed. Twin episodes, one of which irresistibly summons up the other among both the historians and the moralists of antiquity, and whose interdependence is underlined even further by the fact that Cocles and Scaevola, at the conclusion of their exploits, both receive exceptional, and to some extent similar, public recognition – a last vestige, possibly, of the "sovereign" value originally attached to their modes of action and their careers.

Cocles is the one-eyed hero, the famous Horatius, who, when Lars Porsenna is about to take the city by assault, single-handedly holds the enemy in check by his strangely wild behavior, and thus wins the first phase of the war.[8] When the city has finally been besieged and famine threatens, Scaevola is the hero who goes to Porsenna and of his own free will burns his own right hand before him, thus persuading Porsenna to grant the Romans a friendly peace that is the equivalent of a victory.[9] The traditions relating to Odhinn and Tyr give us the key to these two little "historical" mysteries. The selfsame concept is apparent in the guise of mythical tales among the Germans and of historical narratives in Rome: above the equipoise of fortune in an ordinary battle, we have the certain victory gained by the "demoralizing radiance" of someone with "the gift," on the one hand, and, on the other, a war terminated by the heroic use of a legal procedure. Let us examine these two stories more closely.

IV. Cocles[i]

Little inclined as they were to the supernatural, the Romans have nevertheless made it very plain that Cocles, in this combat, was more than an ordinary man; that he mastered his enemies more by the force of his personality and good luck than by any physical means; and that his enemies were unable to get near him.

Polybius, for example (*Histories*, VI, 55), even though he is the only writer to accept that Cocles was badly wounded and died after the battle, is clear on this point, despite his generally rather slapdash wording: "covered with wounds, he [Cocles] stayed at his post and checked the

i On the various Horatii heroes, cf. *Horace et les Curiaces*, p. 89ff. [note added to second edition].

assault, the enemies being less struck (stupefied, καταπεπληγμένων) by his strength than by his courage and his daring."

Livy's account (II, 10) is more circumstantial and gives us a very clear picture of a situation unique in "Roman history." He depicts Cocles, amid the general debacle, rushing to the head of the bridge that is the sole access to Rome, which the Romans, taking advantage of this respite, then begin to demolish. "He stupefied the enemy by this miracle of daring" (*ipso miraculo audaciae obstupefecit hostes*). Then, remaining alone at the entrance to the bridge, he casts terrible and menacing looks at the Etruscan leaders (*circumferens truces minaciter oculos*), challenging them individually, insulting them collectively. For a long while no one dares to attack him. Then they shower him with javelins (*undique in unum hostem tela coniiciunt*); but all stick bristling in his shield, and he, stubborn and unmoved, continues with giant strides to hold the bridge (*neque ille minus obstinatus ingenti pontem obtineret gradu...*). Eventually, they decide to hurl themselves upon him, but just then the thunder of the collapsing bridge and the joyful shouts of the Romans fill them with a sudden fear and stop them in their tracks (*fragor... clamor... pavore subito impetum sustinuit*). Mission accomplished, Cocles commends himself to the god of Tiber, hurls himself fully armed into the river, and swims across it under a hail of ineffective missiles, all of which fail to hit him (*multisque superincedentibus telis incolumis ad suos tranavit*). Thus, in Livy, Cocles controls events throughout, with his terrible grimaces, which paralyze the enemy, and with his good luck, which wards off all weapons.

Dionysius of Halicarnassus (V, 24), who is more verbose and concerned with verisimilitude, at least adds the detail that Cocles was a *iunior*: He also retains this feature: "The Etruscans who pursued the Romans did not dare engage him in hand-to-hand combat (while he was occupying the bridge), regarding him as a madman and as a man in the throes of death" (ὡς μεμηνότι καὶ θανατῶντι). There then follows a lengthy description of the fight, conducted at a distance, during which the unapproachable Roman victoriously returns all the projectiles with which the enemy vainly attempts to overwhelm him.

This unanimity among our authors makes it plain enough that there was something superhuman about Cocles in this battle. Properly speaking, his "gifts" are not, even in Livy, magical "eye-power" and invulnerability; but they are almost that, and they would have been precisely that if the source were not a narrative with historical pretensions, and if we were not in Rome.

It must be remarked upon that this terrible hero who blasts the Etruscans with his gaze, thereby reversing the normal course of battle, is called "Cocles," which is to say (if we follow the usual Roman interpretation), the one-eyed. It is no less remarkable that the mutilation is constantly presented as prior to the exploit. He had lost an eye, all the authors simply tell us, during a previous war. Plutarch alone (*Publicola*, 16), after having quoted this opinion first, adds an extremely interesting variant: "other writers say he owed this appellation [a distortion of the Greek "Cyclops"] to the fact that the upper part of his nose was so flattened, so deeply recessed, that there was no separation between his eyes, and his eyebrows met" (διὰ σιμότητα τῆς ῥινὸς ἐνδεδυκυίας ὥστε μηδὲν εἶναι τὸ διορίζον τὰ ὄμματα καὶ τὰς ὀφρῦς συγκεχύσθαι).

In my *Mythes et dieux des Germains* (p. 105 and n.2), I drew attention to the fact that the great warriors of northern Europe – the Irish Cuchulainn, the Viking chiefs – practiced a heroic grimace that was the certificate of their power, as it were, and the proof of their victory. In Cuchulainn's case, this grimace is only one of the "signs," one of the monstrous "shapes" or "forms" (*delba*) that came upon him immediately after his initiation combat and that were manifest thereafter whenever he was gripped by warlike fury. It took the following form: "he closed one of his eyes," one text says, "until it was no bigger than the eye of a needle, while opening the other until it was as big as the rim of a mead cup" (*iadais indara suil connarbo lethiu indas cro snathaiti, asoilgg alaile combo moir beolu midchuaich*); or, according to a variant, he "swallowed one of his eyes into his head, until even a wild heron could scarcely have brought it back from the depths of his skull to the surface of his cheek," while "the other leapt out and placed itself on his cheek, on the outside" (*imsloic in dara suil do ina chend, issed mod danastarsed fiadchorr tagraim do lar a gruade a hiarthor achlocaind, sesceing a seitig com-boi for a gruad sechtair*: for these texts and other variants see M.–L. Sjoestedt-Jonval, *Etudes Celtiques*, I, 1936, pp. 9, 10, 12, 18; also, analogous data concerning Gallic coins that I interpret differently from the author; cf. E. Windisch, *Tain Bo Cualnge*, 1905, p. 370, n.2).[10] In the case of the Viking Egill, the grimace forms part of a heroic gesture that is, apparently, traditional, since it is understood by the person at whom it is directed. He presents himself in this grimacing shape before the king, who is bound to pay him the wages of his victories, and who, in fact, does continue to pay for as long as the Viking's countenance has not regained its natural composure: "When he sat down, he caused one of his eyebrows to leap down as far as his cheek, and the other up to his hairline; and Egill had black eyes and eyebrows that met" (*er hann sat... tha hleypdhi hann annarri bruninni ofan a kinnina, en annarri upp i harraetr; Egill var svarteygr ok skolbrunn*). It is not until he is satisfied with the payment that he abandons this "shape," and that "his eyebrows return to their places" (*... tha foru brynn hans i lag*: See *Egils Saga Skallagrimssonar*, LV, 9).[11] These grimaces amount to a monstrous widening of one eye, while occluding the other. Both form part of a terrifying mimicry, doubtless based on a principle well known to the Harii, who, according to Tacitus (*Germania*, 43), won battles by terror alone: *terrorem inferunt, nullo hostium sustinente novum ac velut infernum adspectum; nam primi in omnibus proeliis oculi vincuntur* ("they strike terror; no enemy can face this novel and, as it were, hellish vision; in every battle, after all, the feeling of being conquered comes to the eye first"). This "ghostly army" (*feralis exercitus*) of the Harii leads us back to the Einherjar (**Aina-hariya-*) and the *berserkir*, presided over by their prototype, Odhinn (cf. *Mythes et dieux des Germains*, p. 80ff.). It also seems to me probable, albeit unprovable, that Odhinn's ocular disfigurement, of which we have already seen the "civil" magic value, as it were, must also, in "military" actions, have contributed to the paralyzing terror that the *Ynglingasaga* (section 6) attributes to him as his principal weapon. In times of peace, his single eye was the pledge and the proof of his clairvoyance; in times of war, the god undoubtedly cast "the evil eye" upon those whose fate he had quite literally decreed. Ultimately, there seems little doubt that this, too, was one of the objectives shared by the ocular contortions of Egill and Cuchulainn.[12] The congenital, or acquired, malformation attributed by Roman epic literature to its terrorizing champion, Cocles, doubtlessly is maintaining the memory of analogous and very ancient beliefs or practices in the Latin world.[13]

V. Scaevola

Scaevola's links with Fides and Dius Fidius have long been recognized. I cannot do better than to reproduce the reflections of W-F. Otto (Pauly-Wissowa, *Encyclopédie*, VI, 1909, col. 2283, under *Fides*):[14]

> Several scholars have noted that the story of Mucius Scaevola must have been connected, in some way, with the worship of Fides, and particularly with the custom, specific to that cult, of swathing the

> right hand. Ettore Pais has drawn attention to the fact that the temple of Dius Fidius, who is certainly akin to Fides, was located on the *collis Mucialis*, the name of which calls to mind the *gens Mucia*, and he has concluded that the myth of the burnt right hand originated in some variety of ordeal. According to Salomon Reinach (*Le voile de l'Oblation, Cultes, Mythes et Religions*, I, 1905, p. 308; though the work originally dates from 1897),[15] the swathing of the right hand in the cult of Fides is a symbolic offering of that hand to the goddess, and the story of Scaevola would thus refer to a time and a case in which such offerings were still made. This second interpretation seems to me inadmissible; but I cannot resign myself to separating the story of Mucius burning his right hand from the custom of swathing the right hand in the cult of Fides. Although unable to explain the legend, I should like to point out that the tradition concerning Claelia and other hostages, a tradition closely linked with that of Mucius Scaevola, is recounted as outstanding evidence of the *Fides publica populi Romani*....

Basing himself on W-F. Otto, Mr F. Munzer (*op. cit.*, XVI, 1933, col. 417, under *Mucius Scaevola*) has made the following accurate observations:[16]

> Dionysius of Halicarnassus himself, even though his rationalism and incomprehension caused him to suppress Scaevola's self-mutilation, does draw attention to the fact that, when face-to face with Porsenna. Mucius swears an oath forcing himself to tell the truth (V, 29, 2: πίστεις δοὺς ἐπὶ θεῶν), and that he receives a guarantee from Porsenna, also under oath (29, 3: δίδωσιν αὐτῷ δι' ὅρκων τὸ πιστόν). Dionysius also adds that Mucius tricks Porsenna, and that his oath is a ruse, a matter that the other authors leave in the air, failing to make clear whether the revelations that Mucius makes (about the plan drawn up by three hundred young Romans to relay one another, in successive attempts to stab the enemy king – he, Mucius, being only the first to make the attempt, and to fail) are true or false. Here, perhaps, lies the original reason for the loss of Mucius's right hand: out of patriotism, and with full awareness of his action, he swore a false oath and voluntarily received the punishment for his false swearing. Thus, what could have once been celebrated as an act of heroic abnegation later came to lose any clear motivation, or ceased to have any motivation at all, when it began to seem impossible to accept the treachery and the false oath.

It is certain that Münzer is correct here, and that the central thrust of the story was originally as he describes it. But perhaps the "prototype" tradition, on which the historians of Rome were at work, with their varying sets of moral susceptibilities, was even simpler still. Let us remember the mutilation of Tyr: that mythological fiction is easily superimposed on the fragment of epic history we are considering here. For Mucius, as for Tyr, the object is to inspire trust in a threatening enemy, to make him believe something false – in both cases by sacrifice of a right hand – which will persuade that enemy to adopt a stance favorable to their own side. In risking – and thereby inevitably sacrificing – his hand, Tyr gives the gods' enemy the wolf reason to believe that the leash they wish to put on him is not a magic bond (which is false) and thus to agree to the trial. Once bound, the wolf will not be able to free itself, Tyr will lose his hand, but the gods will be saved. By voluntarily burning his hand before Porsenna, Mucius is giving Rome's enemy, the Etruscan king, reason to think that he is being truthful (even if he is lying) when he tells him that three hundred young Romans, all as resolute as himself, could very well have sacrificed their lives in advance and that, in consequence, he, Porsenna, stands every chance of perishing by one of their daggers. The fear, and also the esteem, the king suddenly feels for such a people leads him to conclude the peace treaty that saves Rome. It is true that the "pledge" mechanism is not the same in both cases; the hand that Tyr previously risks is a genuine bailbond for his honesty, whereas the hand that Mucius destroys then and there is a *sample* of Roman heroism. But the result is the same: both hands provide the *guarantee* of an affirmation that, without the hand, would not be believed, and that, by means of the hand, is in fact believed and thus achieves its effect on the enemy's mind.

I hasten to acknowledge that Mucius Scaevola's act, whether sullied by trickery or not, is the nobler of the two (or at least produces nobler effects): Porsenna is not deprived of the capacity, merely of the intention, to do harm. As befits a representative of the series "Mitra-Fides, etc.," Mucius is a true peacemaker who diverts the enemy's mind onto the path of an honorable truce, a durable friendship, so that the treaty concluded between the young Republic and the Etruscan king is certainly not fraudulent, and was even to be famously respected (cf. the story of Claelia), and to serve, as F. Münzer observes after [Theodor] Mommsen (*op. cit.*, col. 423), as a model and reference point for the treaties of friendship that historical Rome was to conclude with foreign sovereigns.

This mythological consonance between Rome and the Germanic world is reinforced by a linguistic one: the Latin *vas* (genitive *vadis*), the legal term for the "pledge that stands surety for," has no corresponding word except in Germanic and Baltic, and there the corresponding word is precisely the one to be found in the Snorri text, quoted earlier: Tyr's hand is placed in the wolf's mouth *at vedhi*, "as surety," so that he will permit himself to be bound. This word (*vedh*, neuter) is the same one that still subsists in the modern German *Wette*, "wager," in the Swedish *staa vad*, "to wager," and even in the French *gage*, *gager*, "pledge, to wager" – a curious contamination of the Latin and Germanic forms. (On *wadium*, *Wette*, etc., on "the amphibology of the wager and the contract," and on the relation between *wadium* and *nexum*, cf. Mauss, *The Gift*, p. 155ff).[17]

VI. Roman mythology[ii]

These two stories – which I have not coupled arbitrarily, since they were always consciously regarded by the Romans themselves as inseparable – are clearly seen to illuminate the Nordic facts. And this fact, in its turn, is justification for the procedure I have adopted of constantly searching in the earliest "Roman history" for the equivalent of what, under other skies, presents itself as "divine myths." It is not my concern here to take sides as to the fundamental veracity of this history. It is of little consequence to me whether, for example, kings named Romulus and Numa actually did exist, whether Romulus was assassinated, whether the Tarquinii were later "driven out," whether Lars Porsenna did besiege Rome, whether the plebeians did secede to the Sacred Hill, and so on. I am not interested in arguing about the reality of Brutus the Consul, or Publicola, or the importance that the gens Horatia and the gens Mucia might or might not have had in distant times. For me, the important thing is that the Romans should have linked certain edifying or symbolic scenes to their epic narratives of these events, and to the biographies of these characters, whatever their degree of historicity; and that the purpose of those scenes is the justification either of periodic feast days

ii Cf. *JMQ I*, p. 36ff.; *Horace et les Curiaces*, p. 61ff.; *Servius et la fortune*, p. 29ff., p. 119ff., p. 12Sff.; *JMQ II*, p. 123ff., and all of Ch. 3 ("Histoire et mythe"). [Note added to second edition. Chapter 3 is actually entitled "Latins et Sabins: histoire et mythe".]

or rites (such as the Lupercalia, the *poplifugium*, the *regifugium*, the festival of Anna Perenna, etc.), or of moral behaviors or "systems of representations" still familiar in the classical era, all of which are naturally very much earlier than the real or fictitious events seen as "establishing themselves" in "history," since they are as old as, and older than, Roman society itself. We must accustom ourselves to the notion that, given such wan gods who are almost wholly lacking in adventures – as Dionysius of Halicarnassus observed in his *Roman Antiquities* (II, 18) – the true Roman mythology, the mythology articulated in narratives, in circumstantiated events, is a mythology of heroes, epic in form, and little different – its weighty concern for verisimilitude apart – from the Irish mythology of the Middle Ages. Let none of my critics attempt to saddle me with the ridiculous thesis that the "Roman-Etruscan" or "Publicola-Porsenna" conflicts were the "historicization" of an ancient mythology of the Indian or Greek type, in which gods struggle against demons. No, Scaevola's opponent has not "taken the place" of a demon! What I do think is that, from its very beginnings, from the time when it acquired those specific characteristics that led to its success, Rome conceived its myths on the terrestrial plane, as a dynamic balance between terrestrial actors and forces.

VII. Nuada and Lug[18]

A moment ago I mentioned Irish mythology; and it is by no means out of place in this investigation, since it too presents us with a version of the "one-eyed sovereign" and the "one-armed sovereign" antithesis. In the epic representation of the successive invasions and settlements of Ireland, the Tuatha De Danann, which is to say, the ancient gods, on whom the Irish concentrated what they had retained of the Indo-European myths, conquered the island from the demonic Fomorians and their allies the Fir Bolg, the Fir Domnann and the Galioin. Their two leaders in this conquest were Nuada and Lug, two ancient and well-known gods. One had been the *Nodens*, *Nodons*, whose name occurs in Latin inscriptions in Great Britain (see above, p. 160/102); the other is the great *Lug samildanach* ("sym-poly-techni-cian"), who gave his name to Lugnasad, the Irish seasonal festival, and to the Gallic city of Lugdunum.

Tradition describes the installation of the Tuatha De Danann in Ireland as occurring in two phases. There were two successive battles, two victories, achieved a few years apart in the same place, on the plain called Mag Tured; the first over the Fir Bolg, the Fir Domnann and the Galioin, and the second over the Fomorians. Philologists, however, are generally of the opinion that this chronology is the result of a late and artificial doubling, and that there was originally only a single battle, that which became "the second." On the face of it, their argument is that the two earliest catalogues of Ireland's epic literature, as well as the "Glossary of Cormac" (about 900 A.D.) and a poem of Cináed hua hArtacáin (died 975 A.D.), mention only "a" battle of Mag Tured, and that it is not until texts of the eleventh century that two battles are mentioned and expressly differentiated (d'Arbois de Jubainville, *The Irish Mythological Cycle*, Dublin, 1903, pp. 84–86; cf., with slight attenuation, *L'Épopée celtique en Irlande*, 1892, p. 396).[19] But the real and underlying reason is that this duality of battles seems, to them, both nugatory and meaningless, and that, in addition, the epic material of the first battle is as jejune and insignificant as that of the second is fertile and original.

The philological argument is a weak one. First, it might well be that the first battle was in fact known at an early date, *without giving rise to autonomous epic narratives* such as those recorded in the early catalogues, and that it was referred to in narratives dealing with the second battle solely in order to clarify a detail or a situation. Second, the *fragment* inserted in the "Glossary of Cormac" does certainly refer to the "second" battle, waged against the Fomorians (d'Arbois de Jubainville, *The Irish Mythological Cycle*, p. 85 n. 3); but how does that prove that the existence of the first battle was unknown in about 900 A.D.? Was Cormac obliged to mention everything? Similarly, the Cináed poem contains a brief allusion to a well-known preliminary of the second battle and situates it, without further clarification, "before the battle of Mag Tured" (*ria cath Maigi Tuired*); but why *should* he specify "before the *second* battle"? Third, a poet contemporary with Cináed, Eochaid ua Flainn (died, 984), was already aware of the first battle, since he says of that battle, in which a hundred thousand warriors were slain, that it ended the royal line of the Tuath Bolg (i.e., clearly, the Fir Bolg). And this presupposes that the division explicitly indicated in the later tradition was already acquired (first battle: Tuatha De Danann versus Fir Bolg; second battle: Tuatha De Danann versus Fomorians).

As for the philologists' underlying reason for eliminating the first battle, the considerations of this present chapter annul it, or rather provide a very serious argument against it. If there are two successive victories at Mag Tured, it is because, as in the war against Porsenna and the exploits of Cocles and Scaevola, there are two types of victorious warrior to be given individual prominence: in the first, Nuada leads his people to victory, but *loses his right arm in so doing* – and this accident is immediately made use of in a ruse based *on the law of war*, which in turn leads to *a compromise peace and a pact of amity* between the adversaries. In the second battle, Lug ensures success for the selfsame people with magic, by circling around his army *while taking on the appearance of a one-eyed man, and this time the victory is total, without compromise.*

The second of these episodes is well known ("The Second Battle of Moytura", ed. W. Stokes, *Revue Celtique*, XII, 1891 p. 96ff.). The Tuatha De Danann are already partially established in Ireland as a result of the first battle, but, feeling themselves oppressed by Bress and the Fomorians (see above p. 161/102), they have shaken off their yoke. The great battle is about to begin. The Tuatha De Danann, who have designated Lug as their commander-in-chief (section 83), are unwilling to place in peril a life and a fund of knowledge so invaluable to them (section 95). Then (section 129), "the Tuatha De Danann, on the other side, rose up, left nine of their comrades to guard Lug, and went to do battle. Then, when the combat had begun, Lug, together with his driver, escaped from the guard under which he had been placed, so that he appeared at the head of the Tuatha De Danann army. A hard and fierce battle was fought between the Fomorians and the men of Ireland. Lug strengthened the men of Ireland (*boi Lug ognertad fer n-Erenn*), exhorting them to fight bravely so that they might live in servitude no longer; it was better for them to meet death defending their country than to live in subjugation and pay tribute, as they had been doing. That is why Lug then sang this song, while he circled the men of Ireland on one foot and with one eye (*conid and rocan Lug an cetul so sios for lethcois ocus letsuil timchall fer n-Erenn*; cf. above p. 172/111, Cuchulainn's one-eyed *delb*): *A battle shall arise....* (Section 130): "The armies let out a great shout as they went into combat, and so on." And then comes victory (sections 131–138), dearly bought but crushing and final, for the army of Lug, who is made king, Nuada having been killed at the very outset.

The first episode is less famous, doubtless because of the prejudice against it noted earlier. Here it is, as recounted in the unique and late manuscript published by Mr J. Fraser (*Eriu*, VIII, 1916, pp. 4–59),[20] which, despite its verbose form conforming to the taste of decadent epic literature, might of course retain early material. The Tuatha De Danann have just landed in Ireland. They have requested that the natives, the

Fir Bolg, cede one half of the island. The Fir Bolg have refused, and a fierce battle ensues. In the course of battle (section 48), the Fir Bolg named Sreng "struck the 'paramount king,' Nuada, with his sword; he cut through the edge of his buckler and the right arm at the shoulder, so that the arm fell to the earth with a third of the buckler" (*dobert Sreang bem cloidimh don airdrigh i do Nuadhaid gur theasg bile an sgeth ogus an laimh ndes ac a ghualaind, gu ndrochair an lamh gu triun an sgeth le for talmain*). The Tuatha De Danann carry Nuada from the battlefield and fight on so valiantly that they end that day victorious. So victorious, apparently, that should the struggle be resumed the next day, the Fir Bolg face certain extermination. During the night, despondent and down cast, the Fir Bolg hold council. Should they leave Ireland? Accept partition? Or fight on (section 57)? They agree on the third option. But Sreng appears to deplore this bloody and futile resistance: "Resistance, for men, is destruction," he says in verse, "the plains of Ireland are filled with suffering; for its forests we have met with misfortune, the loss of many brave men." As a result (section 58), when the two armies are drawn up, Sreng challenges his victim of the previous day, Nuada, to single combat. "Nuada looked at him bravely, as if he were sound in body (*atracht Nuada co nertchalma, amail dobeth slan*), and said to him: 'If what you seek is a fair fight (*comlann comadais*), strap down your right arm, for I no longer have mine (*cengailter luth de laime desi, uair nach fuil sin oramsa*); in this way, the fight will be fair!' Sreng replied: 'Your state implies no obligation on my side (*ni tormaig sin fiacha etir oramsa*), for our first fight has been canceled out (*uair robo comthrom ar cetchomrag*), that is the rule agreed between us!' "This threat to Nuada, this blackmail, as it were, leads the Tuatha De Danann to take the initiative in reaching a compromise that will limit their success. After meeting in council, they offer Sreng the choice of any province in Ireland for himself and his people. Thus peace is concluded, "peace and agreement and friendship" (*sith ogus comand ogus cairdine*). Sreng and the Fir Bolg choose the province of Connaught, the province of the paramount king, which consoles them for their real defeat with the appearance of "success" (*co haindinid aithesach*). As we have seen, Nuada survives, but is forced to give up his kingship to a temporary king (Bress), while he has an artificial arm made in order to reclaim his kingship. Hence, his appellation "*Nuada Airgetlam*," or "Nuada of the Silver Hand."

If we now go back to the diptych of legends that makes up the war of the Romans against Porsenna, the differences between it and the paired Celtic narratives are easily perceived. First, the order of the episodes is reversed: Cocles and his wild eye preceded Scaevola and his burned hand, whereas Nuada and his severed arm precede Lug and his magic grimace. Second, the episodes of Cocles and Scaevola are two episodes in a single war, which, thanks to Scaevola, is definitively ended by the pact of peace and friendship, whereas the Tuatha De Danann fight two successive wars, the first ended by a peace pact, the second by the extermination of their enemy. Third, Scaevola's mutilation is voluntary, calculated; it is Scaevola himself who makes juridical use of it, persuading Porsenna to come to terms, despite his imminent victory; whereas Nuada loses his arm by accident, and the exploitation of that accident is initiated by the Fir Bolg, who are facing disaster, rather than by the Tuatha De Danann, who, while facing a threat to their king's life, are nevertheless in practice already victorious.[iii]

All this is true; but the analogies are no less perceptible. First, the chronological reversal of the episodes in no way alters their meaning. Second, although the Irish epic speaks of two wars, those wars are waged with only a short interval between them, and are merely two

iii In other words, although the "one-armed sovereign," Nuada, is king of the Tuatha De Danann, it is their adversaries who benefit from the legalistic exploitation of that mutilation. In turn, this throws into prominence another situation relating to the "one-eyed sovereign": the other leader of the Tuatha De Danann, Lug, is indeed "one-eyed" as we have seen, but he is so only for a brief period, of his own free will, while assuming a grimace with magic effects. Now, in the battle that is in the offing, Lug's *adversary*, the most terrible of the enemy chiefs (who is, moreover, his own grandfather, whom he will strike down), is "Balar (or Balor) of the piercing gaze" (*Birugderc*), who is authentically one-eyed, and whose power, entirely magical, is linked precisely to that physical disfigurement, which is itself of magic origin. Of his two eyes, the story says (section 133), one, habitually closed, sprang open only on the field of battle, when it shot death at those unfortunate enough to be struck by his gaze. And we are also told the origin of this fearful privilege: one day, when his father's druids were busy concocting spells, Balar came and looked through the window; the fumes of the brew rose so that they reached his eye. (Cf. A.H. Krappe, *Balor with the Evil Eye*, Columbia Univ., 1927.) All these facts seem to indicate that the Irish tradition hesitated, at some point, as to whether the one-eyed and one-armed couple (and the advantages gained by the two mutilations) were to be placed in the Tuatha De Danann camp or in that of their enemies. [The full reference is Alexander Haggerty Krappe, *Balor with the Evil Eye: Studies in Celtic and French Literature* (New York: Institut des Études Françaises, Columbia University), 1927.]

complementary, interdependent episodes in the Tuatha De Danann's settlement of Ireland. Moreover, the second war is declared in the name of liberty (cf. Lug's exhortations to his troops quoted earlier), as the Tuatha De Danann have thrown off the yoke of a semi-alien and wholly tyrannical king, Bress, whom the Fomorians wish to replace – which is precisely the situation of the Romans in relation to Porsenna, who wants to reinstate Tarquinius Superbus (cf. the insults hurled by Cocles at the Etruscans in Livy, II, 10). Third, however dissimilar the "exploitations" of Scaevola's burnt hand and Nuada's severed arm might be, the fact remains that this exploitation takes place, that it culminates in a compromise peace and friendship (as in the case of Porsenna) which is, above all, juridical: using legalistic arguments, and rejecting the case against it formulated by Nuada, Sreng demands his *right in law*, which is to resume the duel begun the day before, with its "score" exactly as it was at the end of the first "set," which he had won, as it were, "hands down." And it is under pressure from this harsh but legitimate requirement that the Tuatha De Danann, after deliberation, make peace with the Fir Bolg.

Therefore, it seems to me that the two battles of Mag Tured are ancient; that, from the viewpoint of a philosophy of sovereignty inherited by the Celts, as by the Latins, from their Indo-European ancestors, they are necessary; and that they preserve, in an original fictional form, the double symbolism of the one-eyed sovereign and the one handed sovereign. Additionally, such a stance also avoids the serious difficulties that arise if one accepts the argument that there originally was only a *single* battle of Mag Tured. I will give one example. Unless we suppose (and where would that lead us?) that the story of the single original battle had a quite different structure from the narrative that has come down to us of the second battle, how are we to situate within that single battle the *mutilation* of Nuada, since he also, we are told, *perishes* in it and must of necessity perish in it? His appellation "of the Silver Hand" clearly requires an interval between the loss of his hand and his death. Yet how can we accept that Nuada survived a battle constructed wholly in honor of Lug, which had as its consequence, both logical in itself and asserted by tradition, that Lug became the new king of the Tuatha De Danann and, therefore, Nuada's successor?

It is from this new point of view we ought to resume the old argument, always conducted on shaky grounds, for and against the linking of "Nuada of the Silver Hand" with the one-handed Tyr (In favor: Axel Olrik, *Aarb. f oldk.*, 1902, p. 210ff.; J. de Vries *Altgerm. Religionsgesch.*, II, 1937, p. 287.[21] Against, with very weak arguments or most improbable hypotheses: K. Krohn, *Tyrs högra hand, Freys svärd*, in *Festsk. H.P. Feilberg*, 1911, p. 541ff.; A.H. Krappe, *Nuada à la main d'argent*, in *Rev. Celt.*, XLIX, 1932, p. 91ff.); the link holds good.[22]

We know that a late Mabinogi conserves, in the form "Lludd of the Silver Hand," *Lludd Llaw Ereint* (a description without explanation today),[iv] the Welsh equivalent of *Nuada Airgetlam*. It is worthy of note that this Mabinogi, *The Adventure of Llud and Llevelys*, (Loth, *Les Mabinogion*, ed. of 1913, I, pp. 231–241)[23] presents Lludd not just on his own, but as a couple, two brother-kings, Lludd (king of Britain) and Llevelys (king of France). King Lludd is a great builder (of London), a fine warrior, a generous distributor of food, but he is unable to solve the problem of three mysterious scourges that invade and lay waste his island. He consults Llevelys, "known for the excellence of his advice and his wisdom," and it is Llevelys who explains to him the magic origin of the three scourges, as well as providing him with the magic means to be rid of them. Ought we to see, concealed by a final distortion behind Llevelys, an equivalent of the Irish Lug (who is certainly to be found in the *Mabinogi of Math*, under the name of *Lleu*)?

iv The epithet Llaw Ereint is applied to Lludd only in another Mabinogi, that of *Kulwch and Olwen*; but the same personage is certainly involved.

CHAPTER X

Savitṛ and Bhaga

I. Sovereignty: The general command[1]

The topic we are exploring does not permit the mind to rest for long upon the states of balance it has glimpsed. Not that the new elements introduced into one's research at each new stage destroy the results of the preceding stage. The contrary is true. But those results can then no longer be viewed as anything but particular cases or as fragments of a much larger ensemble. Thus my analysis of the Luperci, then that of the flamines, at first pursued in isolation, eventually revealed a new perspective: that of the opposition and the "complementarity" of the two types of sacred persons (Chapters I and II). This antithetical couple, in its turn, took its place within an abundant collection of other linked couples – conceptual, ritual or mythical – that together define a bipartite representation of sovereignty (Chapters II and III). The implications of this then led me to look more closely at the Indo-European hierarchy of social functions, and I observed that this "bipartition" was not a specific characteristic of the first function, but that, by a sort of dialectical deduction, the entire social and cosmic hierarchy was made up of similar opposing pairs, successively harmonized into wider and wider concepts (Chapter IV). This view might well have appeared to be definitive, since I only went on to examine the interaction and activities of the sovereign couple within the various settings of sovereignty – in a kind of philosophy of royal histories (Chapter V), in civil law (Chapter VI), in the economic administration of the world (Chapter VIII), in war (Chapter IX);

and also, as a parallel, in the Indo-European areas of the world outside of Rome, India and Iran: among the Greeks (Chapter VII), the Germanic peoples (Chapters VII, VIII, and IX) and the Celts (Chapter IX). At this point, however, a detail from these latest inquiries abruptly forces me to widen the focus yet again.

Mitra and Varuṇa indisputably form a couple. But that couple is not isolated at the head of the divine hierarchy: around it, at the same level, its equal (in dignity if not in vigor), Vedic India, sets a group of singular beings called the Āditya, so that Mitra and Varuṇa are in fact no more than the two most typical, and most frequently invoked, of the Āditya as a whole. Just as my work on Uranos-Varuṇa left in shadow an essential aspect of sovereignty – the aspect of the *couple* – so I can foresee that the present work has left in shadow a whole sheaf of problems: those that pertain to the relations of the couple with the other Āditya, either individually or, it might be, in groups. At the moment, I lack the means to embark upon this immense field of study with any hope of useful results. It must suffice if I draw attention to the fact that several of the Āditya bear names that are certainly very ancient. Aryaman is Indo-Iranian and might have figures corresponding to him in Ireland (the hero Eremon) and in the Germanic world. Bhaga is Indo-Iranian and homophonous with *Bogu*, the noun for "god" in general throughout the Slavonic languages. Further, several of these personages bear abstract names that define their functions, and it is clear that those functions are in fact functions of sovereignty: *Bhaga* and *Aṃśa* are both linked to "distribution"; *Dhātṛ* is a "teacher," *Dakṣa*, "intelligence"; *Aryaman* himself certainly presided over important forms of social or human relations, possibly those linked with "nationality".[i]

The Aməša Spənta, the personified abstractions surrounding the supreme Iranian god, are not homologous with the Āditya. Rather, they are a sublimation of the early hierarchy of Indo-Iranian functional gods, Mitra-Varuṇa, Indra and the twin Nāsatya.[ii] Nevertheless, if we consider, after the Gāthās, the Avesta and Pahlavi literature as a whole, they do form a sort of general command of sovereignty [*d'état major général de la souveraineté*] above the band of the Yazata, and embody, for example,

i See Paul Thieme, *Der Fremdling im Rgveda: Eine Studie über die Bedeutung der Worte* Ari, Arya, Aryaman *und* Ärya, Leipzig: [Deutsche Morgenländische Gesellschaft/F.A. Brockhaus], 1938 [note moved from text].

ii Cf. *JMQ III*, p .86ff. [note added to second edition].

the single high god's various modes of action throughout the tripartite universe and society.[2]

If my analyses of Rome's "historical mythology" are correct, a comparable situation might be discerned there: Romulus and Numa, the two sovereign founders of the city, the worshippers of Jupiter and Fides, are neither its only kings nor even the only two founders of its state institutions. Each of their successors symbolizes, as do Romulus and Numa, a "type" of kingship, perfects some social organ, and is sometimes defined by a predilection for a particular cult. I am thinking in particular here, of Servius Tullius, organizer of the *census* and worshipper of Fortuna, to whom, it is quite true, he owed everything.[iii] But I am also mindful of the warlike Tullus Hostilius, the "manager" of certain forms of combat (Horatius and the Curiatii),[iv] and of the pious Ancus Marcius, who, at least in Livy, is not merely a repeat version of his grandfather, Numa, since the institution of the legal forms of war, of sacred diplomacy, is allotted to him.[v] Roman "history" thus distributed among successive reigns either the secondary provinces of sovereignty – those that do not coincide with the two antithetical provinces already expressed successively in the reigns of Romulus and Numa – or activities carried on in those areas where the two lower functions impinge upon sovereignty.[3]

Let me hasten to make it plain, however, that things are actually even less simple than that: while certainly not "insertable" into the list of Rome's kings, Cocles and Scaevola, as we have seen, nevertheless express two aspects of sovereignty in its relation to combat, to victory. And in India we find a very important being, one who often forms a closely linked couple with the Āditya Bhaga, who is often associated with those other Āditya Varuṇa, Mitra and Aryaman, and who was, nevertheless, not counted in early times as an Āditya himself: I mean Savitṛ.

II. Savitṛ and Bhaga

The twin expressions *Savitii Bhagah* and *Bhagah Savitā* are customary usages in the hymns. It is true that one could regard one of these two names, in either of the two forms, as being a simple epithet describing the other ("the distributing impeller" or "the impelling distributor"), but,

---

iii *Servius et la fortune*, p. 186ff. [note added to second edition].

iv *Horace et les Curiaces*, p. 79ff. [note added to second edition].

v *Tarpeia*, p. 176ff. [note added to second edition].

even reduced in this way, the expressions must attest at least to an affinity between the two personages. And, in fact, not only in the rhetoric of the hymns but also in their ritual use, Savitṛ and Bhaga do appear as complementary figures. The antithesis is less firm and, above all, less rich, than in the case of Varuṇa and Mitra – simply, no doubt, because Bhaga and Savitṛ are less well known to us and play smaller roles – but it is nevertheless clear and also consonant with the etymology of the names.

Savitṛ is an agent-noun in *-tr* formed on the root of Vedic *suváti* (Avestic *hu-nā-(i)ti*), "to excite, to set in motion, to vivify," sometimes "to procure," which is precisely the root used on numerous occasions, either alone or in compound forms, to denote the particular action of this god. J. Muir (*Original Sanskrit Texts*, V, 1870, p. 162ff.)[4] has listed and examined all the strophes or lines of the *Ṛg Veda* in which this propulsive, motivating, animating power is expressed, in its various specific guises. I do not think that present-day Indianists can have much to add to his account. Sometimes – when it comes into the orbit of Prajāpati – this "propulsion" even goes as far as "creation" (see A.A. Macdonell, *Vedic Mythology*, p. 33).[5] Last, there seem to be links, symbolically at least, with night, or with dawn and dusk: Savitṛ is said to be the name of the sun before it rises (Sāyana, *Commentary on the Ṛg Veda*, V, 81, 4), and it is said of him that he "sends to sleep" (*Ṛg Veda*, IV, 53, 6; VII, 45, 1).[6]

Bhaga, on the contrary, neither animates nor creates, but is described as the "distributor" (*vidhartr*), or "apportioner" (*vibhaktr*). He does indeed "give shares" in wealth, and appears, in both rituals and magic hymns, to be linked to "distributive chance or luck," as for instance in the case of marriage ("husband-giver" in *Atharva Veda*, II, 36, etc.) or of agricultural prosperity (*Gobhila Gṛhyasutra*, IV, 4, 28). Lastly, he has undisputed links with dawn ("his sister," *Ṛg Veda*, I, 123, 5) and with morning (Yāska, *Nirukta*, 12, 13).[7]

Thus, in the wake of Varuṇa-Mitra, we find a "motor"-"distributor" couple of which the components are related in an analogous way, and are susceptible, moreover, of taking on the same figurative images (night-day). However, the domains covered by Savitṛ-Bhaga are, needless to say, more circumscribed (in Bhaga's case, they are almost entirely economic), and, "dynamic" though he may be, Savitṛ certainly does not figure as a "terrible" god associated with a "benevolent" one.

Now, it so happens that Bhaga is the god who has lost his eyes and Savitṛ the god who has lost his hands.

III. The god without eyes and the god without hands

The stories that account for these two interdependent disfigurements are not, as among the Germans or the Romans, related to war or to political life. Just as it tended to make the sovereigns Mitra and Varuṇa into master and avenger in the field of ritual and its correct observance, so the sacrificial literature of the brahmans took over Bhaga, Savitṛ and their misadventure: it was on the occasion of a *sacrifice* – something that Savitṛ normally "propels" and Bhaga "apportions" – on the occasion of a very ancient sacrifice, offered by the gods, that the two were mutilated; and it would seem that it was in recompense for those mutilations that they were both subsequently empowered, using "replacement organs," to carry out their functions in the sacrifices offered by mankind.

This orientation of the Indian story does not, however, destroy its analogies with Western legends concerning the one-eyed sovereign and the one-armed sovereign, any more than the fact that the Indian gods, unlike the Western gods or heroes, lose both eyes and both arms. Or, lastly, any more than the fact – quite normal in India, where there is a fondness for "series" – that a third mutilated figure (without teeth) or indeed a whole sequence of them should have been added to the first pair. There is, on the other hand, a more serious difference, one that totally reverses the import of the two mutilations: it is Savitṛ, the propellant god, who loses his hands, and it is Bhaga, the distributive god, who loses his eyes. Of course, it is easy enough to perceive the relationship of these losses with the two gods' functions (the hand drives, the eye allocates; cf. the bandage that we place over Fortune's eyes to signify that she is blind); but in the West it is the "jurist" god (and thus the one akin to, if not homologous with, Bhaga) who is one-armed, by reason of the recognized link between the right hand and good faith, and it is the magician god or the terrible hero who is one-eyed, by reason of the recognized link between the eye and second sight. Thus, the Indians oriented and allotted the elements of the double symbol in a completely different way. Now let me give an account of the various forms the incident took.

The *Kauṣītaki Brāhmaṇa*, VI, 13, links it to the precautions taken by the officiating brahman to consume the *prāśitra*, "the first fruit of the sacrifice." When the gods set out their sacrifice of old, they offered the first fruit to Savitṛ; it cut off his hands (*tasya pāṇī praciccheda*), and they gave him two golden hands, which is why he is called "of the golden hands" (*hiraṇyapāṇiḥ*), an epithet indeed applied to Savitṛ in the *Ṛg Veda*. Then they offered it to Bhaga; it destroyed his two eyes, which is why it is said "Bhaga is blind" (*andhaḥ*). Then they offered it to *Pūṣan*, and it knocked out his teeth, which is why it is said "Pūṣan has no teeth, he eats *karambha*" (a moist flour cake). Then they offered it to Indra, saying: "Indra is the strongest, the most victorious of the gods," and, using the magic formula (*brāhmaṇa*), "he made it gentle." Forewarned by this unpleasant incident from divine prehistory, the brahman who in later times consumed the *prāśitra* took care to say: "I gaze on you with the eye of Mitra," "By permission of the lightfilled Savitṛ, I take you with the arms of the Aśvin, with the hands of Pūṣan," "I eat you with the mouth of Agni." Finally, he rinses his mouth with water, then touches all the parts and orifices of his body, thus restoring any damage done by consumption of the *prāśitra* (cf. a similar formula in which Savitṛ is invoked during the initiation ceremonies of the young *dvija*: *Pāraskara Gṛhyasūtra*, II, 4, 8).

The meaning of the story is clear, and Weber, in *Indische Studien* (II, 1883, pp. 307–308),[8] provides a good explication. Briefly, the *prāśitra* is charged with sacred values, and, so, clearly cannot be jettisoned without catastrophe; but its consumption is likewise a matter of grave peril. This tragic dilemma, from which the gods were once rescued by the devotion of several of their number, is much the same as those from which the Ases and the Romans are rescued by the sacrifices of Tyr and Scaevola. It is simply that here the forces to be confronted and neutralized are purely ritual, reduced entirely to the "sacrificial discharge," whereas the forces threatening Rome and the Ases are those of their enemies – the military force of the Etruscans, the demonic force of Fenrir. Moreover, it is possible that India did have a variant closer to the Western legends, for Mahīdhara, in his commentary on the *Vājasaneyi-Saṁhitā* (I, 16; p. 21 in Weber's edition),[9] in order to explain the epithet "of the golden hands" (*hiraṇyapāṇiḥ*), habitually applied to Savitṛ, says: "It is because the ornaments on his fingers are of gold; or else because Savitṛ's hands, having been cut off by the demons when he was taking the *prāśitra*, the gods made him two more out of gold; that is why it is said that Savitṛ has golden hands (*yad vā daityaih prāśitraharena chinnau Savitṛpānī devair hiranyamayau kṛtāv iti savitur hiranyapānītvam iti*).

Other texts recount the incident much as it occurs in the *Kausītaki Brāhmaṇa*, but sometimes with variants. Although the *Gopatha Brāhmaṇa* (II, 1, 2)[10] reproduces the same sequence of mutilations, albeit with Bhaga preceding Savitṛ, the *Śatapatha Brāhmaṇa* (I, 7, 4, 6–8) restricts mutilation to Bhaga (*andhaḥ*, "blind" because he looked at the *prāśitra*) and Pūṣan (*adantakaḥ*, "toothless" because he tasted it), and it is Bṛhaspati, thanks to the "animator" Savitṛ, and not Indra, who succeeds in taming the perilous portion without injury. In general, the episode comes at the end of a "terrible" story (e.g., *Śatapatha Brāhmaṇa* I, 7, 4, 1–5): Prajāpati, the Lord of Creatures, the Creator, was guilty of having conceived a love for his own daughter. The angry gods asked Rudra, king of the beasts, to pierce him with an arrow. Rudra shot his arrow, and Prajāpati fell. Their anger stilled, the gods tended him and drew out Rudra's arrow, but, "Prajāpati being the sacrifice," a little sacrificial matter remained stuck to the arrow, and it was this that constituted the prototype of the fearsome *prāśitra*.

Fictionalized in a different form, this is the story, famous in the epic literature, of the "sacrifice of Dakṣa." Dakṣa – one of the ancient Āditya, whose name appears to mean "intelligence, skill," and who assimilated very early on into Prajāpati as universal father – offers a sacrifice to which, for a variety of reasons, he fails to invite Śiva (assimilated to Rudra, etc.). Śiva appears in a fury, bow in hand, and scatters the sacrifice and mutilates the gods who are present. The *Mahābhārata*, for example (X, 18), says that "Rudra cut off both Savitṛ's hands and, in his anger, put out both Bhaga's eyes, and smashed in Pūṣan's teeth with the curved end of his bow; then the gods and the various elements of the sacrifice fled..." (slokas 801–802). Eventually, this terrible Great God is appeased: "He gave back his two eyes to Bhaga, his two hands to Savitṛ, and his teeth to Pūṣan, and to the gods their sacrifice," of which they hurriedly hand over to him, as his share, "the totality" (slokas 807–808).

Other texts present slightly different versions, often omitting Savitṛ and his hands, while, on the contrary, decapitating Dakṣa, who then receives a ram's head as compensation. But occasionally one comes across a direct echo of the "warning formulas" of the *Kausītaki Brāhmaṇa*. In the *Bhāgavata Purāṇa* (IV, 7, 3–5), for example, when the terrible god is appeased and is making good the injuries he has inflicted, he tells Bhaga to look upon his share of the sacrifice "through the eye of Mitra" (*Mitrasya cakṣuṣā*), and, without mentioning Savitṛ's specific mutilation, the compensation he offers for it is precisely that found in the ancient ritual text: "Let those who lost arms and hands find arms again by the arms of the Aśvin, by the hands of Pūṣan!" (*bāhubhyām asvinoh pūṣno hastābhyaṃ kṛtabāhavaḥ bhavantu*!).[vi]

---

vi Cf. the formula that, from Vedic times onward, precedes so many ritual gestures: *devasya savituh prasave aśvinor bāhubhyām pūsno hastābhyām* "in the propulsion of the god Savitṛ, by the arms of the Aśvin,

Such were the ways in which the twin mutilations of the ancient sovereign gods evolved in the epic literature and the Puranas. And note should be taken of Bhaga's compensation for his blinding: he will see "with the eye of Mitra." This link, this two-way connection between the "distributor" and the "punctilious" is not surprising, and echoes that which is sometimes observed – in a purely ritual context – between the "propeller" and the "terrible," between Savitṛ and Varuṇa (e.g., *Śatapatha Brāhmaṇa*, XII, 7, 2, 17). It also lends full significance to the fact that Mithra, in one part of Iran, seems to have been honored under the name *Baga* (whereas, elsewhere, *Baga* became, as in Slavonic, a generic term for "gods").

IV. The Cyclopes and the hundred-handed giants

Thus, with a reversal of the relations and an amplification of the details that alter neither the framework nor the general import of the episode, India, like the West, was no stranger to the theme of the coupled sovereign gods, or coupled "agents of sovereignty," one with mutilated eyes, the other with mutilated hands. Such agreement leads one to think that this theme was customary in the symbolism and mythology of cosmic sovereignty, as early as the time of the Indo-European community. And one is then tempted to attribute both importance and antiquity to a detail in the Uranides story. Let me just quote the beginning of Apollodorus's *Bibliotheca.*

> "Uranos was the first sovereign of the universe (Οὐρανὸς πρῶτος τοῦ παντὸς ἐδυνάστευσε κόσμου). He married Gaia and had as first children those called the 'hundred-hands,' Briareos, Gyes, Kottos, all without rivals in their stature and strength, furnished with a hundred arms (χεῖρας μὲν ἀνὰ ἑκατὸν) and fifty heads. Then came the Cyclopes, Arges, Steropes, Brontes, each with one eye in his forehead (ὧν ἕκαστος εἶχεν ἕνα ὀφθαλμὸν ἐπὶ τοῦ μετώπου). These last

---

by the hands of Pūṣan!" (see the index of Weber's ed. of *Taitt. Samh.*, and L. von Schroeder's of *Maitr. Samh*). [Note added to second edition. These are abbreviations to standard editions. Albrecht Weber (ed.), *Die Taittirīya-Saṃhitā* (Leipzig: Brockhaus, 2 volumes, 1871–72); Leopold von Schroeder (ed.), *Maitrāyaṇī saṃhitā* (Leipzig: F.A. Brockhaus, 4 volumes, 1881–86).]

Uranos chained, and hurled them into Tartarus (τούτους μὲν Οὐρανὸς δήσας εἰς Τάρταρον ἔρριψε), a place of darkness in Hades, as far from earth as earth is from heaven. Then he begot, with Gaia, sons who are called Titans: Oceanos, Koios, Hyperion, Krios, Iapetos and, last of all, Kronos, as well as daughters who are called Titanides, Tethys, Rhea, Themis, Mnemosyne, Phoibe, Dione, Theia.

"Outraged by the loss of her children who were cast into Tartarus, Gaia persuaded the Titans to attack their father and gave Kronos a steel scythe. Oceanos excepted, the Titans attacked their father, and Kronos cut off his genitals and hurled them into the sea. The Erinyes, Alekto, Tisiphone, and Magaera were born from the drops of blood that fell. Having toppled Uranos from power, the Titans brought their brothers back from Tartarus and gave Kronos power.

"But he chained them once more, and sent them back to Tarturus (ὁ δὲ τούτους μὲν ἐν τῷ Ταρτάρῳ πάλιν δήσας καθεῖρξε), then married his sister, Rhea. Kronos swallowed all those who were born to him, Hestia first, then Demeter and Hera, then Pluto and Poseidon, because Gaia and Uranos had prophesied that power would be taken from Kronos by his own son. Angered, Rhea journeyed to Crete, for she was pregnant with Zeus, and gave birth in Dikte's cave. [Then follows the usual story of Zeus's childhood, the stone given to the father and swallowed as a substitute, etc.]

"When Zeus was grown, he secured the aid of Metis, daughter of Oceanos, who caused Kronos to drink a drug that made him vomit up the stone, and then all the children he had swallowed. Then Zeus waged war against Kronos and the Titans. They fought for ten years. Gaia prophesied victory for Zeus if he won the allegiance of those who had been cast into Tartarus (ἡ Γῆ τῷ Διὶ ἔχρησε τὴν νίκην, τοὺς καταταρταρωθέντας ἂν ἔχῃ συμμάχους). Zeus killed Kampe, who tended their shackles, and unbound them (ὁ δὲ τὴν φρουροῦσαν αὐτῶν τὰ δεσμὰ Κάμπην ἀποκτείνας ἔλυσε). Then the Cyclopes gave thunder and lightning to Zeus, the skin helmet to Pluto, the trident to Poseidon. Thus armed, these three overcame the Titans, and, having imprisoned them in Tartarus, set the hundred-hands over them as their keepers (καθείρξαντες αὐτοὺς ἐν τῷ Ταρτάρῳ τοὺς ἑκατόγχειρας κατέστησαν φύλακας). They, themselves, drew lots for power: Zeus received sovereignty over the sky, Poseidon over the sea, and Pluto over Hades."

I am happy to reproduce this text here for several reasons. First, in the light of all the documentary evidence so far assembled relating to the *bond*, to the importance of the bond as a symbol and as a weapon of the terrible sovereign, as opposed to both the warrior god and the jurist-sovereign (for Varuṇa, see my *Ouranós-Vāruṇa*, pp. 50–51, and *Flamen-Brahman*, pp. 67–68; for *Wôdhanaz, see my *Mythes et dieux des Germains* pp. 21, 26–27, and above; for Romulus, see above pp. 113ff/67ff, 113 n. 1/67 n. i). I hope that certain Hellenists will not continue to regard the verb δεῖν, the substantive δεσμός, and the verb λύειν, which occur so regularly in this narrative, as mere "everyday" words. The literary trustee of a tradition whose former breadth and scope I have never claimed he was aware of, Apollodorus makes the contrast as clear as possible between two modes of struggle: that of the terrible sovereigns, Zeus's predecessors, and that of Zeus himself. Uranos – and this is partly true of his doublet, Kronos, too – does not fight and has no weapon. No mention is made of any resistance to his violence, and, yet, at least some of his victims are said to be "without rivals for their stature and their strength." This is as if to say that resistance to Uranos is inconceivable, as is attested again by the very scenario of his fall: he cannot be attacked, nor even accosted, except through the use of guile and ambush. When he takes the initiative, "he binds," and that is that. Zeus, on the contrary, is a combatant, one who fights for ten years and more against savage resistance, one who acquires weapons, and who, in order to recruit allies, "unbinds" those "bound" by Uranos, after first killing the tender of their "bonds." This opposition is in perfect conformity with that observed in India, between the magician-sovereign Varuṇa, who binds without combat, and the combatant Indra, who is only too ready to unbind Varuṇa's victims (see above p. 125/76); with that observed in Germany, between binding magician, *Wôdhanaz, and the combatant, Thor; and with that observed in Rome, between the binder Romulus (who has his *lictores* bind instantly all those he points out) and either the unbinding *flāmen dialis* or the consul of the legend of the *nexi soluti* (see above, p. 130/79–80). It is the symbolic expression of an opposition between the natures of two types of leader. And since the very names of Uranos and Varuṇa seem to be linked, according to Indian tradition, to a root that means "to bind," it is not possible for me, either by way of comparative research or simple textual analysis, to allow this extremely articulate document to be ruled out on the pretext of a mere subjective impression of "everydayness."[vii]

vii Cf. Ch.VI [p. 113/67] [note added to second edition].

However, I have quoted the Uranides story for another reason. I have been led to the conclusion that the Indo-Europeans symbolized two aspects of sovereignty in beings – major or minor sovereign gods, or auxiliaries to the sovereign gods – one of whom had only one eye (or no eyes at all), and the other only one hand (or no hand at all); and this deformity, usually acquired but sometimes congenital, is precisely what fits them both for their sovereign function (see the discussion on Cocles, according to Plutarch's alternative explanation, above, p. 171/111).

Now, the story of the Uranides – and not in Apollodorus alone – brings into play, first as children and as victims of the terrible Uranos, then as "givers of sovereignty" allied with Zeus, *two symmetrical groups of beings, one of which has only one eye and the other a hundred hands*. Yes, I know that there is a difference between a hundred and one. Nonetheless, it is striking that Zeus's sovereignty should be assured by the cooperation of coupled sets of abnormal beings whose abnormalities relate to the eyes, in one case, and to the hands, in the other. Perhaps there even remains, between these two groups, something of an early allocation of "secondary sovereign functions" comparable to that seen elsewhere, with those functions simply downgraded, becoming mere craft-level magic for one set, and police or prison-officer work for the other. For it is the metalworking Cyclopes who, in fact, make the supernatural weapons that assure Zeus and his principal officers of their victory, and the hundred hands who are then used by the triumphant Zeus as his jailers. And – whereas prison-officers need to be strong, and higher-ranking servants of the law, like Tyr or Scaevola, above all need to instill trust in their word – it is conceivable that these monsters have each received an additional ninety-eight hands, rather than losing one, to make them more fitted to their humbler duties.[viii]

Therefore, it seems that the story of the Uranides is more archaic and more coherent than I was hitherto aware, and that, in a fanciful, fictional form, and with the alterations usual in traditions that no longer have any religious value proper, it preserves a complex system of representations, a whole interplay of concepts and symbols, an entire theory of sovereignty.

viii On the Cyclopes and the hundred-hands, cf. also *Tarpeia*, p. 221ff. [note added to second edition].

Conclusion

The analysis of couples conforming to the Mitra-Varuṇa type will have to be extended, no doubt, to areas I have not yet suspected. We already know enough about such couples, however, to be sure that this bipartition was very important. Enough, also, to define their limits and originality. And it is on these last two points that I now wish to lay stress.

Faced with certain tendencies in Indian thought, the reader might in fact have received the impression that oppositions of this type had a limitless field of application, that they constituted a method of division that could be used for all the concepts comprised in representations of the world. Seeing day and night (India, Rome) and autumn and spring (Iran) drawn into this classificatory current, some might have called to mind that fundamental couple found in Chinese classifications, *yin* and *yang*. And perhaps, indeed, the thought of the Indo-Europeans might well have found, in the facts we are dealing with here, both the material and the instrument for a Chinese-style systematization. In practice, however, it did not venture very far along that path. Even so, the comparison is an instructive one.

Marcel Granet (*La Pensée Chinoise*, pp. 115–148) has investigated the uses of the terms *yin* and *yang* in the earliest texts, those from the fifth to the third centuries B.C. and even that early their applications are very widespread indeed.[1] They are found in astronomical, geographical and musical texts, and the "male-female" orientation is more than suggested. (The primacy of this last aspect is not very probable, however, since the two corresponding characters are formed with the mound radical, whereas any notion that is essentially, primitively feminine as opposed to masculine would contain the woman radical. It began to emerge very early, however, under the influence, Granet thinks, of hierogamic representations such as Earth-Heaven, Water-Fire and the like, which are so important in all Chinese speculation.) Whatever the origin of the words and their graphic representations, however, concrete universe and abstract universe alike were very quickly distributed between *yin* and *yang*. Points and segments of time and space, social functions, organs, colors, sounds, were all divided into antithetical dyads with the aid of massive or exiguous correspondences, of symbolic interactions, of mathematical artifice or dialectical analogy. And that, according to Granet's analysis, is the primary characteristic of this couple: it has no clear definition other than as a principle of classification, as a form of thought. Its material, the attributes it connotes, which are in any case limitless, are of less importance. It corresponds to a type of mind that pushes to the extreme the recognition and use of *contrasts*. A second characteristic is also common to at least a very large number of these contrasts: they are not only antithetical, they are also *rhythmic*, which is to say, subject to a system of alternations, of which the seasons provide the most typical natural example.

Perhaps I have not attached enough importance to this notion of rhythm in our Indo-European couples: the double alternation that constitutes the series of Rome's first four kings (the Lupercus Romulus; the king-priest Numa; Tullus, who reacts against Rome's "senescence" under Numa; Ancus, who restores the regime of Numa); myths such as those of Othinus and Mithothyn, Othinus and Ollerus; the periodicity of the Lupercalia; the annual swing from the spring festival of Naurōz (Ahura-Mazdāh) to the autumn festival of Mihrjān (Mithra): all these facts, and several others, should be examined anew from this fresh point of view.

Similarly, the analogy with *yin* and *yang* frees me from the task of defining our Indo-European coupling exactly in terms of its material: it too, being essentially a mode of thought, a formal principle of classification, evades such definition. At the most, one can provide samples and say, for instance, that one of the two components (Varuṇa, etc.) covers that which is inspired, unpredictable, frenzied, swift, magical, terrible, dark, demanding, totalitarian, *iunior*, and so on; whereas the other (the Mitra side) covers that which is regulated, exact, majestic, slow, juridical, benevolent, light, liberal, distributive, *senior*, and so on. But it would be futile to start from one element in these lists of "contents" in the hope of deducing the others from it.

Can the analogy be pushed any further?[2] Did the "sovereign concepts" couple evolve, like *yin* and *yang*, toward a sexed interpretation, toward a "male-female" pairing? If we take the Indo-European world as a whole, it appears not. In Rome, Fides is a feminine divinity only because she is a personified abstraction, and she is so little opposed to *Iupiter* as female to male that she is in fact doubled with a masculine equivalent, Dius Fidius. In reality, within each of the two types of representations, there is room, should it be required, for both sexes, in which case the types of relations between the sexes are then radically opposed (the behavior of the Luperci toward the anonymous women they whip, as opposed to the holy and personal union of *flāmen dialis* and *flāminica*, etc.). But the most precociously philosophical of the Indo-European regions, India, did indeed set out along the path of the sexed couple, and did so, it appears, like the Chinese, under the influence of their powerful hierogamic representation of heaven and earth:[i] is Varuṇa not "the other world" and also, albeit not in any stable way, heaven (cf. οὐρανὸς), whereas Mitra is "this world"?[ii] But a fact that seems very odd at first glance, and contradicts the Chinese system (heavenly *yang*, earthly *yin*), as well as a Greek development (Uranos, the "male" of Gaia) – a fact doubtless to be explained by the passive character often taken on by what Mircea Eliade terms the "hierophanies of heaven" (*Dyauh*, "heaven" is, after all, constructed grammatically in many Vedic texts as if it were feminine) – is that it is Varuṇa who is endowed with feminine values, those of *yin*, and Mitra who takes on the powers of the male, of *yang*.[3] The *Śatapatha Brāhmaṇa* (II, 4, 4, 19), says that "Mitra ejaculated his seed into Varuṇa" (*mitro varuṇe retaḥ siñcati*). The same *Brāhmaṇa* (XII, 9, 1, 17), though contrasting him this time with Indra as the male, confirms that "Varuṇa is the womb" (*yonir eva varuṇaḥ*). This sexual primacy of Mitra's, and this sexual impregnation of Varuṇa by Mitra, indeed link up nicely with Mitra's conceptual primacy and Varuṇa's conceptual impregnation by Mitra which are expounded, for example, in *Śatapatha Brāhmaṇa*, IV, 1, 4,[iii] an important text in which

i Cf. A.K. Coomaraswamy, *Spiritual Authority and Temporal Power in the Indian Theory of Government*, 1942, p. 50ff. [Note added to second edition. This discussion is on pp. 50–51.]

ii Certainly Indo-Iranian notions, and no doubt Indo-European: see Coomaraswamy, [*Spiritual Authority and Temporal Power*], p. 85 [note added to second edition].

iii Translated into French by M.L. Renou in his *Anthologie sanskrite*, [*Textes de l'Inde ancienne*, Paris: Payot] 1947, pp. 32–33 [note added to second edition].

Mitra and Varuṇa are successively opposed as the *kratu* (who formulates desire) and the *dakṣa* (who executes desire), as the *abhigantṛ* ("conceiver") and the *kartṛ* ("actor"), as *brahman* and *kṣatra* (more or less, as we say, "spiritual power" and "temporal power"). This text explains that Mitra and Varuṇa were once distinct (*agre nānevāsatuḥ*); but that, whereas Mitra (*brahman*) could subsist apart from Varuṇa (*kṣatra*), the reverse was not the case, and that, consequently, Varuṇa said to Mitra: "Turn toward me (*upa māvartasva*), so that we maybe united (*saṃsṛjāvahai*); I assign you priority (*puras tvā karavai*)." In this light, I believe it becomes easier to understand the origin of certain concepts in later Indian philosophy. The *sāṃkhya* system, which holds the universe to be collaboration between a spectator "self" which it calls *Purașa*, "the male principle," and the *prakrti*, an active, multiform, female "nature," felt that its *Purașa* and its *prakṛti* were antithetical in the same way as Mitra and Varuṇa (*Mahābhārata*, XII, 318, 39; *Mitram puruṣaṃ Varuṇam praktṛiṃ tatha*).[4] In the other great Indian philosophic system, the Vedanta, the two antithetical components are *Brāhma* and *Māyā*, and they, too, are divided in accordance with the same system: on the one hand, the celestial projection – masculine – of the brahman (and remember that the old liturgical texts, when contrasting him with Varuṇa, say that "Mitra is the brahman"); on the other, the creative illusion (and *maya* in the Veda is the great technique of the magician Varuṇa).[5] I leave historians of philosophy to evaluate these coincidences, and to decide whether they are mere chance or whether the two dualistic philosophies developed in part from the early myth of bipartite cosmic sovereignty. I have already expressed my opinion (*Flamen-Brahman*, appendix I: *la carriere du brahman céleste*)[6] that the concept of Brahmā the creator, of Brahmā taking himself as sacrificial victim at the beginning of time in order to constitute the world order, did not spring into being as the mere fancy of one thinker, but as an amplification and stylization of early rituals of human sacrifice, the purpose of which was the periodic renewal or maintenance of social and world order, and in which the victim was normally a terrestrial brahman. Similarly, it is also probable that the triads of "qualities" that played so large a role in Indian speculations are not wholly different in kind from the early theory of the threefold division of social and cosmic functions. Nor, indeed, is there anything exceptional in a myth that gives rise to a philosophy.

Yin and *yang* determine a general bipartition of the universe, at all its levels. Is the same true of the Indo-European pairing of sovereign concepts? Assuredly not, since, in the Indo-European system, sovereignty is only the first of the three levels of both universe and society, so that the dualist formula characterizing it is adapted to that level alone. It is quite true that the other levels, that of the warrior and that of the third estate, that of victory and that of prosperity, are also, either occasionally or regularly, presided over by paired divinities. For example, at the morning pressing of the soma sacrifice, we find Indra-Vayū on the second level juxtaposed to Mitra-Varuṇa, then the twin Aśvin or Nāsatya on the third (*Śatapatha Brāhmaṇa*, IV, 1, 3–5). But it is easy to establish that the intention, the stability and the inner mechanism of these dualist formulas are very different from those of the Mitra-Varuṇa coupling: far from being antithetical and complementary, the two Aśvin are interdependent and equivalent to the point of being indistinguishable; and as for the association of Indra with Vayū, it is merely one of the very numerous associations to which Indra is prone, associations that are so numerous precisely because they are the products of particular occasions and never make any profound inroads into the unitary, unipolar, solitary structure of the fighter-god. Of course, India would not be India if these straight forward analyses did not encounter an exception: the fundamental hierogamic representation, heaven-earth, has, on occasion, exerted its influence on these various couples: "the Aśvin are in truth heaven and earth," we read, for example, in *Śatapatha Brāhmaṇa*, IV, 1, 5, 16 (and even as early as *Ṛg Veda*, VI, 72, 3); but that does not entail any sexual consequence for them, one does not "ejaculate his seed" into the other, and they remain undifferentiated. In short, this fleeting assimilation has no more importance than when *Ṛg Veda* (I, 109, 4) invokes Indra-Agni as Aśvin, or (X, 61, 14–16) again assimilates Agni and Indra to the Nāsatya; or, again, *when Śatapatha Brāhmaṇa* (X, 4, 1, 5), interprets the Indra-Agni couple as the equivalent of the *kṣatra-brahman* couple. These are simply the customary and conscious games of Vedic "confusionism."

It will be interesting to confront the Indo-European mechanism isolated here with mechanisms other than that of *yin* and *yang*. Analogies will be found – as will differences, of which I can give one important example. One might be tempted to compare the "good" Mitra alongside the "terrible" Varuṇa with certain forms of messianism known in the ancient Near East, or with the great Christian dogma of the "son" as intercessor and savior juxtaposed to the avenging, punishing father. It does not seem, however, that any development in this direction was initiated in any region – except Iran, where Plutarch (*Isis and Osiris*, 46) was able to take Mithra as being a μεσίτης, a "mediator" (but, even then, a very specific type of mediator between the principle of good and the principle of evil), and which, above all, provided the Mediterranean world with the elements of "Mithraism," a salvation religion that proved capable of almost tipping the scales against Christianity for a period. But this particular development is doubtless to be explained by Iran's geographical position, its particular neighbors, and the probable contacts that resulted, at a very early stage, between its own religions and others that were centered around a suffering and triumphant savior. Moreover, it was a development that did not take on any precise form, significantly enough, until that moment when the religion of Mithra had in fact become detached from Iran.

APPENDIX I

"Nuada and Balar"

Seventh section of Chapter IX, first edition, pp. 124–8, translated by the editor

Nous venons de parler de l'Irlande : elle n'est pas déplacée dans cet exposé puisqu'elle présente elle aussi, sous une forma aberrante, l'opposition du « Souverain Borgne » et du « Souverain Manchot ». Mais ici il faut parler d'opposition au sens le plus fort : duel, et duel à mort. Par cette affabulation, l'Irlande est donc – en la dépassant même par la rigueur – d'accord avec la Germanie contre Rome, contre l'Iran, contre l'Inde (cf. ci-dessus, pp. 88 et 96). Son Manchot est le roi des « bons ». Tuatha Dê Danann, dont il a déjà été question (p. 108), son Borgne est le roi des « mauvais » Fômoré, ennemis des Tuatha Dê Danann : ainsi l'antithèse qui, dans l'Inde avec Varuṇa et Mitra, à Rome avec Romulus et Numa, Jupiter et Fides, etc., n'est que l'antithèse abstraite de deux formes également bonnes de la	A moment ago I mentioned Ireland: it is not out of place in this reading since it too presents, in an aberrant form, the opposition of the "One-eyed Sovereign" and the "One-armed Sovereign." But here we must speak of opposition in the strongest sense: duel, and duel to the death. By this fabrication, Ireland is thus—even exceeding it in rigour—in agreement with Germania against Rome, against Iran, against India (cf. above, pp. 134–5/84–85 and 145/91). Its one-armed is the king of the "good." Tuatha De Danann, already mentioned (p. 160/102), its one-eyed king is the king of the "bad" Fomorians, enemies of the Tuatha De Danann: thus the antithesis which, in India with Varuṇa and Mitra, in Rome with Romulus and Numa, Jupiter and Fides, etc., is merely the abstract antithesis of two equally good forms of

Souveraineté, se résout ici dans une lutte concrète entre une forme bonne et une forme mauvaise de la Souveraineté. Évolution qui n'a rien d'extraordinaire, étant donné la violence, parfois la cruauté, qui caractérise les concepts du type Varuṇa, Romulus, Jupiter, etc. Évolution dont l'Inde, d'ailleurs, offre partiellement l'équivalent puisque, après les *Veda*, le « grand Asura » Varuṇa n'a pu rester un être « bon », un « dieu », qu'en rompant toute solidarité avec les Asura, qui, eux, se tournaient franchement en démons, et puisque les rois du type *Gandharva*, tels que Purūravas et Nahuṣa (cf. ci-dessus, pp. 63 et suiv.), finissent au moins comme des rois « mauvais ». La vieille collaboration « sorcier-prêtre » (« illusionniste-juriste », etc.) tend souvent, par la stabilisation des sociétés, à évoluer en conflit, avec déchéance du sorcier.	Sovereignty, is resolved here in a concrete struggle between a good and an evil form of Sovereignty. This is not an unusual development, given the violence, sometimes cruelty, that characterises concepts like Varuṇa, Romulus, Jupiter, etc. India offers a partial equivalent of this development, since after the Veda, the "great Asura" Varuṇa could only remain a "good" being, a "god," by breaking all solidarity with the Asura, who, in turn, transformed directly into demons, and since the kings of the Gandharva type, such as Purūravas and Nahuṣa (cf. above, pp. 103 ff/60ff), end up at least as "bad" kings. The old collaboration of the "sorcerer-priest" ("illusionist-lawyer," etc.) often tends, through the stabilisation of societies, to evolve into conflict, with the sorcerer's downfall.
Le caractère de deux personnages est bien assuré : le Manchot (qui a perdu son main « dans une bataille antérieure » comme Cocles a perdu son œil, – ce qui signifie peut-être simplement que, dans l'un et l'autre cas, une origine plus précise et plus pittoresque a été oubliée). Nuada « à la main d'argent (*Airgellâm*), c'est le prince juste et réglé, ainsi qu'il ressort suffisamment du comportement contraire de son « intérimaire » Bress, dans le récit qui a été étudié plus haut (p. 109) ; en effet, contre Bress, il représente la forme particulière de justice et de liberté économiques, de propriété inviolable, qui semble avoir été l'idéal des Celtes insulaires, et c'est parce qu'il représente « ce droit »	The character of two persons is well assured: the One-armed king (who lost his hand "in a previous battle" as Cocles lost his eye—which may simply mean that in both cases a more precise and picturesque origin has been forgotten). Nuada "of the silver hand" (*Airgellâm*) is the just and regulated prince, as is sufficiently evident from the contrary behaviour of his "temporary replacement," Bress, in the account which was studied above (p. 161/102); indeed, against Bress, he represents the particular form of economic justice and freedom, of inviolable property, which seems to have been the ideal of the island Celts, and it is because he represents "this right" that the Tuatha De Danann are

que les Tuatha Dê Danann lui sont attachés, lui rendent le trône et se battent pour lui contre les Fômoré qui soutiennent « l'étatiste » Bress. Le Monoculaire, Balar « au regard transperceur » (*Birugderc*), le plus terrible des chefs des Fômoré protecteurs de Bress, c'est au contraire le prince au pouvoir magique, et justement sa magie est logée dans sa disgrâce, dont l'origine est également magique : de ses deux yeux, dit le récit sur *la Seconde Bataille de Mag Thured*, §133, l'un, habituellement fermé, ne s'ouvrait que sur le champ de bataille et jetait la mort sur les malheureux que son regard atteignait ; et nous savons, cette fois, et en détail, d'où vient ce redoutable privilège : « Un jour que les druides de son père étaient occupés à cuire des charmes, Balar vint et regarda par la fenêtre ; la fumée de cette décoction l'atteignit de sorte que la fumée de la décoction lui vint sur l'œil. »	attached to him, return the throne to him, and fight for him against the Fômoré who support the "statist" Bress. The one-eyed Balar "of the piercing gaze" (*Birugderc*), the most terrible of the chiefs of the Fomorians, protectors of Bress, is on the contrary the prince with magical power, and his magic is precisely lodged in his disgrace, whose origin is also magical: Of his two eyes, says the account of the *Second Battle of Moytura*, §133, one, usually closed, opened only on the battlefield and cast death on the unfortunate ones its gaze reached; and we know, this time, and in detail, from where this fearsome privilege comes: "One day when his father's druids were busy making charms, Balar came and looked through the window; the smoke of this potion reached him so that the smoke of the potion came upon his eye."
Ainsi nous tenons ici encore, en opposition, le souverain garant du Droit distributif et réglé, – qui est le Manchot ; et souverain terrible à action magique – qui est le Borgne. Mais si, pour le second, la disgrâce physique est étroitement liée au caractère et au mode d'action du personnage, et cela dans analogue à ce qui a été vu dans le cas du magicien Odhinn et de l' « épouvantable » Cocles, pour le premier, la seule forme attestée de la tradition n'établit aucun lien de cette sorte. En particulier, en fait de technique de guerre, si Balar, opère bien surnaturellement, avec son « mauvais ceil » (cf. A.H. Krappe, *Balar with the Evil Eye*, Columbia Univ., 1927),	Thus we have here again, in opposition, the sovereign guarantor of distributive and regulated Law—who is the one-armed king; and the terrible sovereign with magical action—who is the one-eyed king. But if, for the latter, the physical disgrace is closely linked to the character and his mode of action, and this analogous with what we have seen in the case of the magician Odhinn and the "dreadful" Cocles, for the former, the only attested form of the tradition establishes no such link. In particular, in terms of warfare, while Balar does operate supernaturally, with his "evil eye" (cf. A.H. Krappe, *Balar with the Evil Eye*, Columbia Univ., 1927),

Nuadu ne se distingue nullement des combattants ordinaires et si, plus anciennement, la perte de sa main a été en rapport avec une manière « juridique » de gagner une guerre, rien ne subsiste plus de ce thème. Cette lacune n'empêche pas, pensons-nous, le symbolisme de rester clair.	Nuadu in no way differs from ordinary combatants, and while the loss of his hand was earlier related to a "legal" way of winning a war, nothing remains of this theme. This lacuna does not, I believe, prevent the symbolism from remaining clear.
Nous disions que l'Irlande avait poussé à l'extrême l'opposition des deux personnages : en effet, non seulement ils représentent des modes d'action, des conduites contraires, non seulement ils commandent chacun à l'un des peuples qui s'affrontent, mais, sur le champ de bataille même, ils se rencontrent et c'est le Borgne – qui tue le Manchot, – pour succomber bientôt, lui-même à une pierre de fronde adroitement lancée dans son mauvais œil par le personnage le plus original des systèmes mythologiques des Celtes, Lug. Lug est l'Inventeur, « le Technicien de toutes les techniques » ; c'est lui que César appelle Mercurius et qui est, en Gaule, le principal des dieux, au-dessus même du souverain célèste. Dans ce récit de la *Bataille de Mag Thured*, il est l'allié, le soutien, le vengeur de Nuadu le Manchot et, comme lui, l'adversaire du terrible Borgne. Ces positions rappellent (avec, en plus, la position privilégiée et le triomphe de l'Inventeur) celles qui s'observent chez les Scandinaves entre les trois dieux homologues : le Borgne Ödhinn, le Magicien terrible, n'est pas seulement l'antithèse de Tŷr le Manchot, le Juriste, mais aussi celui de Ullr, qui semble bien, outre ses valeurs juridiques, être le Technicien, l'Inventeur de techniques par excellence.	I said that Ireland had pushed the opposition of the two characters to the extreme: indeed, not only do they represent opposing modes of action, opposing behaviours, not only do they each command one of the warring peoples, but, on the battlefield itself, they meet, and it is the one-eyed king who kills the one-armed—only to succumb to a sling stone deftly thrown into his evil eye by the most original character in the mythological systems of the Celts, Lug. Lug is the Inventor, "the Technician of all techniques"; the one Caesar calls Mercurius and who is, in Gaul, the chief of the gods, above even the celestial ruler. In this account of the *Battle of Mag Thured*, he is the ally, the supporter, the avenger of Nuadu the one-armed and, like him, the opponent of the terrible one-eyed god. These positions are reminiscent (with, in addition, the privileged position and triumph of the Inventor) of those observed among the Scandinavians between the three homologous gods: the one-eyed Ödhinn, the terrible Magician, is not only the antithesis of Tŷr the one-armed, the Jurist, but also that of Ullr, who seems to be, in addition to his juridical values, the Technician, the Inventor of techniques par excellence.

Chez les Gallois, Nuadu et Balar ont des équivalents depuis longtemps remarqués : d'une part le « bon » roi *Lludd à la Main d'Argent* (qualificatif qu'aucune tradition n'explique plus) d'autre part le « terrible » *Yspaddaden Penkawr* dont le mauvais œil opère exactement comme celui de Balar. Mais ils apparaissent dans deux *Mabinogion* différents, sans point de contact, possibilité de collaboration ni de lutte. Peut-être cependant, en dehors d'Yspadden et dans le *Mabinogi* propre de Lludd (Loth, *Les Mabinogion*, éd. de 1913, I, *Mab. de Lludd et Llevelys*, pp. 231–241), y a-t-il trace des oppositions qui nous intéressent. Lludd en effet est un généreux, « distribuant largement nourriture et boisson à ceux qui en demandent ». Sous son règne, l'île de Bretagne est en proie à trois fléaux dont il vient à bout ; or le troisième est un « magicien puissant » qui, par sa magie, endort tout le monde et enlève régulièrement du palais royal, en une fois, toutes les provisions si considérables soient-elles de nourriture et de boisson : on reconnaît un thème comparable à cela du bon Nuadu opposé à Bress, l'avide et l'avare, « l'enleveur de biens », du palais de qui chacun sortait affamé. Or l'histoire se termine par un duel furieux : Lludd à la Main d'Argent résiste au sommeil, voit le Magicien entrer et entasser les provisions dans un panier qui ne s'emplit jamais ; il l'assaille, le renverse – et lui accorde finalement merci moyennant un pacte de réparation : « Tout ce que je t'ai fait perdre, dit le magicien vaincu, je saurai t'en dédommager complètement ; je ne ferai plus rien de pareil et

Among the Welsh, Nuadu and Balar have equivalents that have long been noted: on the one hand, the "good" King Lludd of the Silver Hand (a term that no tradition explains any more) and, on the other hand, the "terrible" *Yspaddaden Penkawr*, whose evil eye operates in exactly the same way as that of Balar. But they appear in two different *Mabinogion*, without any point of contact, possibility of collaboration or struggle. Perhaps, however, outside Yspadden and in Lludd's own *Mabinogi* (Loth, *The Mabinogion*, ed. 1913, I, *Mab. of Lludd and Llevelys*, pp. 231–41), there are traces of the oppositions that interest us. Lludd is indeed a generous man, "distributing food and drink widely to those who ask for it." During his reign, the island of Brittany is beset by three plagues which he overcomes; the third is a "powerful magician" who, by his magic, puts everyone to sleep and regularly removes from the royal palace, at once, all the provisions, however considerable, of food and drink: here we recognise a theme comparable to that of the good Nuadu opposed to the greedy and avaricious Bress, "the remover of goods," from whose palace everyone came out hungry. The story ends with a furious duel: Lludd of the Silver Hand resists sleep, sees the Magician enter and pile provisions into a basket that never fills up; he assaults him, knocks him down—and finally grants him mercy in return for a pact of reparation: "All that I have made you lose," says the defeated magician, "I will know how to compensate you completely; I will do nothing of the kind again and I

je serai désormais pour toi un vassal fidèle. » Cette conclusion pacifique s'accorde avec celle de l'histoire de l'Irlandais Bress : fait prisonnier à la fin de la bataille de Mag Thured après la mort de Nuadu, de Balar, etc., Bress obtient des Tuatha Dê Danann et de Lug la vie sauve moyennant un pacte réparateur : il assurera dorénavant la prospérité et l'abondance (les vaches d'Irlande auront toujours du lait, il y aura une moisson à chaque saison...). L'adversaire du généreux roi Lludd, le « magicien dépouilleur », semble tenir et de Bress (parce qu'il confisque la nourriture et finalement doit « dédommager »), et de Balar (parce qu'il a la puissance non certes de tuer avec son regard, mais d'immobiliser l'adversaire en l'endormant). Les différences sont donc importantes, mais elles sont celles qu'on attend dans le traitement romanesque et littéraire et, dans le cas présent, fort tardif – d'une ancienne mythologie, et qu'on observe même dans les parties les plus mythologiques des *Mabinogion* : le magicien n'est pas borgne, et n'a pas proprement le « mauvais œil »; et surtout rien ne permet de le considérer comme un souverain, comme un rival égal de Lludd à la Main d'Argent, comme Bress d'une part, Balar d'autre part le sont de Nuadu à la Main d'Argent. Nous devions verser au dossier ce document gallois, mais il est évidemment décomposé et peu utilisable.

will henceforth be a faithful vassal to you." This peaceful conclusion is consistent with the story of the Irishman Bress: taken prisoner at the end of the battle of Mag Thured after the death of Nuadu, Balar, etc., Bress obtains from the Tuatha De Danann and Lug his life in return for a reparative pact: he will henceforth ensure prosperity and abundance (the cows of Ireland will always have milk, there will be a harvest in every season...) The opponent of the generous King Lludd, the "robber magician," seems to take after both Bress (because he confiscates the food and ultimately has to "compensate") and Balar (because he has the power not only to kill with his stare, but to immobilise his opponent by putting him to sleep). The differences are therefore important, but they are what one expects in a novelistic and literary treatment—and in this case, a very late one—of an ancient mythology, and which we observe even in the most mythological parts of the *Mabinogion*: the magician is not one-eyed, nor does he have the "evil eye"; and above all, there is no reason to consider him as a sovereign, as an equal rival of Lludd of the Silver Hand, as Bress on the one hand, and Balar on the other, are of Nuadu of the Silver Hand. We had to add this Welsh document to the file, but it is obviously degraded and not very usable.

APPENDIX II

Variant passage from Conclusion, first edition, pp. 145–6, translated by the editor

Ces ressemblances sont compensées par deux graves différences.	These similarities are offset by two serious differences.
Mitra-Varuṇa, et tous les couples apparentés, ne sont strictement valables que dans le domaine de la Souveraineté. Rien, du moins au point où en est notre étude, ne permet de dire qu'ils vaillent encore, qu'ils aient encore un sens aux autres échelons de l'organisme social, par exemple dans les représentations relevant des combattants non-souverains ou des pasteurs agriculteurs : quelques faits relevés au chapitre VI (Indra contre Varuṇa, les *nexi soluti*) donnent au contraire à penser que l'intervention du « militaire » change entièrement la perspective, même dans le domaine propre de la Souveraineté. Autrement dit, loin d'être le cadre primaire et général du monde, ce dualisme s'insère comme une subdivision dans un cadre tout différent.	Mitra-Varuṇa, and all related pairs, are strictly valid only when it comes to Sovereignty. There is nothing, at least at this point of our study, to suggest that they are still valid, that they still make sense at other levels of the social organism, for example in representations pertaining to non-sovereign warriors or agricultural pastoralists: on the contrary, some of the facts noted in Chapter VI (Indra against Varuṇa, the *nexi soluti*)[1] suggest that the intervention of the "military" changes the perspective entirely, even in the domain of Sovereignty proper. In other words, far from being the primary, general framework of the world, this dualism is inserted as a subdivision in a completely different framework.

Puis, sur aucun domaine, les oppositions du type Mitra Varuṇa ne prennent la forme – si importante dans le cas du couple *yâng-yin*, qu'elle y soit primaire ou secondaire – d'une opposition « mâle-femelle ». *Fides* n'est une divinité féminine que parce qu'elle est une abstraction personnifiée, mais elle s'oppose si peu à *Iupiter* en tant que femelle à mâle qu'elle se double d'un masculin équivalent, *Dius Fidius*. En réalité, à l'intérieur de chacun des deux types de représentations, il y a place éventuellement pour les deux sexes, – les types de rapports entre les sexes s'opposant alors radicalement (le comportement des Luperques envers les femmes anonymes qu'ils fouettent ; l'union sainte et personnelle du *flāmen dialis* et de la *flāminica*, etc.). Néanmoins, des recherches ultérieures peuvent réserver des surprises : la philosophie sāmkhya, qui voit dans l'univers la collaboration d'un « Moi » spectateur qu'il appelle Puruṣa, « le (principe) mâle », avec une « nature », actrice multiforme, la *prakrti*, a senti que son *Purusa* et sa *prakrti* s'opposaient comme Mitra et Varuṇa (*Mahābhārata*, XII, 318, 39 ; *Mitram purusam Varuṇam prakrtim tathā*), mais peut-être l'auteur de ces assimilations signifiait-il par là les aspects *passif* et *actif*, calme et créateur, etc. plutôt que le caractère ici mâle, là femelle des deux entités ; car, si cette valeur sexuelle dominait, on s'expliquerait mal comment Varuṇa aurait pu être assimilé à l'élément mobile, créateur ou illusionniste. Il est remarquable que dans l'autre grand système philosophique de l'Inde, dans le vedānta, les deux principes	And then, in no domain do oppositions of the Mitra Varuṇa type take the form—so important in the case of the *yin-yang* couple, whether primary or secondary—of a "male-female" opposition. *Fides* is a female deity only because she is a personified abstraction, but she is so little opposed to *Iupiter* as female to male that she is doubled with a male equivalent, Dius Fidius. In reality, within each of the two types of representation, there is eventual room for both sexes—the types of gender relations then being radically opposed (the behaviour of the Lupercians towards the anonymous women they whip; the holy and personal union of the *flāmen dialis* and the *flāminica*, etc.). Nevertheless, later research may hold surprises: Sāmkhya philosophy, which sees in the universe the collaboration of a spectator "I" which it calls Puruṣa, "the male (principle)," with a "nature," a multiform actor, the *prakrti*, felt that its *Puruṣa* and its *prakrti* were opposed like Mitra and Varuṇa (*Mahābhārata*, XII, 318, 39; *Mitram purusam Varuṇam prakrtim tathā*).[2] But perhaps the author of these assimilations meant by this the passive and active, calm and creative aspects, etc. rather than the character here male, there female of the two entities; for, if this sexual value were dominant, it would be difficult to explain how Varuṇa could have been assimilated to the mobile, creative or illusionary element. It is remarkable that in the other great philosophical system of India, the vedānta, the two antithetical principles are *Brahmā* and *Māyā*; they too are divided along the same lines: on the one hand, the celestial

antithétiques soient *Brahmā* et *Māyā* ; eux aussi se répartissent selon le même principe : d'une part la projection céleste du *brahman* (or « Mitra est le *brahman* », disaient les vieux textes liturgiques en l'opposant à *Varuṇa*), d'autre part l'Illusion créatrice (or dans les Veda la *māyā* est la grande technique du magicien Varuṇa).	projection of Brahman ("Mitra is Brahman," as the the old liturgical texts said, opposing him to Varuṇa), on the other hand the creative Illusion (in the Veda *māyā* is the preferred technique of the magician Varuṇa).

AFTERWORD

Mitra-Varuna: The Ongoing Life of a Concept

Veena Das

Johns Hopkins University

If the criteria of success and failure may be applied at all to the intellectual life of a concept, then the success of Dumézil's writing on Mitra-Varuna[1] lies, not so much in resolving problems once and for all, but in the influence it continues to wield on reshaping questions in contemporary discussions on sovereignty across many disciplines. I single out three issues: the problem of sovereignty and how to think of it beyond the right to kill; the tripartite division of functions that are seen to constitute the underlying ideology of the Indo-European world; and the significance of multiplicity of gods that bypasses the standard classification into monotheism, polytheism, or pantheism. The importance of the pairing of gods is evident everywhere in the Indo-European world, as Dumézil says, but I have been able to give attention only to the missing female figures, though it remains an important question as to how pairs and couples relate to larger groupings of gods. I do not claim that there are any definitive answers to how we should receive a book like *Mitra-Varuna* today, but if anthropology has any conceit that it is hospitable to other modes of thought and their salience for "provincializing Europe," the texts we allow into the canon must be raked for their potential for the future they might have as much as for their past. My discussion is heavily oriented to the Indian texts that I know best, but Dumézil shows us that the relevance of these texts is not confined to the local.

The opening paragraph of the first edition of *Mitra-Varuna*, from 1940, states:

> This essay investigates a certain bipartite conception of sovereignty that appears to have been present among the Indo-Europeans, and that dominated the mythologies of certain of the peoples who spoke Indo-European languages at the time of the earliest documents. In my earlier work, mostly devoted to the mechanisms and representations of sovereignty, I had already encountered some of the elements that interest me here; but I had previously understood their relations only very imperfectly. In this work, it is the broad system of those relations that I try to elucidate.

Dumézil then goes on to say:

> The system is truly inherent in the material. It may be observed, always the same, in the most diverse sets of facts – in all those sets of facts, one might say, that fall within the province of sovereignty … there has been no need for me to reconstruct or to interpret anything whatsoever: those who used the myths, rituals and formulas were quite conscious of the system; my sole task has been to make clear its scope and its antiquity.[2]

It is interesting to see the steps by which Dumézil came to see what he describes as the transparency of the system[3] informed by the tripartite division of the social world into three functions, viz., the priestly function combining the juridical and magical, the warrior function, and the function related to production of material prosperity and fecundity. Of these three functions, it is the first and the second which influenced the discussion on sovereignty in later literature. In the book on Mitra-Varuna and the series of lectures on this theme at the Collège de France from 1938 and 1939, Dumézil drew attention to other pairs, such as Numa and Romulus, Tyr and Odhinn, comparing them to Mitra-Varuna to establish an ideology of the dual character of sovereignty as expressed in the mythology of the Indo-European world. Although his earlier work on the relations between Centaurs, Gandharvas, and Luperci, which he published in 1929, as well as on the correspondences between Ouranos and Varuna, in 1934, or on the similarities between Brahman and flamen, in 1935, did not receive the same attention as *Mitra-Varuna*, these earlier works contributed to his stunning breakthrough on the internal partition in the domain of sovereignty. Conceptually important in *Mitra-Varuna* was that the two gods were seen to represent a *relation*, rather than being treated as a collection through aggregation. Equally significant is the fact that the second warrior function represented in the mythology of the Vedic god, Indra, was seen as lying "outside" the domain of sovereignty. As the representation of the warrior, Indra is a transgressive figure who sometimes violates the law of the sovereign in the domains of sexuality and economics, but also offers a different picture of justice than that represented in the penal power of Varuna. We shall see that the idea of "outside" is not a simple one. We may ask, for instance, if Indra's being outside the split domain of the sovereign is symmetrical to the *śūdra* being outside the *varna* system. Indra in his warrior function challenges the force wielded by Varuna as much as he disrupts the pact-making functions of Mitra, whereas, lying outside the tripartite functions, the śūdra seems to disappear from the text. Does Dumézil's method of constructing hierarchy as a succession of binary oppositions rather than a linear distribution through application of a single measure help determine what lies inside a domain and what falls outside? Let us look at Dumézil 's mapping of the tripartite partition of functions on the varna hierarchy, which he takes to be equivalent to social hierarchy.

> The Indians' social hierarchy, like the system of ideas that sustains it, is linear in appearance only. In reality it is a sequence, rather Hegelian in character, in which a thesis summons an antithesis then combines with it in a synthesis that becomes in turn a further thesis, thus providing fresh material enabling the process to continue. For example, *brāhmna*, *kṣatriya* and *vaiśya* (priest, warrior and herdsman-cultivator) are not to be numbered "one, two, three." The *brāhmna* is defined at the outset in opposition to the *kṣatriya*; then the two are reconciled and collaborate in a new notion, that of "power" (*ubhe virye*, "the two forces," is the eloquent dual expression in some texts), which is then immediately defined in opposition to *vaiśya* (e.g., Manu, IX, 327), an opposition itself resolved by a synthesis into the *dvija*, "the twice-born," which is then confronted by the appearance of the *śūdra*.[4]

It is to be noted that, while the first function, referring to the sovereign, has two occupants or figures, and the warrior function receives attention as the figuration of force outside the control of the sovereign, there is not much discussion on the *vaiśya* as the one who sustains the material order. This is at least partly due to the fact that the category of the householder as the one who sustains everyday life and maintains the sacrificial fire receives no attention because of the kinds of texts that are excluded from consideration (e.g., the *Grhya Sutras*) and partly because once the śūdra is excluded from the "twice-born" status, it is assumed that he is excluded from religious life altogether. The elaboration of what it would mean to say that the category of the twice-born is *confronted* by the category of the śūdra is left hanging in the air. While I cannot elaborate this point further here, I simply note that the theme of the extinction of the kṣatriyas as a varna is explicit in the epics, and the possibility of śūdra kings, their purification, and the legitimacy they acquire through the ritual participation of some Brahman castes is a matter of discussion in the mythic register.[5] Would a further discussion on the dilemmas posed by śūdra *kings* have illuminated other, darker aspects of sovereignty for the varna ideology and the tripartite functions? Let us turn to Louis Dumont[6] for some questions on the double-headed hierarchy within sovereignty from a different angle, though Dumont pays very little attention to the non-normative kings who appear temporarily in myths such as Nahuṣa who replaces Indra as the ruler of heaven but is killed because of his sexual infringements against Indra's wife.

In his magnum opus, Dumont (1998 [1970]) starts with the distinction between *jatis* and varnas, a distinction that M.N. Srinivas had mapped on the "field-view" of caste and the "book-view" of caste.[7] But while Srinivas thought that there was a bias in Indian studies toward privileging texts over the messy empirical realities that accounted for the dominance of the varna model in scholarly literature on caste, Dumont detected an opposition between two different principles underlying the systems of jati and varna. In his analytical frame, inter-caste relations at the level of jatis were expressed in such practices as exchange of food, ritual services provided to higher castes, particularly with regard to removal of pollution, and the attribution of higher or lower rank to castes within the *local* hierarchy. Such relations of exchange, which lay at the heart of the jati system, he famously argued, were governed by the overarching opposition between pure and impure that provided the criteria for assigning higher or lower status to different castes, especially those in the middle rungs of the hierarchy. At this level there was consensus on the highest and lowest rung of the caste hierarchy, but disputes occurred on the middle level as specific castes strived to change their practices for claiming higher status. The principle of hierarchy in the case of the varna system, despite its enumeration of *four* varnas, was much more concerned with the relation between priesthood and power, represented in the relation between the Brahman and the king. It is the intersections and overlaps between the two systems, that of jati and that of varna, and the positing of a structural homology between them that allows Dumont to resolve the vexing question of the place of power in determining caste hierarchy. After all, if it is the opposition of pure and impure that determines the position of a caste in relation to other castes, how would one account for the fact the Brahman caste, which is the purest, is dependent on the kṣatriyas, who wield temporal power? Dumézil's theory of a divided sovereignty became decisive in enabling Dumont to keep his theory of the dominance of the purity–pollution opposition intact against the challenge that was posed by material dependence of Brahmans on patrons who were lower on the criteria of purity but wielded power. If the opposition of pure and impure was primarily a religious opposition, Dumont asked, could one generate a theory of power that relied equally on religious principles? Here is a crucial citation from Dumont:

> Once hierarchy has been isolated as purely a matter of religious values, it naturally remains to be seen how it relates to power, and how authority is to be defined. In the previous chapter, we linked the principle of hierarchy with the opposition between the pure and the impure. Now we cannot but recognize that this opposition, a purely religious one, tells us nothing about the place of power in society. On this question we must resort to a traditional Hindu theory which, while not dealing with caste *(jati) stricto sensu,* yet has an intimate bearing on it.[8]

Thanks to Hocart and more precisely to Dumézil the hierarchy of the varnas can be seen not as a linear order, but as a series of successive dichotomies or inclusions . . .the Kshatriya may order a sacrifice as may the Vaishya, but only the Brahman may perform it. The king is thus deprived of any sacerdotal function… It can be seen that the series of dichotomies on which this hierarchy rests is formally somewhat similar to caste hierarchy, and it is also essentially religious; but it is less systematic, and its principles are different.[9]

My interest in this Afterword is not to engage with the merits or the blind spots in Dumont's overarching arguments, on which I have offered my criticisms elsewhere.[10] However I think it is important to pay some attention to the way Dumézil's work is incorporated to overcome an impasse that sovereign power poses for Dumont and his claim that caste hierarchy is based on the religious principles of purity and impurity. Dumont was not interested in the representations of sovereignty through Mitra-Varuna or in what lay outside the domain of the sovereign through the figure of Indra, the warrior god. None of these themes play any part in his argument. His insistence that in India the religion of gods is secondary and the religion of castes is primary[11] causes him to miss the richness of Dumézil's discussion on sovereignty and power. Yet Dumont's demonstration that the principles underlying the jati system are different from the principles underlying the varna system invites us to think further on the transformations that happen to the figures of Indo-European mythology as they journeyed to other places and interacted with other ideologies. Though he expresses much admiration for Dumézil, Dumont does not engage with the Vedic gods as representations of sovereignty. In the field of religious studies and Indo-European Studies, these questions remain very much alive.

Mitra-Varuna and Their Traces

In a variant passage reproduced in Appendix II of the present volume, Dumézil noted:

> Mitra-Varuṇa, and all related pairs, are strictly valid only when it comes to Sovereignty. There is nothing, at least at this point of our study, to suggest that they are still valid, that they still make sense at other levels of the social organism, for example in representations pertaining to non-sovereign warriors or agricultural pastoralists: on the contrary, some of the facts noted in Chapter VI (Indra against Varuṇa, the *nexi soluti*) suggest that the intervention of the "military" changes the perspective entirely, even in the domain of Sovereignty proper. In other words, far from being the primary, general framework of the world, this dualism is inserted as a subdivision in a completely different framework.[12]

Let us take the first part of this observation and ask how to take further the question " … [do] they still make sense at other levels of the social organism?" Bhrigupati Singh's compelling analysis of precisely this issue starts with the relation between current practices of devotion to a minor deity, Thakur Baba, by members of the Saharia community he studied in a district in Rajasthan, India, a low-status group which occupies the fuzzy boundary between caste and tribe on the lower rungs of the caste hierarchy.[13] Small wayside shrines of Thakur Baba and other minor deities or spirits dot the landscape of every village of the region, and when asked who Thakur Baba was, villagers often told Singh that he was a Rajput (a member of the warrior caste) who died in battle, continuing to fight even after his head was cut off. Singh takes Thakur Baba to be the sovereign over the area in which he presides and finds, in the Mitra-Varuna division of the sovereign function, the ambivalence and duality that Thakur Baba establishes with his devotees. Comparable to the great force exercised by Varuna, Thakur Baba sometimes strikes down those who defy him. But like Mitra, he also makes pacts with his devotees, receiving offerings and granting boons to resolve their difficulties or to fulfill their aspirations and desires.

For Singh, Dumézil provides an alternative that enables a much more nuanced model of sovereignty than the vastly admired and prevalent model based on the figure of *homo sacer* in Roman law. However a puzzle remains for Singh as it did for Dumézil, viz., that it is hard to locate the horse-bound heroic figure of the Rajput warrior in the current politics of India. As Singh writes: "Where could I locate the power that Thakur Baba expresses? Unless we look to the tourist brochures of Indian heritage hotels, it would be impossible to find a present-day Rajput who embodies the martial ethos of a horse-bound warrior's death. And yet in many areas of Rajasthan and central India, the deified specter of Thakur Baba subsists among high and low castes, and tribes, former generations of whom may have lived under the rule of Rajputs. Why do these social groups preserve this 'feudal' figure among spirits, even though he is materially outmoded … ?" [14] Singh does well in answering this question to show that a bipolar notion of sovereignty allows one to think of sovereignty not as a unipolar concentrated power manifested in the right to kill, but as a negotiable contract between sovereign and subject.[15] There are gradations of sovereignty, but Singh conceptualizes these gradations to become active over different thresholds of life rather than at different levels of social organization. Two questions remain. First, it is not entirely clear from Singh's discussion whether the Rajputs dispossessed of their right to rule might not have moved into the category of the warrior, the second function in Dumézil's tripartite division, which he places outside sovereignty. In that case, one would need to think of varna categories as mobile, and Singh's discussion of the negotiations over offerings (through substitutions) whereby villagers have slowly shifted to offerings which do not require the killing of an animal demonstrates the pact-making aspect of sovereignty.

This negotiation between deity and devotees not only bears the traces of Mitra but also nicely incorporates the dimension of time into contract. It also calls for the relation between the first and second functions to be fleshed out much more than is usual (on which more later). But Singh's ethnographic eye shows us how and where to find traces of the Vedic deities in current ritual and devotional practices, and this might be a very rewarding issue to pursue.

The Warrior Function

The complementary relation of Mitra-Varuna finds a new iteration in the discussion by Deleuze and Guattari in *A Thousand Plateaus: Capitalism and Schizophrenia*.[16] Thinking of the war machine, the authors argue that the war machine is exterior to the State apparatus and that this exteriority is first attested to in mythology, epic, drama, and games, as Dumézil had shown through his method. The Mitra-Varuna opposition, Deleuze and Guattari argue, when set against the actions of Indra, who represents the warrior function, shows which kind of violence the State has at its disposal. The authors are emphatic that war is not contained within the State apparatus: "*Either* the State has at its disposal a violence that is not channeled through war—either it uses police officers and jailors in place of warriors, has no arms and no need of them, operates by immediate, magical capture, 'seizes' and 'binds' preventing all combat—*or* the State acquires an army, but in a way that presupposes a juridical integration of war and the organization of a military function."[17] As Dumézil had perceptively argued, Indra as war god has the opposite qualities of being the rogue god outside the laws of sexuality and of economics who could show both extraordinary cruelty and paradoxically extraordinary compassion. "And the warrior especially, because of his position either on the fringe of or even above the code, regards himself as having the right to clemency; the right to break, among other things, the mandates of 'strict justice'; the right, in short, to introduce into the terrible determinism of human relations that miracle: humanity." Deleuze and Guattari use this insight to develop a more elaborate theory in which the war machine remains exterior to the apparatus of the State but in some circumstances becomes confused with the two heads of the State apparatus. In their words, "[i]n short whenever the irruption of war power is confused with the line of State domination, everything gets muddled; the war machine can then be understood only through the categories of the negative, since nothing is left that is outside the State. But returned to the milieu of externality, the state power is seen to be of another nature, of another origin." The absolute irreducibility and exteriority of the warrior function is revealed only in flashes, since it becomes visible momentarily as it passes between the two heads, the jural and the magical force, the peaceful pole and the terrible pole, represented by Mitra and Varuna and other similar pairs within the Indo-European ideology. I cannot go into a detailed discussion of the specificity of Deleuze and Guattari's argument here since the point is not to provide a measure of how close or distant their formulations are to Dumézil's arguments but to show the various directions in which Dumézil's insights could move social theory or philosophical thought. I will, however, allow myself one final thought, which complicates the already complex relation between sovereignty and the warrior function.

Force Inside the Law, Outside the Law

In section IV, Chapter VI of *Mitra-Varuna*, Indra is shown primarily in his battles against the bonds of Varuna. There are two myth fragments in which Indra steps in to prohibit the blind following of a law of sacrifice that would be legal but cruel and rescues the victims bound by Varuna for having broken the laws of sacrifice. In the first case, Manu is making preparations to sacrifice his wife. He is tricked into this act by the word he has given to two demonic priests. At that moment, Indra steps in, halts the sacrifice, and ordains that Manu will still get the benefits of the sacrifice.

The second case, as Dumézil tells it, is of Śunaḥśepa, in which a king has been seized by Varuna because he did not keep his promise to sacrifice his son to Varuna.[18] The king is a righteous king, and though Varuna wants to release him from the obligation to sacrifice his son, he himself is bound by the law and cannot break it. However Varuna consents to a substitution of the victim by another human victim. A Brahman boy, the middle son of a highly regarded Brahman ascetic in the grip of poverty and hunger, is bought and substituted for the king's son as the sacrificial offering. Terrified, the boy approaches various gods; each god expresses his own helplessness in the face of Varuna's might and passes him to another in a kind of relay. Śunaḥśepa is finally released through the force of a prayer given to him by the goddess Dawn. Though it is the goddess Dawn who finally gives him the *mantra* that releases him from the bonds of Varuna, Dumézil draws from other stories to suggest that this story is an instantiation of the compassion shown by Indra in his warrior function.[19]

Another allusion to this story, taken from an incident mentioned in Valmiki's *Ramayana*, is relevant here. It refers to the moment when Rama, having vanquished Ravana, the Brahman demon king of Lanka, returns victorious to his capital where he is crowned with great pomp and splendor. He wishes to perform the *rājasūya yajna* to proclaim his lordship over the entire earth. However Rama is dissuaded from performing this sacrifice by his two younger brothers, who urge him to perform the horse sacrifice instead, since the *rājasūya yajna* would entail the risk of extinguishing the entire kṣatriya race and could even destroy the earth. Rama praises his brothers for their wisdom and releases a black horse that would roam the earth unchallenged and thus proclaim Rama's sovereignty over the entire earth before being sacrificed in the *aśvamedha* ritual sacrifice. Dumézil comments that it is "that very *aśvamedha*, respectful of human life, that was originally instituted by Indra." Furthermore we have seen how Deleuze and Guattari, too, see the glimmer of a human sympathy that originates in the warrior's opposition to the cruelty of human sacrifice. However the story does not lend itself so easily to the interpretation of Indra the warrior as displaying here a great compassion and the miraculous advent of humanism to which Dumézil assumes it gives expression. So let us consider what Lakshmana says to Rama to persuade him to perform the horse sacrifice instead of the human sacrifice. It should be noted that Lakshmana speaks after his younger brother, Bharata, has spoken, and Rama has already been convinced by Bharata that performing the *rājasūya yajna* entails a great risk of extermination of the kṣatriya varna altogether. The implication is that, challenged by the humiliation of publicly having to accept Rama's overlordship, they might wage battle against him and die, and that the earth itself might be destroyed by continuing battles. So in speaking next, what has Lakshmana added to this conversation? Lakshmana says: "It is heard from the older texts that, sullied by the sin of killing a Brahman, Vasava was again purified by performing a horse sacrifice." The reference to Indra as Vasava here is an allusion to his being the head of the vasus and having killed Vritra by stealth. The evocation of this incident reminds us that Indra had committed the sin of killing a Brahman, perhaps the most heinous act; but Lakshmana's words are also aimed at Rama, who was himself guilty of the same sin of *brahmahatyā,* the killing of a Brahman, for Ravana, though a demon, was also a learned Brahman.

Dumézil's discussion of this episode credits Indra for having instituted the sacrifice of a horse in place of the sacrifice of a human being: "And doubtless his [Indra's] intervention was more decisive still in the less 'priestly' forms of the story,[20] since later writings were to contrast the ancient ritual of royal consecration instituted by Varuṇa (the *rājasūya*), stained from the outset by human blood (as the Śunaḥśepa story presupposes and several details confirm), with that which has no human victim, instituted by Indra (*aśvamedha*). ... Rama yields to his brother's argument and unhesitatingly renounces 'the greatest of all the sacrifices (the *rājasūyāt krattutamāt nivartayāmi*),' because 'an act detrimental to the world ought not be performed by wise men (*Llokapīḍakararṃ karma na kartavyaṃ vicakṣaṇaiḥ*) ...'. In its place, he celebrates the no less efficacious, no less glorious *aśvamedha*, that very *aśvamedha*, respectful of human life, originally instituted by Indra."[21]

Originally instituted by Indra? Respectful of human life? In both cases taken as instantiations of Indra's compassion, something is surely missing. First of all, it was the goddess Dawn (Ushas) who caused Varuna's bonds to dissolve and, second, Lakshmana's words were meant to remind Rama that not only did he not need any further affirmation of his dominion over the whole earth, but also that, having committed *brahmhatyā*, Rama was himself in need of purification *just as Indra had once been* in such need after the killing of Vritra. The evasion of the role of the female, whether as goddess Dawn in this story or as the grammatical and terrifying feminine that the act of killing a Brahman (brahmhatyā) releases,[22] or the neglect of women who show compassion to Indra, including his wife, as Allen shows (see note 9), means that the question of the feminine in the pairings of the gods may need to go further in the direction of the she-gods. The relation between the warrior and the sovereign, the outside and the inside, is still open for discussion from the angle of the feminine.[23]

That a book such as *Mitra-Varuna* can continue to open so many lines of inquiry, so many ways of inheriting it, shows its potency and unmatched creativity. The feminine enters in this text on Mitra-Varuna almost by stealth, but as a tribute to the possibilities of further expansion of the insights in *Mitra-Varuna*, one hopes that the elusive feminine figures of these early texts will find their own specificity and felicitous attention in years to come.

Editor's Notes

Notes to the Introduction

1. Georges Dumézil, *Mitra-Varuna: Essai sur deux representations indo-européennes de la souverainété* (Paris: Presses Universitaires de France, 1940); second edition (Paris: Gallimard, 1948); *Mitra-Varuna: An Essay on Two Indo-European Representations of Sovereignty*, trans. Derek Coltman (New York, NY: Zone Books, 1988). Subsequent references give the pages of two French editions separated by /; followed by the page of the original English edition and the current text in the same way.
2. François [Franz] Bopp, *Grammaire comparée des langues indo-européennes*, trans. Michel Bréal, five volumes (Paris: Imprimerie Nationale, 1866–74); *A Comparative Grammar of the Sanskrit, Zend, Greek, Latin, Lithuanian, Gothic, German and Sclavonic* [sic] *Languages*, ed. H.S. Wilson, three volumes (Cambridge: CUP, 2009 [1843–50]).
3. Alfred Ernout and Antoine Meillet, *Dictionnaire étymologique de la langue latine: Histoire des mots*, revised fourth edition (Paris: Klincksieck, 2001). Ernout had taught Dumézil at the *lycée* de Troyes.
4. This was an additional round, organised because of war-time disruption.
5. Georges Dumézil, *Entretiens avec Didier Eribon* (Paris: Gallimard, 1987), pp. 46–47. See Marco V. García Quintela, *Dumezil: une introduction*, trans. Marie-Pierre Bouyssou (Crozon: Armeline, 2001), p. 18; Daniel Dubuisson, *Twentieth-Century Mythologies: Dumézil, Lévi-Strauss, Eliade*, trans. Martha Cunningham, second edition (London: Routledge, 2006), p. 8. This is an updated version of *Mythologies du XX*[e] *siècle (Dumézil, Lévi-Strauss, Eliade)* (Lille: Presses Universitaires de Lille, 1993).
6. Georges Dumézil, *Le Festin d'immortalité: Étude de mythologie comparée indo-européenne* (Paris: Librairie Orientaliste Paul Geuthner,

1924); *Le Crime des Lemniennes: Rites et légendes du monde égéen* (Paris: Librairie Orientaliste Paul Geuthner, 1924); revised edition, ed. Bernadette Leclerq-Neveu (Paris: Macula, 1998).

7. Dumézil, *Entretiens avec Didier Eribon*, pp. 54–55, 60; see Dubuisson, *Twentieth-Century Mythologies*, p. 8.
8. Lucien Febvre supported Baruzi in this election. See his letters in *Marc Bloch, Lucien Febvre et les Annales d'Histoire économique et sociale, Correspondance,* Tome premier: *1928–33*, ed. Bertrand Müller (Paris: Fayard, 1994), pp. 345 and 345, n. 74, 350, 353.
9. These papers are archived at the Collège de France: 4 AP 531-l, "Proposition de M. Émile Benveniste pour la création d'une chaire de Civilisation indo-européenne," available at https://salamandre.college-de-france.fr/archives-en-ligne/ark:/72507/r19960z48f8jpk/f1?context=ead::FR075CDF_00RAP001_de-273 and 14 CDF 20-d1, "Exposé par M. Émile Benveniste des titres de M. Georges Dumézil et de M. Emmanuel Laroche, candidat à la chaire de Civilisation indo-européenne," available at https://salamandre.college-de-france.fr/archives-en-ligne/ark:/72507/r19964zjvxshfk/f1?context=ead::FR075CDF_00RAP001_de-535 For a longer biographical sketch, see Claude Lévi-Strauss, "Réponse de M. Claude Lévi-Strauss au discours de M. Georges Dumézil," in *Discours prononcé dans la séance publique tenue par l'Académie française pour la réception de M. Georges Dumézil le jeudi 14 juin 1979* (Paris: Firmin-Didot et Cie, 1979), pp. 21–37; and Gérard Fussman's "Hommage" for the Collège de France in 1987, available at https://www.college-de-france.fr/site/georges-dumezil/Hommage.htm
10. A longer study of his contribution can be found in C. Scott Littleton, *The New Comparative Mythology: An Anthropological Assessment of the Theories of Georges Dumézil*, third edition (Berkeley, CA: University of California Press, 1982), which remains the only book-length introduction in English; though see Dubuisson, *Twentieth-Century Mythologies*, Part I, pp. 7–102; and the highly technical Wouter W. Belier, *Decayed Gods: Origin and Development of Georges Dumézil's Idéologie Tripartite* (Leiden: Brill, 1991). A good introduction in his own words is the interview "Myth, Ideology, Sovereignty," in Richard Kearney, *Debates in Continental Philosophy: Conversations with Contemporary Thinkers* (New York: Fordham University Press, 2004), pp. 53–61. In French the key studies are Jean-Claude Rivière, *Georges Dumézil à la découverte des Indo-Européens* (Paris: Copernic, 1979); García Quintela, *Dumezil*; and Michel Poitevin, *Georges Dumézil, un naturel comparatiste* (Paris: L'Harmattan, 2002). As well as the valuable *Entretiens avec Didier Eribon*, there is a briefer interview: Georges Dumézil and François Ewald, "Le Messager des dieux," *Magazine littéraire* 229, pp. 16–21.

11. Georges Dumézil, *Le Festin d'immortalité*; *Le Problème des Centaures: Étude de mythologie comparée indo-européenne* (Paris: Librairie Orientaliste Paul Geuthner, 1929).
12. Dumézil, *Mitra-Varuna*, p. -/13; 12/xxxv (see note 1 for explanation; not in first edition).
13. Georges Dumézil, *Ouranós-Váruṇa: Étude de mythologie comparée indo-européenne* (Paris: Adrien Maisonneuve, 1934); *Flamen-Brahman* (Paris: Librairie Orientaliste Paul Geuthner, 1935).
14. Cited in Arnaldo Momigliano, "Georges Dumézil and the Trifunctional Approach to Roman Civilization," *History and Theory* 23 (3), 1984: 312–30, p. 315; also reported by Dumézil in Georges Dumézil, Jacques Bonnet, and Didier Pralon, "Entretien," in *Georges Dumézil: Cahiers pour un temps* (Paris: Centre Georges Pompidou, 1981), pp. 15–44, p. 40.
15. Lévi-Strauss, "Réponse," p. 25. See Dumézil and Ewald, "Le Messager des dieux," p. 17, where Dumézil recounts this story, but initially says Lévi-Strauss discouraged him from contacting him.
16. Georges Dumézil, "Préface," Marcel Granet, *La Religion des Chinois* (Paris: Éditions Imago, 1980), pp. v–viii. Granet's book was first published in 1922. Dumézil's preface does not appear in *The Religion of the Chinese People*, trans. Maurice Freedman (Oxford: Basil Blackwell, 1975), though he is thanked by the translator (p. vii).
17. Georges Dumézil, "La Préhistoire des flamines majeurs," *Revue de l'Histoire des religions* 118, 1938: 188–200, reprinted in *Idées romaines* (Paris: Gallimard, 1969), pp. 155–66. For an analysis of this text, see Dubuisson, *Twentieth Century Mythologies*, pp. 79–91.
18. Dumézil, "La Préhistoire des flamines majeurs," p. 189.
19. Dubuisson, *Twentieth-Century Mythologies*, p. 85.
20. Georges Dumézil, *Mythes et dieux des Germains: Essai d'interprétation comparative* (Paris: Librairie Ernest Leroux, 1939).
21. Georges Dumézil, *L'Oubli de l'homme et l'honneur des dieux et autres essais: Vingt-cinq esquisses de mythologie (51–74)* (Paris: Gallimard, 1984), p. 307; *Entretiens avec Didier Eribon*, p. 67.
22. Georges Dumézil, "XVII.—Mythologie comparée," *École Pratique des Hautes Études, Section des Sciences religieuses, Annuaire 1939–40*, pp. 83–84. See also Dumézil, *Entretiens avec Didier Eribon*, pp. 67–68.
23. Fonds Georges Dumézil, Collège de France, DMZ 56.3, "Mythes et rites relatifs à l'initiation des guerriers dans diverses sociétés indo-européennes; DMZ 56.4, "Études de quelques notions religieuses indo-européennes."
24. Georges Dumézil, *Aspects de la fonction guerrière chez les Indo-Européens* (Paris: Presses Universitaires de France, 1956). This book was developed from Collège de France lectures in 1951–52 and 1952–53.
25. DMZ 45.5 has some notes, newspaper clippings, and correspondence relating to the book.

26. Dumézil's notes on Caillois's presentations are in DMZ 56.4.
27. Roger Caillois, *L'Homme et le sacré* (Paris: Librairie Ernest Leroux, 1939); second edition (Paris: Gallimard, 1950); *Man and the Sacred*, trans. Meyer Barash (Glencoe, IL: The Free Press of Glencoe, 1959).
28. Caillois, *L'Homme et le sacré*, second edition, p. 19; *Man and the Sacred*, p. 15.
29. Dumézil, *Mitra-Varuna*, pp. x–xi/19; 19/xl–xli.
30. Dumézil, *Mitra-Varuna*, p. 49/85; 72/47.
31. Available at https://www.gallimard.fr/Catalogue/GALLIMARD/La-montagne-Sainte-Genevieve/Mitra-Varuna
32. Dumézil, *Entretiens avec Didier Eribon*, pp. 68, 70–72; see Alexandre Toumarkine, "Dumézil en Turquie (1926–1940)," in Güneş Işiksel, and Emmanuel Szurek, eds., *Turcs et Français: Une histoire culturelle, 1860–1960* (Presses Universitaires de Rennes, 2014), pp. 271–84, pp. 283–4; García Quintela, *Dumézil*, p. 19; Dubuisson, *Twentieth-Century Mythologies*, pp. 8–9.
33. For a much fuller account, and valuable documentary sources, see Didier Eribon, *Faut-il brûler Dumézil? Mythologie, science et politique* (Paris: Flammarion, 1992), pp. 214–41.
34. Georges Dumézil, *Jupiter, Mars, Quirinus: Essai sur la conception indo-européenne de la société et sur les origines de Rome* (Paris: Gallimard, 1941); *Naissance de Rome: Jupiter, Mars, Quirinus* II (Paris: Gallimard, 1944); *Naissance d'archanges—Essai sur la formation de la théologie zoroastrienne: Jupiter, Mars, Quirinus* III (Paris: Gallimard, 1945); *Horace et les Curiaces* (Paris: Gallimard, 1942); *Servius et la fortune: Essai sur la fonction sociale de louange et de blâme et sur les éléments indo-européens du cens romain* (Paris: Gallimard, 1943); *Tarpeia: Essais de philologie comparée indo-européenne* (Paris: Gallimard, 1947). On the general cultural context of this period, see Daniel Lindenberg, *Les Années souterraines 1937–1947* (Paris: La Découverte, 1990).
35. Available at https://www.gallimard.fr/Catalogue/GALLIMARD/La-montagne-Sainte-Genevieve/Mitra-Varuna; Hervé Coutau-Bégarie, *L'Œuvre de Georges Dumézil: Catalogue raisonné* (Paris: Economica, 1998), p. 37.
36. Georges Dumézil, *Jupiter, Mars, Quirinus* IV*: Explication de textes indiens et latins* (Paris: Presses Universitaires de France, 1948); *Loki* (Paris: GP Maisonneuve, 1948).
37. Lévi-Strauss, "Réponse," p. 30.
38. Georges Dumézil, *L'Héritage indo-européen à Rome* (Paris: Gallimard, 1949).
39. Editorial note to Georges Dumézil, *Mythes et dieux des Indo-Européens*, ed. Hervé Coutau-Bégarie (Paris: Flammarion, 1992), p. 13; see Dumézil, *L'Héritage indo-européen à Rome*, p. 10.

40. Georges Dumézil, *Recherches comparatives sur le verbe caucasien* (Paris: Librarie Ancienne Honoré Champion, 1933); *Introduction à la grammaire comparée des langues caucasiennes du nord* (Paris: Librarie Ancienne Honoré Champion, 1933).
41. García Quintela, *Dumézil*, p. 26. On this period, see Toumarkine, "Dumézil en Turquie (1926–1940)."
42. Nicolai S. Trubetzkoy, "I: *Dumézil, Georges: Études comparatives sur les langues caucasiennes du nord-ouest*.... II: *Recherches comparatives sur le verbe caucasien*...," *Orientalistische Literaturzeitung* 37 (10), 1934, cols. 629–35.
43. N.S. Trubetzkoy to Roman Jakobson, January 25, 1935. Trubetzkoy's correspondence with Roman Jakobson first appeared largely in Russian as *N.S. Trubetzkoy's Letters and Notes*, ed. Roman Jakobson, with assistance of H. Baran, O. Ronen, and Martha Taylor (Berlin: Mouton, 1985), p. 319. There is no complete English translation, but see *Correspondance avec Roman Jakobson et autres écrits*, ed. Patrick Seriot, trans. Patrick Seriot and Margarita Schönenberger (Lausanne: Éditions Payot, 2006), p. 368. This letter is partly excerpted in N.S. Trubetzkoy, *Studies in General Linguistics and Language Structure*, ed. Anatoly Liberman (Durham, NC: Duke University Press, 2001), p. 256.
44. Georges Dumézil, *Méthodes et mœurs de la linguistique caucasienne: Réponse au Prince Troubetskoy* (Paris: Adrien Maisonneuve, 1934).
45. On this debate, see Eribon, *Faut-il brûler Dumézil?* pp. 314–21 and especially Stefanos Geroulanos and Jamie Philips, "Euroasianism versus IndoGermanism: Linguistics and Mythology in the 1930s' Controversies over European Prehistory," *History of Science* 56 (3), 2018: 343–78.
46. Georges Dumézil, *La Langue des Oubykhs* (I: *Grammaire*; II: *Textes traduits et commentés*; III: *Notes de vocabulaire*) (Paris: Librairie Ancienne Honoré Champion, 1931).
47. Georges Dumézil with Tevfik Esenç, *Le Verbe oubykh: Études descriptives et comparatives* (Paris: Imprimerie Nationale/Librairie C. Klincksieck, 1975), p. 6; and the accounts in Dumézil, *Entretiens avec Didier Eribon*, pp. 56–58, pp. 84–90; "Georges Dumézil 2: 'Une grammaire, pour moi, c'est un roman'," in Roger-Pol Droit, *La Compagnie des contemporains* (Paris: Odile Jacob, 2002), pp. 247–51, p. 250. See Rieks Smeets, in A. Sumru Özsoy, ed., *Proceedings of the Conference on Northwest Caucasian Linguistics, 10–12 October 1994,* Studia Causoligca III (Oslo: Novus Forlag, 1997), pp. 37–62, p. 38; Rohan S.H. Fenwick, *A Grammar of Ubykh* (Munich: Lincom Europa, 2011), p. 10.
48. See, among others, Georges Dumézil, *Études oubykhs* (Paris: Libraire Adrien Maisonneuve, 1959); *Documents anatoliens sur les langues et les traditions du Caucase* III: *Nouvelles Études oubykhs* (Paris: Institut d'Ethnologie, 1965); Dumézil with Esenç, *Le Verbe oubykh.*

49. Hans Vogt, *Dictionnaire de la langue oubykh avec introduction phonologique* (Oslo: Universitetsforlaget, 1963).
50. Dumézil, *Nouvelles études oubykhs*, pp. 197–259. See also https://circassianworld.wordpress.com/2013/09/04/tevfik-esenc-the-last-person-able-to-speak-the-ubykh-language/
51. The story of the Dumézil-Vogt relation, and his own project of a dictionary, is recounted in Georges Charachidzé, "Le Dernier Dictionnaire de la langue oubykh," in Özsoy, ed., *Proceedings of the Conference on Northwest Caucasian Linguistics*, pp. 11–19. See also his "Ubykh," in B. George Hewitt, ed., *The Indigenous Languages of the Caucasus, 2: North West Caucasus* (Delmar, NY: Caravan Books, 1989), pp. 357–459. Dumézil had originally agreed to write this chapter, but it passed to Charachidzé after Dumézil's death. See B.G. Hewitt, "Preface," p. 7, and "In Memoriam Georges Charachidzé (1930–20 February 2010)," available at https://abkhazworld.com/aw/abkhazians/language/567-in-memoriam-georges-charachidze
52. Fenwick, *A Grammar of Ubykh*, p. 10.
53. Fenwick, *A Grammar of Ubykh*. Some recordings are archived at https://pangloss.cnrs.fr/corpus/Ubykh?lang=en&mode=pro For more on the language, see https://www.omniglot.com/writing/ubykh.htm
54. Arnaldo Momigliano, "Premesse per una discussion su Georges Dumézil," *Opus: Revista internazionale per la storia economica e sociale dell'antichità* II (2), 1983: 329–42, p. 331; "Introduction to a Discussion of Georges Dumézil," *Studies on Modern Scholarship*, ed. G.W. Bowersock and T. J. Cornell (Berkeley, CA: University of California Press, 1994), pp. 286–301, p. 289. Momigliano was critical of Dumézil's work as a whole. See "Georges Dumézil and the Trifunctional Approach to Roman Civilization," p. 315: "Any unbiased reader of the first edition of the book by Dumézil, *Mythes et dieux des Germains*, which appeared in 1939, is bound to find in it sympathy with Nazi ideologies."
55. Momigliano, "Premesse per una discussion su Georges Dumézil," p. 331; "Introduction to a Discussion of Georges Dumézil," p. 289.
56. Riccardo Di Donato, "Materiali per una biografia intellettuale di Arnaldo Momigliano, 1: Libertà e pace nel mondo antico," *Athenaeum* 83(1), 1995: 213–44; W.V. Harris, "The Silences of Momigliano," *The Times Literary Supplement*, April 12, 1996, pp. 6–7; Louis Rose, *Psychology, Art, and Fascism: Ernst Kris, E.H. Gombrich, and the Politics of Caricature* (New Haven, CT and London: Yale University Press, 2016), p. 262, n. 94. See also Marco V. García Quintela, "Dumézil, Momigliano, Bloch: Between Politics and Historiography," *Studia Indo-Europea* 2 (2002–2005): 1–18.
57. Dumézil, *L'Oubli de l'homme*, pp. 299–318, especially pp. 307, 310.
58. Carlo Ginzburg, "Mitologia germanica e nazismo: Su un vecchio libro di Georges Dumézil," *Miti emblemi spie: Morfolgia e storia* (Torino: Einaudi,

1986), pp. 210–38; "Germanic Mythology and Nazism," in *Clues, Myths and the Historical Method*, trans. John and Anne C. Tedeschi (Baltimore, MD: The Johns Hopkins University Press, [repaginated] 2013 [1989]), pp. 114–31. The article was originally published in Italian in 1984, and in French as "Mythologie germanique et nazisme. Sur un ancien livre de Georges Dumézil," *Annales: Histoires, sciences sociales* 40 (4), 1985: 695–715. References are to the Italian and English books.

59. Dumézil, *Mythes et dieux des Germains*, pp. 156; see Ginzburg, "Mitologia germanica e nazismo," p. 213; "Germanic Mythology and Nazism," pp. 116–17.
60. Dumézil, *Mythes et dieux des Germains*, pp. 90–91.
61. Ginzburg, "Mitologia germanica e nazismo," p. 214; "Germanic Mythology and Nazism," p. 117.
62. Littleton, *The New Comparative Mythology*, p. 63.
63. Ginzburg, "Mitologia germanica e nazismo," p. 234, n. 7; "Germanic Mythology and Nazism," p. 197, n. 7.
64. Ginzburg, "Mitologia germanica e nazismo," p. 214; "Germanic Mythology and Nazism," p. 117.
65. Marc Bloch, "Georges Dumézil, *Mythes et dieux des Germains*," *Revue historique* 188/189 (2): 274–6.
66. Ginzburg, "Mitologia germanica e nazismo," p. 212; "Germanic Mythology and Nazism," p. 116.
67. L.F. [Lucien Febvre], "Religions, littérature et vie sociale," *Annales d'histoire sociale* 3 (3), 1941: 98–106, pp. 98–99.
68. Georges Dumézil, "Jeunesse, éternité, aube: Linguistique comparée et mythologie comparée indo-européennes," *Annales d'histoire économique et sociale* 10 (52), 1938: 289–301.
69. Quoted by Hervé Coutau-Bégarie, "Dumézil rattrapé par la politique," in Coutau-Bégarie, *L'Œuvre de Georges Dumézil*, pp. 199–208, p. 208. This article was originally published in *Histoire, économie et société* 14 (3), 1995: 533–54.
70. Georges Dumézil, "Science et politique. Réponse à Carlo Ginzburg," *Annales: Histoire, sciences sociales* 40 (5), 1985: 985–8.
71. Dumézil, "Science et politique," p. 985.
72. Dumézil, "Science et politique," pp. 985–6.
73. Dumézil, "Science et politique," p. 987.
74. Dumézil, "Science et politique," pp. 987–8.
75. Dumézil, "Science et politique," p. 988.
76. Cristiano Grottanelli, *Ideologie, miti, massacre: Indoeuropei di Georges Dumézil* (Palermo: Sellerio, 1993); Bruce Lincoln, *Theorizing Myth: Narrative, Ideology, and Scholarship* (Chicago, IL: University of Chicago Press, 1998). See also Cristiano Grottanelli, "Ancora Dumézil: addenda e

corrigenda," *Quaderni di storia* XX (39), 1994: 195–207, which picks up on the debate between Eribon and Ginzburg.

77. Eribon, *Faut-il brûler Dumézil?*; Dean A. Miller, "Georges Dumézil: Theories, Critiques and Theoretical Extensions," *Religion* 30 (1), 2000: 27–40.
78. García Quintela, *Dumézil*, Part III, pp. 121–98. For a wider audience, see also Jean-François Philippe, "Le Cas Dumézil," *L'Histoire* 159, 1992: 52–53.
79. Coutau-Bégarie, "Dumézil rattrapé par la politique," p. 201.
80. Georges Dumézil, *Les Dieux des Germains: Essai sur la formation de la religion scandinave* (Paris: Presses Universitaires de France, 1959).
81. Georges Dumézil, *Gods of the Ancient Northmen*, ed. and trans. Einar Haugen (Berkeley, CA: University of California Press, 1973).
82. Ginzburg, "Mitologia germanica e nazismo," pp. 211, 234, n. 4; "Germanic Mythology and Nazism," pp. 115, 197, n. 4.
83. Coutau-Bégarie, "Dumézil rattrapé par la politique," p. 205.
84. See Eribon, *Faut-il brûler Dumézil?* pp. 119–44 and Coutau-Bégarie, "Dumézil rattrapé par la politique," p. 206.
85. García Quintela, *Dumézil*, p. 27.
86. See Coutau-Bégarie, *L'Œuvre de Georges Dumézil*, p. 6, n. 2.
87. See also García Quintela, *Dumézil*, p. 28.
88. Pierre Gaxotte, *La Révolution française* (Paris: Arthème Fayard, 1928).
89. Dumézil, *Entretiens avec Didier Eribon*, p. 205; Dubuisson, *Twentieth-Century Mythologies*, p. 8.
90. Stéphane Giocanti, *Charles Maurras: Le Chaos et l'ordre* (Paris: Flammarion, 2006), p. 269.
91. Giocanti, *Charles Maurras*, pp. 323–4. See also Pierre-Jean Deschodt, "Introduction," in Pierre-Jean Deschodt, ed., *Cher Maître: Lettres à Charles Maurras de l'Académie française* (Paris: Christian de Bartillat, 1995), pp. 9–40, p. 21.
92. Dumézil to Maurras, May 18, 1925; Dumézil to Maurras, September 21 [1925]; both cited in Giocanti, *Charles Maurras*, p. 323. The first is in Deschodt, ed., *Cher Maitre*, p. 301 and Coutau-Bégarie, *L'Œuvre de Georges Dumézil*, p. 210. See also Coutau-Bégarie, "Dumézil rattrapé par la politique," pp. 205–6.
93. Lincoln, *Theorizing Myth*, p. 135; discussing Dumézil, *Mitra-Varuna*, pp. 114/166–67; 142/86–87.
94. In *Mitra-Varuna*, Dumézil references both Stig Wikander, *Der arische Männerbund: Studien zur indo-iranischen Sprach- und Religionsgeschichte* (Lund: Ohlsson, 1938); and Otto Höfler, *Kultische Geheimbünde der Germanen* (Frankfurt-am-Main: Verlag Moritz Diesterweg, 1934).
95. On his work and reception, see Courtney Marie Burrell, "Otto Höfler's Männerbund Theory and Popular Representations of the North,"

Nordeuropaforum Zeitschrift für Kulturstudien 2020, pp. 228–66; and her "Otto Höfler's *Männerbünde* and *Völkisch* Ideology," in Nicholas Meylan and Lukas Rösli eds., *Old Norse Myths as Political Ideologies: Critical Studies in the Appropriation of Medieval Narratives* (Turnhout: Brepols, 2020), pp. 91–115.

96. Burrell, "Otto Höfler's Männerbund Theory," p. 233.
97. Ginzburg, "Mitologia germanica e nazismo," p. 227; "Germanic Mythology and Nazism," p. 126. Ginzburg discusses Höfler's work in some detail, and this uncritical use is a large part of his charge against Dumézil.
98. See notably Mircea Eliade, *Shamanism: Archaic Techniques of Ecstasy*, trans. Willard R. Trask (London: Arkana, 1989); *Zalmoxis—The Vanishing God: Comparative Studies in the Religions and Folklore of Dacia and Eastern Europe*, trans. Willard R. Trask (Chicago, IL: University of Chicago Press, 1972), pp. 5–11.
99. Burrell, "Otto Höfler's Männerbund Theory," pp. 248–9.
100. Dumézil, *Entretiens avec Didier Eribon*, pp. 93–94; Mircea Eliade, *Autobiography*, Vol. II: *1937–1960 Exile's Odyssey*, trans. Mac Linscott Ricketts (Chicago, IL: University of Chicago Press, 1988), pp. 104, 113; *The Portugal Journal*, trans. Mac Linscott Ricketts (Albany, NY: State University of New York Press, 2010), p. 97. Eliade's autobiography and his journals furnish much material for tracing the connections between him and Dumézil. On the period in France, see also Mircea Eliade, *Ordeal by Labyrinth: Conversations with Claude-Henri Rocquet*, trans. Derek Coltman (Chicago, IL: University of Chicago Press, 1982), pp. 87–101; and Mircea Eliade and Raffael Pettazzoni, *L'Histoire des religions a-t-elle un sens? Correspondance 1926–1959*, ed. Natale Spinetto (Paris: Les Éditions du Cerf, 1994). Eliade reviewed the 1948 edition of *Mitra-Varuna* for *Critique* in 1949, reprinted in Eliade, *Briser le toit de la maison: La Créativité et ses symboles* (Paris: Gallimard, 1986), pp. 297–306. On their relation, see Julien Ries and Natale Spineto, eds., *Deux explorateurs de la pensée humaine: Georges Dumézil et Mircea Eliade* (Turnhout: Brepols, 2003).
101. See, for example, Philip Ó Ceallaigh and Bryan Rennie, "Mircea Eliade and Antisemitism: An Exchange," available at https://lareviewofbooks.org/article/mircea-eliade-and-antisemitism-an-exchange/ A good summary is Robert Ellwood, *The Politics of Myth: A Study of C.G. Jung, Mircea Eliade and Joseph Campbell* (Albany, NY: SUNY Press, 1999). For the wider context, see Cristina A. Bejan, *Intellectuals and Fascism in Interwar Romania: The Criterion Association* (London: Palgrave, 2019).
102. Eliade, *The Portugal Journal*.
103. Dubuisson, *Twentieth-Century Mythologies*, Part III.

104. Robert A. Segal, "Foreword," in Dubuisson, *Twentieth-Century Mythologies*, pp. ix–xiii, p. xiii
105. "Préface de Georges Dumézil," Mircea Eliade, *Traité d'histoire des religions* (Paris: Payot, 1975 [1949]), pp. 5–9; "Avant-Propos," Mircea Eliade, *Images et symboles: Essais sur le symbolisme magico-religieux* (Paris: Gallimard Tel, 1980 [1952]), pp. 7–9. Neither appears in the English translations of Eliade's texts.
106. Guillaume Ducœur, "'Nous avons combattu ensemble': correspondance de Georges Dumézil et Jan de Vries de 1949 à 1964," *Deshima: Revue d'histoire globale des pays du Nord* 9, 2015: 99–176.
107. Otto Höfler, "Zur Einführung", in Georges Dumézil, *Loki*, trans. Ingo Köck (Darmstadt: Wissenschaftliche Buchgesellschaft, 1959); pp. xi–xv.
108. Dumézil, "Vorwort," *Loki*, pp. xvii–xx, p. xx.
109. Georges Dumézil, "Attila entre deux trésors," in Helmut Birkhan, ed., *Festgabe für Otto Höfler zum 75. Geburtstag* (Vienna: Braumüller, 1976), pp. 121–7. I owe the clue to look at the *Festgabe* to Ginzburg, "Mitologia germanica e nazismo," p. 235, n. 28; "Germanic Mythology and Nazism," p. 198, n. 28.
110. "Georges Dumézil et les études indo-européennes," *Nouvelle École* 22–23, 1972–73.
111. Alain de Benoist, "Georges Dumézil répond aux questions de Nouvelle École," *Nouvelle École* 10, 1969: 41–44.
112. Rivière, *Georges Dumézil à la découverte des Indo-Européens.*
113. On this, see Stefan Arvidsson, *Aryan Idols: Indo-European Mythology as Ideology and Science*, trans. Sonia Wichmann (Chicago, IL: University of Chicago Press, 2006), pp. 304–6. For the journal's account, see Alain de Benoist, "Nécrologie: Georges Dumézil," *Nouvelle I* 45, 1988–89: 136–9.
114. Ginzburg, "Mitologia germanica e nazismo," pp. 219–20; "Germanic Mythology and Nazism," p. 121.
115. Dumézil, Bonnet, and Pralon, "Entretien," p. 39; see Maurice Olender and Georges Dumézil, "Les Festins secrets de Georges Dumézil," *Le Nouvel Observateur*, January 14–28, 1983, pp. 50–54, p. 53. Ginzburg's other reference is to Jean-Claude Rivière, "Actualité de Georges Dumézil," *Éléments* 32, 1979 (November–December): 15–17.
116. Olender and Dumézil, "Les Festins secrets de Georges Dumézil," p. 53.
117. Dumézil, *L'Héritage indo-européen à Rome*, p. 242.
118. Georges Dumézil, *Leçon inaugurale faite le Jeudi 1er Décembre 1949 par M. Georges Dumézil* (Nogent-le-Rotrou: Collège de France, 1950); reprinted in *Mythes et dieux des Indo-Europeens*, ed. Hervé Coutau-Bégarie (Paris: Flammarion, 1998), pp. 13–36, p. 32.
119. Georges Dumézil, *Les Dieux des Indo-Européens* (Paris: Presses Universitaires de France, 1952). See p. 3 for the note on its provenance.

120. Following lectures in the 1950s, this was summarised in Georges Dumézil, *L'Idéologie tripartie des Indo-Européens* (Brussels: Latomus, 1958); largely reprinted in *Mythes et dieux des Indo-Européens*.
121. Georges Dumézil, *Les Dieux souverains des Indo-Européens* (Paris: Gallimard, 1977), 55–85.
122. Georges Dumézil, *Mythe et épopée,* I*: L'Idéologie des trois fonctions dans les épopées des peuples indo-européens* (Paris: Gallimard, 1968). See Coutau-Bégarie, *L'Œuvre de Georges Dumézil*, p. 56.
123. Georges Dumézil, *Mythe et épopée,* II*: Types épiques indo-européens: Un héros, un sorcier, un roi* (Paris: Gallimard, 1971); *The Stakes of the Warrior*, ed. Jaan Puhvel, trans. David Weeks (Berkeley and Los Angeles, CA: University of California Press, 1983); *The Plight of a Sorcerer*, eds. Jaan Puhvel and David Weeks (Berkeley and Los Angeles, CA: University of California Press, 1986), and *The Destiny of a King*, trans. Alf Hiltebeitel (Chicago, IL: University of Chicago Press, 1973).
124. Georges Dumézil, *Mythe et épopée,* III*: Histoires romaines* (Paris: Gallimard, 1973); *Camillus: A Study of Indo-European Religion as Roman History*, ed. Udo Strutynski, trans. Annette Aronowicz and Josette Bryson (Berkeley, CA: University of California Press, 1980).
125. Georges Dumézil, *Heur et malheur du guerrier: Aspects mythiques de la fonction guerrière chez les Indo-Européens* (Paris: Presses Universitaires de France, 1969), p. 5; *The Destiny of the Warrior*, trans. Alf Hiltebeitel (Chicago, IL: University of Chicago Press, 1970), p. xiv.
126. Udo Strutynski, "Bibliographical Note," in Dumézil, *Camillus*, pp. 257–61, 260; see Dumézil, *Les Dieux souverains des Indo-Européens*, pp. 10–12.
127. Dumézil, *La Religion romaine archaïque* (Paris: Payot, 1974 [1966]), p. 12; *Entretiens avec Didier Eribon*, p. 100. For some of the challenges, see Dumézil, Bonnet, and Pralon, "Entretien," p. 37; Dumézil and Ewald, "Le Messager des dieux," p. 18; Dumézil, *Entretiens avec Didier Eribon*, pp. 167–73. *Tarpeia* may be the best substitute. See Coutau-Bégarie, *L'Œuvre de Georges Dumézil*, p. 12.
128. Strutynski, "Bibliographical Note," p. 260. Georges Dumézil, *Du mythe au roman: La Saga de Hadingus (Saxo Grammaticus I, v–viii) et autres essais* (Paris: Presses Universitaires de France, 1970); *From Myth to Fiction: The Saga of Hadingus*, trans. Derek Coltman (Chicago, IL: University of Chicago Press, 1973). This text is a revision of *La Saga de Hadingus (Saxo Grammaticus I, v–viii): Du mythe au roman* (Paris: Presses Universitaires de France, 1953).
129. Georges Dumézil, *Idées romaines*; *Fêtes romaines d'été et d'automne* suivi de *Dix questions romaines* (Paris: Gallimard, 1975); and the more substantial part of *Mariages indo-européens* (Paris: Payot, 1979), entitled "Quinze questions romaines," pp. 119–336.

130. Georges Dumézil, *Romans de Scythie et d'alentour* (Paris: Payot, 1978); *Contes et légendes des peuples du Caucase*, Vol. 1: *Textes avars, tatars, tchétschènes et ingouches, lazes, tcherkesses, abkhazes, et arméniens* (Lisieux: Lingva, 2017). Though the latter was billed as Volume 1, no other volumes have yet appeared. The plan was for a second volume of Ubykh texts (Viktoriya and Patrice Lajoye, "Georges Dumézil et le Caucase," in Dumézil, *Contes et legendes des peuples du Caucase*, pp. 5–8, p. 7.
131. Strutynski, "Bibliographical Note," p. 260.
132. Dumézil, *Gods of the Ancient Northmen*; *From Myth to Fiction*; *Mythes et dieux de la Scandinavie ancienne*, ed. François-Xavier Dillmann (Paris: Gallimard, 2000).
133. "Complément bibliographique," in Dumézil, *Mythes et dieux de la Scandinavie ancienne*, pp. 369–74, p. 372.
134. Strutynski, "Bibliographical Note," p. 260.
135. Dumézil, *Heur et malheur du guerrier*, p. 5; *The Destiny of the Warrior*, p. xiv. See p. 54 n. 1/54 n. 3 for a description.
136. Georges Dumézil, *Archaic Roman Religion* (Chicago, IL: University of Chicago Press, 1970), two volumes; reprinted (Baltimore, MD: The Johns Hopkins University Press, 1996), Vol. I, p. xix.
137. Dumézil, *Les Dieux souverains des Indo-Européens*, pp. 10–11; see Coutau-Bégarie, *L'Œuvre de Georges Dumézil*, p. 67.
138. Coutau-Bégarie, *L'Œuvre de Georges Dumézil*, p. 75.
139. Available at https://www.gallimard.fr/Catalogue/GALLIMARD/Bibliotheque-des-Sciences-humaines/Les-dieux-souverains-des-Indo-Europeens
140. Dumézil, *Entretiens avec Didier Eribon*.
141. Coutau-Bégarie, *L'Œuvre de Georges Dumézil*.
142. Georges Dumézil, *Loki* (Paris: GP Maisonneve, 1959); *Loki* (Paris: Flammarion, 1986); reprinted in 1999 and 2010.
143. Georges Dumézil, *La Religion romaine archaïque*; second edition; *Archaic Roman Religion*.
144. Georges Dumézil, *Los Dioses de los Indoeuropeos* (Barcelona: Seix Barral, 1970).
145. Littleton, *The New Comparative Mythology*, p. 243. Coutau-Bégarie, in *L'Œuvre de Georges Dumézil*, p. 38, reports he was originally supposed to have translated *Mitra-Varuna*, too.
146. Dumézil, *Archaic Roman Religion*, p. xix; "Bibliographie raisonnée," in *Georges Dumézil: Cahiers pour un temps*, pp. 339–49, p. 343; "Bibliographie," *Magazine littéraire* 229: 51–52, p. 52.
147. Georges Dumézil, *The Riddle of Nostradamus: A Critical Dialogue*, trans. Betsy Wing (Baltimore, MD: The Johns Hopkins University Press, 1999); a translation of "*…Le Moyne noir en gris dedans Varennes,*" *Sotie*

nostradamique suivie d'un *Divertissement sur les dernières paroles de Socrate* (Paris: Gallimard, 1984).

148. Alf Hiltebeitel, "Mitra-Varuna: An Essay on Two Indo-European Representations of Sovereignty," *The Journal of Religion* 70 (2), 1990: 295–6, p. 296.
149. N.J. Allen, "Mitra-Varuna: An Essay on Two Indo-European Representations of Sovereignty, by Georges Dumézil," *Man*, new series 25 (1), 1990: 155. The reference to correcting earlier work is to Dumézil, *Du mythe au roman*, p. 103, n. 1; *From Myth to Novel*, p. 103, n. 16.
150. In 1959, for example, he suggests that the whole last chapter of the present work should be cut or deleted (*supprimer*) as he recognises Bhaga is blind, not one-eyed as he argues here. See "La Transposition des dieux souverains mineurs en héros dans le *Mahābhārata*," *Indo-Iranian Journal* 3 (1): 1–16, p. 9 and p. 9, n. 22. For a more balanced assessment, see Georges Dumézil, "'Le Borgne' and 'Le Manchot': The State of the Problem," in Gerard James Larson with C. Scott Littleton and Jaan Puhvel, eds., *Myth in Indo-European Antiquity* (Berkeley, CA: University of California Press, 1974), pp. 17–28; *Mythe et épopée,* III, pp. 267–81.
151. Dumézil, *L'Héritage indo-européen à Rome*, pp. 250–1, part-translated in Dubuisson, *Twentieth-Century Mythologies*, p. 67.
152. Dubuisson, *Twentieth-Century Mythologies*, pp. 66–67.
153. For a longer discussion of the relation, see Didier Eribon, *Michel Foucault et ses contemporains* (Paris: Fayard, 1994); my books on Foucault, especially *The Early Foucault* (Cambridge: Polity, 2021); "The Yoke of Law and the Lustre of Glory: Foucault and Dumézil on Sovereignty," in Martina Tazzioli and William Walters, eds., *Handbook on Governmentality* (Cheltenham: Edward Elgar, 2023), pp. 38–53; and "Foucault and Dumézil on Antiquity," *Journal of the History of Ideas*, 85 (3), 2024: 571–600.
154. Dumézil, *Servius et la fortune*, pp. 9–14.
155. Georges Canguilhem, "Mort de l'homme ou épuissement du cogito?" *Œuvres complètes,* Tome V: *Histoire des sciences, épistémologie, commemorations (1966–1995)*, ed. Camille Limoges (Paris: Vrin, 2018), pp. 189–214, pp. 192–3; "The Death of Man, or Exhaustion of the Cogito?" trans. Catherine Porter, in Gary Gutting, ed., *The Cambridge Companion to Michel Foucault* (Cambridge: Cambridge University Press, 1994), pp. 71–91, pp. 72–73. For a longer discussion, see Stuart Elden, "Canguilhem, Dumézil, Hyppolite: Georges Canguilhem and his Contemporaries," *Revue internationale de philosophie*, 307, 2024: 27–48.

Editorial Note

1. N.J. Allen, "Mitra-Varuna: An Essay on Two Indo-European Representations of Sovereignty, by Georges Dumézil," *Man*, new series 25 (1), 1990: 155; Alf Hiltebeitel, "Mitra-Varuna: An Essay on Two Indo-European Representations of Sovereignty," *The Journal of Religion* 70 (2), 1990: 295–6, 296.

Notes to Preface to the Second Edition

1. This is a reference to the works listed at the end of the second paragraph.
2. It is actually the seventh section of Chapter IX, which is rewritten. The first-edition texts and translations are provided in Appendices I and II of the present edition.
3. All these works were published by Gallimard. *Horace et les Curiaces*, *Servius et la fortune*, and *Tarpeia* comprised a series on *Les Mythes romains*. A fourth volume of *Jupiter, Mars, Quirinus*, *Explication de textes indiens et latins*, was published by Presses Universitaires de France in 1948.
4. The closest Dumézil comes to this vision is *Mythe et épopée*, published by Gallimard in three volumes in 1968, 1971, and 1973, and reprinted as a single volume in 1995. For a brief discussion, see the editor's Introduction.
5. Georges Dumézil, *Le Festin d'immortalité: Étude de mythologie comparée indo-européenne* (Paris: Librairie Orientaliste Paul Geuthner, 1924).
6. Georges Dumézil, *Le Problème des Centaures: Étude de mythologie comparée indo-européenne* (Paris: Librairie Orientaliste Paul Geuthner, 1929).
7. This sentence is missing from the earlier English translation: "Cela demandait du temps, et quelque liberté."
8. Georges Dumézil, *Ouranós-Váruṇa: Étude de mythologie comparée indo-européenne* (Paris: Adrien Maisonneuve, 1934).
9. The course records were published as Georges Dumézil, "XVII.— Mythologie comparée," *École Pratique des Hautes Études, Section des Sciences religieuses. Annuaire 1939–1940*, pp. 83–84. For the description of the courses and a brief discussion, see the editor's Introduction.
10. Dumézil treats these questions in more detail in *Aspects de la fonction guerrière chez les Indo-Européens* (Paris: Presses Universitaires de France, 1956), revised as *Heur et malheur du guerrier : Aspects de la fonction guerrière chez les Indo-Européens* (Paris: Presses Universitaires

de France, 1969); *The Destiny of the Warrior*, trans. Alf Hiltebeitel (Chicago, IL: University of Chicago Press, 1970).

11. These are themes of the *Jupiter, Mars, Quirinus* series, particularly Volumes II and III.
12. See *Marie-Louise Sjoestedt (1900–1940). In Memoriam,* suivi de [Marie-Louise Sjoestedt] *Essai sur une littérature nationale, la littérature irlandaise contemporaine* (Paris: E. Droz, 1941). Dumézil's homage is found on pp. 44–45.
13. "Mme Pintelon" was listed as one of the regular attendees of this course, in Dumézil, "XVII.— Mythologie comparée," p. 84. Pierre Pintelon is one of those listed on the attendance sheet found in DMZ 56.4, leçon 1. I have been unable to find further information.
14. See Lukian Prijac, "Déborah Lifszyc (1907–1942): Ethnologue et linguiste (de Gondar à Auschwitz)," *Aethiopica* 11: 148–72.

Notes to Preface to the First Edition

1. This is indeed the case in the first edition. The footnotes here are either those he added to the second edition or some of the more cumbersome in-text references, which have been moved to notes.
2. Georges Dumézil, "La Préhistoire des flamines majeurs," *Revue de l'Histoire des religions* 118, 1938: 188–200.
3. First edition, p. xi: "among the Indo-Iranians and among the Italo-Celts [*chez les Indo-Iraniens et chez les Italo-Celts*]."
4. One paragraph of the first edition preface (p. xii) is not included in the second: "The method of our research will be evident from the presentation. However we would like to refer you to the clarification we have made (and which we hope will appear soon) at the beginning of the section that has been entrusted to us (Religion des Indo-Européens) in the *Histoire des Religions*, edited by Gorce and Mortier with Quillet. [*La méthode de nos recherches ressortira assez de l'exposé. Nous nous permettons cependant de renvoyer à la mise au point que nous avons faite (et qui, nous l'espérons, paraîtra bientôt) en tête de la partie qui nous a été confiée (Religion des Indo-Européens) dans l'Histoire des Religions que dirigent à la librairie Quillet MM. Gorce et Mortier*]." The work was published as *Histoire générale des religions*, ed. Maxime Gorce and Raoul Mortier (Paris: Librairie Aristide Quillet, 1948–52), five volumes; Volume 1 had the subtitle *Introduction générale, les primitifs, l'ancien Orient, les Indo-Européens*; Dumézil's contribution was "Religion et mythologie préhistoriques des Indo-Européens," pp. 443–53.

Notes to Chapter I

1. Despite the way the references appear, these are books not articles. Georges Dumézil, *Flāmen-Brahman* (Paris: Librairie Orientaliste Paul Geuthner, 1935); *Le Problème des Centaures*: *Étude de mythologie comparée indo-européenne* (Paris: Librairie Orientaliste Paul Geuthner, 1929).
2. First edition, p. 1 adds: "We have dealt with it in several paragraphs of our contribution to the *Histoire des religions* edited by Gorce and Mortier (in press, Quillet, section on Religion des Indo-Européens); the present chapter will develop this preliminary sketch. [*Nous l'avons abordée dans plusieurs paragraphes de notre contribution à l'Histoire des Religions que dirigent MM Gorce et Mortier (sous presse, librairie Quillet, section sur la Religion des Indo-Européens); le présent chapitre développera cette première esquisse*]." This is the work cited in note 4 of the "Preface to the First Edition."
3. The *Lex Iulia Municipalis*, also known as the Tabula Heracleensis, is a set of municipal laws including regulations for vehicles allowed inside Rome's walls. The Latin text can be found at https://droitromain.univ-grenoble-alpes.fr/Leges/heracleensis_crawford.html; and an English translation at https://droitromain.univ-grenoble-alpes.fr/Anglica/heracleensis_johnson.html
4. First edition, p. 2 adds: "for example on that fateful day of the Lupercalia when they both pass their power to the terrible Runners [*par exemple en ce jour pathétique des Lupercales où tous deux passent leur pouvoir aux terribles Coureurs*]."
5. First edition, p. 2 adds: "are only brought together, in historical times, for these inaugurations [*ne sont plus réunis, à l'époque historique, que pour procéder à ces inaugurations*]."
6. Dumézil regularly refers to "Manu," meaning the text also known as *The Laws of Manu*, the *Institutes of Hindu Law*, or *The Ordinances of Manu.*
7. The most-widely circulated English-language version is *The Institutes of Vishnu*, trans. Julius Jolly (Oxford: Clarendon Press, 1880).
8. Dumézil refers to XXVIII, 146; I have amended to XXVIII, 40.
9. First edition, p. 5 has "the strictest morals [*les mœurs les plus rigoureuse*] in place of "the strictest decorum [*la tenue la plus rigoureuse*]."
10. Henri D'Arbois de Jubainville, *Cours de littérature celtique,* VI: *La Civilisation des Celtes et celle de l'épopée homérique* (Paris: Albert Fontemoing, 1899). The references in this note are: "Whitley Stokes, *The Tripartite Life*, T. II, pp. 325–6; Hogan, *Vita sancti Patricii*, p. 83; *Analecta Bollandiana*, T. II, p. 61. Cf. Pline, I, XVI, §251; d. Ian, T. III, p. 45." Whitley Stokes, *The Tripartite Life of Patrick: With Other Documents Relating to that Saint,* two volumes (London: Eyre and Spottiswoode,

1888); Edmund Hogan, *Vita Sancti Patricii Hibernorum Apostoli* (Bruxellis, Typis Polleunis, 1882); E. Hogan, "Tirechani Collectanea de Sancto Patricio ex Libro Armachano," *Analecta Bollandiana* II, 1883, pp. 35–68. The reference to the edition of Pliny's *Natural History* is not clear, but it presumably means the edition by Ludwig von Jan in five volumes (Lipsiae: Teubner, 1854–60). Dumézil's references to Pliny are XVI, 49; XXIV, 103. I have changed these to the more common references of XVI, 95 and XXIV, 62.

11. Text cut from first edition pp. 6–7: "As for the root, which may be found, secularised, in Armenian (cf. our note on arm. *Batjat* 'to desire strongly', *Rev*[ue]. *des Études Indo-Européennes*, I, 2–4, Bucharest, 1938), it surely has to do with sacrificial operations; no doubt it had a value of the type: 'to work at realising a desire, shamanistically or religiously, by means of sacrificial manipulation and speech'. [*Quant à la racine, qui se retrouve peut-être, laïcisée, en armenien (c.f. notre note sur arm.* batjat *'désirer vivement,'* Rev. des Études Indo-Européennes, *I, 2–4, Bucarest, 1938), elle a sûrement rapport aux opérations sacrificielles; sans doute avait-elle une valeur du type: 'travailler à réaliser un désir, chamanistiquement ou religieusement, par la manipulation et par la parole sacrificielles*'.]" Dumézil's piece was entitled "Arménien ԲԱՂՁԱԼ, ԻՂՁ," *Revue des Études indo-européennes* I (2–4): 377–80. The Benveniste reference is probably to "Esquisse d'une théorie de la racine," *Origines de la formation des noms en indo-européen* (Paris: Adrian Maisonneuve, 1935), pp. 147–73; translated by Theodore M. Lightner as "Sketch of a Theory of the Root," *Paper in Linguistics* 10 (1–2): 101–34.
12. First edition, p. 7: simply says "Once a year, in the month of February, the last of the year" [*Une fois l'an, au mois de februarius, le dernier de l'année*]."
13. First edition, p. 7: "Now, on this *dies februatus* which is the 15th of *februarius*, *rēx* and *flāmen dialis* hand over the *februa* to the *pontifices* and thus set off the rites, perhaps collaborating in them (Ovid, *Fastes* II, 21–22, 27–28, and 282). But the rites… [*Or, en ce* dies februatus *qu'est le 15 de* februarius, rēx *et* flāmen dialis *remittent bien aux* pontifices *les* februa *et déclenchent ainsi les rites, y collaborant peut-être (Ovide,* Fastes, II, 21–22, 27–28 et 282*) Mais les rites...*]."
14. First edition p. 8 has "brutal [*brutal*]" in place of "scabrous [*scabreux*]."
15. The references are to Joseph Vendryes, "La Famille du latin *mundus* 'monde'," *Mémoires de la Société de linguistique*, XVIII, 1913: 305–10 and "Remarques sur quelques faits de vocabulaire," *Revue celtique* 40, 1923: 428–41.

Notes to Chapter II

1. First edition, p. 15 adds: "on the very morning of the Lupercalia, as we have seen, the great command of the Social Order – *rēx, flāmen* and *flāminica, pontifices* – met in full to perform a kind of 'transmission of powers' to open the field to the violence of the runners-flagellants (it is probable that the verse in *Fastes* II, 282, simply alludes to this 'setting in train' of the rites [*le matin même des Lupercales, on l'a vu, le grand état-major de l'Ordre Social* – rēx, flāmen *et* flāminica, pontifices – *se réunissait au complet pour accomplir une sorte de « transmission de pouvoirs », pour ouvrir le champ aux violences des coureurs-flagellateurs (il est probable que le vers des* Fastes *II, 282, fait simplement allusion à cette « mise en train » des rites)*]."
2. Dumézil's reference of VIII, 66, 5 is incorrect. I have replaced with VIII, 77, 5.
3. First edition, p. 16 references the first edition of Georg Wissowa, *Religion und Kultur der Römes* (Munich: C.H. Beck, 1902), p. 85, n. 6 and 7.
4. Alfred von Domaszewski, *Abhandlungen zur Römischen Religion* (Leipzig and Berlin: B.G. Teubner, 1909).
5. Georges Dumézil, "Jeunesse, eternité, aube: Linguistique comparée et mythologie comparée indo-européennes," *Annales d'histoire économique et sociales* 52 (July), 1938: 289–301.
6. Émile Benveniste, "Expression indo-européenne de l' 'éternité'," *Bulletin de la Société de linguistique de Paris* 38 (1), 1937: 103–12.
7. Dumézil's reference to XIV, 4, 3, 7 is incorrect. The Gandharva are described as Varuṇa's people in *Śatapatha Brāhmaṇa* XIII, 4, 3, 7.
8. This sentence is missing from the original translation [*Les quatres chapitres qui suivent sont consacrés à inventorier ces nouvelles acquisitions. D'autres se proposeront ensuite d'elle-mêmes*].

Notes to Chapter III

1. Dumézil gives the reference as II, 75, but this is II, 65 in the Loeb edition, online at https://penelope.uchicago.edu/Thayer/E/Roman/Texts/Dionysius_of_Halicarnassus/2C*.html
2. The final clause of this sentence and reference to Claudian is added to the second edition.
3. The passage in parentheses is added to the second edition.
4. The full references are Sylvain Lévi, *La Doctrine du sacrifice dans les Brāhmaṇas* (Paris: Ernest Leroux, 1898), pp. 108ff; Antoine Meillet, "A propos de Avestique *arazdā*," *Mémoires de la Société de linguistique* XVIII, 1913: 60–64; Joseph Vendryes, "A propos du verbe 'croire' et

de la 'croyance'," *Revue celtique* XLIV, 1927: 90–96; A. Ernout, "Skr. *Çraddhā*, lat. *credo*, irl. *Cretim*," in *Mélanges d'indianisme offerts par ses élèves à M. Sylvain Lévi* (Paris: Ernest Leroux, 1911), pp. 85–89; A. Meillet, "Du nominatif et de l'accusatif," *Memoires de la Société de linguistique* XXII, 1922: 49–55.

5. The full references are Henri Hubert and Marcel Mauss, "Essai sur la nature et la fonction sociale du sacrifice," *L'Année sociologique* II, 1899: 29–138; reprinted as a book by Presses Universitaires de France, 2016; *Sacrifice: Its Nature and Functions*, trans. W.D. Halls (Chicago, IL: University of Chicago Press, 1964); and "Origine des pouvoirs magiques dans les societes australiennes: Étude analytique et critique de documents ethnographiques," *Annuaire de l'École Pratique des Hautes Études, Sciences religieuses* (1904): 1–55.
6. Lévi, *La Doctrine du sacrifice dans les Brāhmaṇas*, pp. 120–1: "Manu est vraiment le héros de la çraddhā; il a la folie du sacrifice comme les saints du boudhisme ont la folie du dévouement."
7. This passage is transliterated and translated in J. Muir, *Original Sanskrit Texts on the Origin and History of the People of India, their Religion and Institutions,* Vol. I: *Mythical and Legendary Accounts of the Origin of Caste, with an Enquiry into its Existence in the Vedic Age*, second edition (London: Trübner & Co, 1868), pp. 189–90.
8. Dumézil references Book V of the *Fastes*, but the passage is in Book III.

Notes to Chapter IV

1. First edition, p. 44: "A Mitanien treaty" [*Un traité mitanien*].
2. Abel Bergaigne, *La Religion védique d'après les hymnes du Rig-Veda* (Paris: F. Vieweg, 1878–83). The second volume was in two parts, published in 1883; a third was published in 1897.
3. Antoine Meillet, "Le Dieu indo-iranien Mitra," *Journal asiatique* 10, 1907: 143–59.
4. Georges Davy, *La Foi jurée, étude sociologique du problème du contrat, la formation du lien contractuel* (Paris: Librairie Félix Alcan, 1922).
5. First edition, p. 47: "Hâvamâl (Paroles du Très Haut)." In the English book *The Gift*, these appear on pp. 1–3 (Routledge) or pp. 55–57 (Hau). "Sayings of the High One" is the second part of the *Poetic Edda.*
6. First edition, p. 47 numbers these 39, 41, 42, 43, 46; corrected in the second edition.
7. First edition, p. 47 adds "root which is probably found in Celtic in the name of the *dru-(v)id-* [*racine qui se retrouve sans doute en celtique dans le nom du* dru-(v)id-]."

8. Alfred Ernout and Antoine Meillet, *Dictionnaire étymologique de la langue latine: Histoire des mots*, revised fourth edition (Paris: Klincksieck, 2001), p. 737. First edition, p. 48 specifies "*uindex.*"
9. This sentence and reference are added to the second edition. Rudolf Thurneysen, "Aus dem irischen Recht III, 4: Die falschen Urteilssprüche Caratnia's," *Zeitschrift für celtische Philologie* XV, 1925: 303–76, the discussion of section 17 is on pp. 325–7.
10. First edition, p. 49: "raw butter [*le beurre brut*]."
11. The phrase "can be explained only in accordance with an Italic origin (cf. *curia, quirites*)" is not in the first edition (p. 50).
12. First edition, p. 50: "formule de composition" is in quotes.
13. S. Weinstock, "Summanus," *Paulys Real-encyclopädie der classischen Altertumswissenschaft*, eds. Georg Wissowa, Wilhelm Kroll, and Karl Mittelhaus, Zweite Reihe (R–Z), Siebter Halbband, Stoa–Symposion (Stuttgart: J.B. Metzlerscche Verlagsbuchhandlung, 1931), col. 898. The reference to Thulin is to C.O. Thulin, *Die etruskische Disziplin*, three volumes (Göteborg: Wald Zachrissons Boktryckeri, 1906–1909.
14. Dumézil references II, 138; I have amended to the more common location.
15. J. Muir, *Original Sanskrit Texts on the Origin and History of the People of India, their Religion and Institutions*, Vol. V: *Contribution to a Knowledge of the Cosmology, Mythology, Religious Ideas, Life and Manners, of the Indians in the Vedic Age* (London: Trübner & Co, 1870), pp. 58–76. The references to Sayana's commentary, the *Taittirīya Brāhmaṇa*, and the *Taittriya Saṁhitā* all follow Muir.
16. Dumézil references *Maitrāyaṇī Saṁhitā* V, 2, 5, which is incorrect. There is a discussion of the colour of sacrifices to Mitra and Varuṇa in II, 5, 7. (It appears Dumézil transposed the first two numbers: V, 2 instead of II, 5.) It is also a two-coloured animal, for the symbolism Dumézil indicates, not that there are two separate animals.
17. Dumézil's reference is to *Corpus Inscriptionum Latinarum*, Vol. VI, Part I: *Inscriptiones Urbis Romae Latinae* (Berlin: Georg Reimer, 1876), p. 576, where it appears as "Summan Pat Verb Atros." The inscription can also be found in Guil. [Wilhelm] Henzen, *Acta Fratrum Arualium* (Berlin: Georgii Reimeri, 1874), p. 146.
18. Dumézil references Hésiode, *Théogonie, Les Travaux et les jours, Le Bouclier*, trans. Paul Mazon (Paris: Les Belles Lettres, 1928); the English uses Hesiod, *The Works and Days, Theogony, The Shield of Herakles*, trans. Richard Lattimore (Ann Arbor, MI: University of Michigan Press, 1959).
19. Jean Przyluski, "Totémisme et végétalisme dans l'Inde," *Revue de l'Histoire des religions* 96, 1927: 347–64.

Notes to Chapter V

1. This passage is included in J. Muir, *Original Sanskrit Texts on the Origin and History of the People of India, their Religion and Institutions* (London: Trübner & Co, 1870), Vol. I, p. 186, which gives the reference as *Taittiriya Brāhmaṇa* I, 1, 4, 4.
2. A. Otto, *Die Sprichwörter und sprichwörtlichen Redensarten der Römer* (Stuttgart and Leipzig: B.G. Teubner, 1890), pp. 208–9. Dumézil uses the following edition: *Sexti Pompei Festi, De Verborum Significatu quae supersunt cum Pauli Epitome*, ed. Wallace M. Lindsay (Lepizig: B.G. Teubner, 1913). The quote is from p. 135.
3. Dumézil gets the year wrong. The correct reference is André Vaillant, "Slave *mǫžb*," *Revue des Études slaves* 18 (1–2), 1938: 75–77. An offprint of this is found in DMZ 56.4, leçon 2.
4. This seems to be a reference to A. Cuny, "Les Thèmes subsidiaires en *-u-*," *Revue de Philologie, de littérature et d'histoire anciennes* 4, 1930: 5–24.
5. Frederik Muller Jzn, *Altitalisches Wörterbuch* (Göttingen: Vandenhoeck & Ruprecht, 1926), p. 254. Frederik Muller in first edition, p. 63.
6. Muir, *Original Sanskrit Texts*, Vol. I, pp. 306–7.
7. Dumézil's source is Muir, *Original Sanskrit Texts*, Vol. I, p. 307.
8. The reference is to Sylvain Lévi, "Problèmes indo-hébraiques," *Mémorial Sylvain Lévi* (Paris: Paul Hartmann, 1937), pp. 314–18. This is a collection of Lévi's articles; pp. 316–18 of this piece is entitled "II. Le Roi Nahuṣa metamorphose en serpent."
9. This is the text referenced previously: Geo Widengren, *Hochgottglaube im alten Iran: eine religionsphänomenologische Untersuchung*, Uppsala Universitets Årsskrift 6 (Uppsala: Lundequist, 1938).
10. Herman Lommel, chair of Indo-European Studies at the Goethe University Frankfurt. Major works include *Die Religion Zarathustras, nach dem Awesta dargestellt* (Tübingen: J.C.B. Mohr, 1930); *Die alten Arier: Von Art und Adel ihrer Götter* (Frankfurt-am-Main: Vittorio Klostermann, 1935); and *Die arische Kriegsgott* (Frankfurt-am-Main: Vittorio Klostermann, 1939).
11. Al-Biruni, *The Chronology of Ancient Nations: An English Version of the Arabic Text of the Athâr-ul-Bâkiya of Albîrûnî, Or "Vestiges of the Past,"* trans. C. Edward Sachau (London: William H. Allen, 1879), p. 208. Dumézil translates the English translation into French; Coltman retranslates into English. Sachau's translation of this passage reads "because at Mihrajân that which grows reaches its perfection and has no more material for further growth and because animals cease from sexual intercourse. In the same way they make Naurôz a sign for the beginning of the world, because the contrary of all these things happens on Naurôz."

12. Al-Tha'alibl, *Histoire des Rois de Perses*, bilingual Arabic-French version, ed. and trans. H. Zotenberg (Paris: Imprimerie Nationale, 1900), p. 13.

Notes to Chapter VI

1. Alfred Ernout and Antoine Meillet, *Dictionnaire étymologique de la langue latine: Histoire des mots*, revised fourth edition (Paris Klincksieck, 2001), pp. 358 and 172.
2. This is a reference to Antoine Meillet, "Le Dieu indo-iranien Mitra," *Journal asiatique* 10, 1907: 143–59.
3. First edition, p. 74: "successfully separated *ius* from *fas* [*a su séparer le* ius *du* fas]."
4. Ernout and Meillet, *Dictionnaire étymologique de la langue latine*, p. 435.
5. The passage in parentheses is added to the second edition. The reference is to Raymond Monier, *Manuel élémentaire de droit romain*, third edition, Vol. II : *Les Obligations* (Paris: Éditions Domat-Montchrestien, 1944), p. 21.
6. First edition, p. 77 has "d'échange plus équilibrée"; second edition, p. 122 "plus équilibrée d'échange."
7. Stig Wikander, *Der arische Männerbund: Studien zur indo-iranischen Sprach- und Religionsgeschichte* (Lund: Ohlsson, 1938).
8. Otto Höfler, *Kultische Geheimbünde der Germanen* (Frankfurt-am-Main: Verlag Moritz Diesterweg, 1934). This had the designation "I. Band," but no other volumes were published.
9. *Zend-Avesta*, trans. James Darmesteter (Oxford: Oxford University Press, 1884–87), three volumes; reprinted as Vol. II, pp. 120–1 (Delhi: Motilal Banarsidass, 1965). It seems Darmesteter translated as "ruffian," while "*bandit*" is Dumézil's translation of this choice.
10. The first edition p. 83 has "Marcel Granet, who is studying the same phenomenon in the Chinese domain, has accustomed us, in his books, in his lectures and in his remarks… [*M. Marcel Granet qui étudie le même phénoméne sur le domaine chinois, nous a habitués, dans ses livres, dans ses Leçons et dans ses propos…*]." Marcel Granet died in November 1940. He was the author of several books on Chinese civilisation and thought. Dumézil wrote a preface to the reedition of his Marcel Granet, *La Religion des Chinois* (Paris: Éditions Imago, 1980 [1922]), pp. v–viii, and cites his *La Pensée chinoise* (Paris: La Renaissance du Livre, 1934), in this book's conclusion.

Notes to Chapter VII

1. The cross-reference is added to the second edition.
2. First edition, p. 88: "Servius-Brutus."
3. E.N. Setälä, "Ein altes arisches Kulturwort im finnischen und lappischen," *Finnisch-Ugrische Forschungen: Zeitschrift von finnisch-ugrische Sprach und Volkskunde* 8, 1908: 77–80.
4. Bernhard Geiger, *Die Aməša Spəntas: Ihr Wesen und ihre ursprüngliche Bedeutung*, Sitzungsberichte der Philosophisch-Historischen Classe der Kaiserlichen Akademie der Wissenschaften in Wien, 176, Bd 7 (Vienna: Alfred Hölder, 1916).
5. First edition, p. 91 simply reads: "It is probable that this Iranian state of things is the result of an evolution. In the first place, it must fall to the particular form of relations there between warrior power and the royal administration. [*Il est probable que cet équilibre des faits iraniens est l'effet d'une évolution; il doit répondre à la forme particulière qu'ont revêtue là les rapports entre la force guerrière et l'administration royale.*]"
6. First edition, p. 93: "the one chaotic and the other δικαιος... the one monstrous and the other merely superhuman [*l'un désordonné et l'autre* δικαιος... *l'un monstreux et l'autre seulement surhumain*]."
7. Lucien Gerschel was a long-time student in Dumézil's classes and wrote about his work. See, for example, "Georges Dumézil's Comparative Studies in Tales and Traditions," trans. Archer Taylor, *Midwest Folklore* 7 (3), 1957: 141–8.
8. First edition, p. 94: "Indo-Iranian, Italo-Celtic data. We have marked how the absence... [*des faits indo-iraniens, italo-celtiques. Nous avons marqué comment l'absence...*]."
9. Jan de Vries, *Altgermanische Religionsgeschichte*, 2 volumes (Berlin and Leipzig: Walter de Gruyter, 1935), Vol. I, pp. 212–16.
10. De Vries, *Altgermanische Religionsgeschichte*, Vol. I, pp. 166–79.
11. "The Second Battle of Moytura," ed. and trans. Whitley Stokes, *Revue celtique* 12, 1891: 52–130, available at https://celt.ucc.ie/published/T300011.html. Dumézil translates the Irish *Cath Maige Tuired* as "Battle of Mag Tured," whereas a more common English rendering is Moytura. Apart from references, the translation follows Dumézil's choice.
12. Magnus Olsen, *Hedenske Kultminder i norske Stedsnavne*, Skrifter utget av Videnskapsselskaptet (Kristiana/Oslo: J. Dybwad, 1915), pp. 104ff.
13. Jan de Vries, *Contributions to the Study of Othin Especially in his Relation to Agricultural Practices in Modern Popular Lore*, Folklore Fellows Communications 94 (Helsinki: Suomalainen tiedeakatemia, Societas [i.e. Academia] scientiarum fennica, 1931), p. 31. Dumézil's quotations are not exact, though he does not distort the sense. De Vries describes the

term as "furious, in a highly excited movement, as when the storm, the sea or the fire are called *ôdhr.*"

14. Although this quotation is in English in Dumézil's text, de Vries actually says "the being possessed by a spiritual force, being in the state of a *daimonius*… the being possessed by a divine force" (*Contributions to the Study of Othin*, p. 31).

Notes to Chapter VIII

1. Wilhelm Ranisch, *Eddalieder mit Grammatik, Übersetzung und Erläuterungen*, Sammlung Gösche 171 (Berlin and Leipzig: Vereinigung wissenschaftlicher Verleger, 1920), p. 111, n.
2. J. Grimm, *Deutsche Rechtsaltertümer* (Leipzig: Dieterich'sche Verlagsbuchhandlung Theodor Weichner, 1899), Vol. II, p. 7, n.
3. Magnus Olsen, *Ættegård og helligdom: Norske stedsnavn sosialt og religionshistorisk belyst* (Oslo: Institutted for sammenlignende kulturforskning, 1926); *Farms and Fanes of Ancient Norway: The Place-names of a Country Discussed in their Bearings on Social and Religious History*, trans. Theodor Gleditsch (Oslo: H. Aschehoug & Co., 1928).
4. "The Prose Tales in the Rennes Dindshenchas," ed. Whitley Stokes, *Revue celtique* 15, 1894: 272–336, 418–84, p. 439, available at https://www.ucd.ie/tlh/text/ws.rc.15.002.text.html; Henri d'Arbois de Jubainville, *The Irish Mythological Cycle and Celtic Mythology*, trans. Richard Irvine Best (Dublin: Hodges, Figgis & Co. Ltd, 1903).
5. "The Second Battle of Moytura", ed. and trans. Whitley Stokes, *Revue celtique* 12, 1891: 52–130, 306–8, available at https://celt.ucc.ie/published/T300011.html

Notes to Chapter IX

1. The French is *le Borgne et le Manchot*.
2. The *Völuspâ* is a text in the *Poetic Edda*, usually translated as the prophecy of the sibyl, seeress, or wise-woman.
3. The *Ynglingasaga* is the first part of Snorri Sturluson's *Helmskringla*, a history of the Kings of Norway.
4. The *Gylfaginning* is the first part of Snorri Sturluson's *Prose Edda*.
5. First edition, p. 12 adds: "We do not think that our thesis is entirely irreconcilable with that which Mr. Aa. Ohlmark, *Heimdalls Horn und Odins Auge*, I, Lund and Copenhagen, 1937, seems to want to develop; but we must wait for the rest of the work to be published. ["(*Nous ne pensons*

pas que notre thèse soit entièrement inconciliable avec celle que M. Aa. Ohlmark, Heimdalls Horn und Odins Auge, I, *Lund et Copenhagen, 1937, parait vouloir développer ; mais nous devons attendre que la suite de l'ouvrage soit publiée.*)."] The reference is to Åke Ohlmarks, *Heimdalls Studien zur nordischen und vergleichenden Religionsgeschichte,* Erstes Buch (I–II): *Heimdallr und das Horn* (Lund: C.W.K. Gleerup and Kopenhagen: Levin & Munksgaard, 1937). It does not seem that further volumes were published.

6. The references are added to the second edition. At least some editions of the *Gylfaginning* have the Tyr and the wolf story in section 34. The *Lokasenna* (Loki's Quarrel or Duel) is in the *Poetic Edda.*
7. The first edition, p. 112 has "the dwarves of Alfheimr [*les nains de l'Alfheimr*]."
8. The phrase "the famous Horatius" is not in the French, but rather Coltman's useful gloss. He is also known as Publius Horatius Cocles.
9. Scaevola is the cognomen of Gaius Mucius Cordus. Cocles and Scaevola are crucial to the defence of Rome from Clusium, led by their king Lars Porsenna.
10. The references are to Marie-Louise Sjoestedt-Jonval, "Légendes épiques irlandaises et monnaies gauloises: Recherches sur la constitution de la légende de Cuchullainn," *Études celtiques* 1, 1936: 1–77, pp. 9, 10, 12, 18; Ernst Windisch, *Die altirische Heldensage, Táin bó Cúalnge* (Leipzig: S. Hirzel, 1905), p. 370, n. 2.
11. There are multiple translations as *Egil's Saga*, or the story of Egil Skallagrimsson.
12. First edition, p. 119 adds: "as in the 'magical pose' of the god Lug, at the beginning of the second battle of Mag Thured (§129), when 'standing on one foot, closing one eye and holding the other open' he circles the army he commands, exhorting it to fight [*comme encore de la 'pose magique' du dieu Lug, au début de la second bataille de Mag Thured (§129), lorsque 'debout sur un pied, fermant un œil et tenant l'autre ouvert,' il fait le tour de l'armée qu'il commande en l'exhortant au combat*]."
13. First edition, p. 119–20 adds: "(The comparison between Cocles the Cyclops and Lug closing one eye is all the more opportune as the political situations in which they operate are the same: the Romans here, the Tuatha De Danann there, have expelled their foreign tyrant, Tarquin the Etruscan, Bress the Fomorite there; an enemy army, here of Etruscans, there of Fomorites, is approaching to re-establish the tyrant's power; finally, Cocles and Lug save their threatened people. This analogy of situations means that the words attributed here to Cocles insulting the Etruscans – Livy, II, 10 – and there to Lug exhorting his warriors – *Battle of M. T.*, § 129 – are more or less equivalent and are based on the theme 'Long live liberty!' It is therefore possible that both legends, the Irish

and the Roman, are ancient myths of *regifungium.*) [*(Le rapprochement de Cocles le Cyclope et de Lug fermant un œil est d'autant plus opportun que les situations politiques où ils opèrent sont les mêmes: les Romains ici, là les Tuatha Dê Danann, ont expulsé leur tyran étranger, ici Tarquin l'Étrusque, là Bress le Fômoré; une armée ennemie, ici d'Étrusques, là de Fômoré, s'approche pour rétablir le tyran dans son pouvoir ; enfin Cocles et Lug sauvent leur peuple menacé. Cette analogie de situations fait que les paroles attribuées ici à Cocles injuriant les Étrusques – Tite-Live, II, 10 – et là à Lug exhortant ses guerriers – Bat de M. T., § 129 – sont à peu près équivalentes et roulent sur le thème 'Vive la liberté !' Il est donc possible que les deux légendes, l'irlandaise comme la romaine, soient d'anciens mythes de* regifungium.)"]
The reference is to The Battle of Mag Thured/Moytura.

14. W.F. Otto, "Fides," *Paulys Real-Encyclopédie*, 1909, Vol. IV, col. 2281–6, 2283.
15. Salomon Reinach, "Le Voile de l'oblation," *Cultes, mythes et religions* I, 1905: 299–311, p. 308
16. The reference is slightly incorrect: F. Munzer, "Mucius Scaevola," *Paulys Real-Encyclopédie*, Vol. 31, 1933, col. 412–59, 423.
17. Again, the reference is to the original article. See Mauss, *Sociologie et anthropologie* (Paris: Presses Universitaires de France, 1950), pp. 253–5; *The Gift: Forms and Function of Exchange in Archaic Societies*, trans. W.D. Halls (London: Routledge, 1990), pp. 79–80; *The Gift: Expanded edition*, trans. Jane I. Guyer (Chicago: Hau), 2016, pp. 172–4.
18. This entire section is new to the second edition, replacing the first edition's "Nuada and Balor." For the text and translation of the first edition, see Appendix I.
19. d'Arbois de Jubainville, *The Irish Mythological Cycle and Celtic Mythology*, pp. 84–86; d'Arbois de Jubainville, *L'Epopée celtique en Irlande* (Paris: Ernest Thorin, 1892), p. 396. Coltman's translation omits "and a poem of Cináed hua hArtacáin (died 975 A.D.)."
20. John Fraser, "The First Battle of Moytura," *Ériu* 8, 1916: 1–63; also available at http://www.maryjones.us/ctexts/1maghtured.html
21. Axel Olrik, "Om Ragnarok," *Aarbøger for Nordisk Oldkyndighed og Historie* (København: G.E.C. Gad's Universitesboghandet, 1920), pp. 157–292; Jan de Vries, *Altgermanische Religionsgeschichte*, 2 volumes (Berlin and Leipzig: Walter de Gruyter, 1935), Vol. II, p. 287.
22. K. Krohn, "Tyrs högra hand, Freys svärd," in *Festskrift til H. F. Feilberg: Fra Nordiske Sprog- og Folkemindeforskere* (Stockholm: P. A. Norstedt and Soner, 1911), pp. 541–7; Alexander Haggerty Krappe, "Nuada à la main d'argent," *Revue celtique* 49: 91–95.
23. "Lludd et Llevelys," *Les Mabinogion du Livre Rouge de Hergest avec les variants du Livre Blanc de Rhydderch*, ed. and trans. J. Loth, two volumes

(Paris: Fontemoinf et Cie, 1913), Vol. I, pp. 231–41. For an English version, see "Lludd and Llefelys," *The Mabinogion*, trans. Sioned Davies (Oxford: Oxford University Press, 2008), pp. 111–5.

Notes to Chapter X

1. The French is "L'État-major de la souveraineté." Coltman translates this as "general staff" or, below, "*une sorte d'état-major général de la souveraineté*" as "general staff or board of management of sovereignty." Both capture something of the sense intended by Dumézil, but I have amended to the more natural "general command."
2. This paragraph replaces a different passage in the first edition pp. 130–1: "The Aməša Spənta, the personified abstractions surrounding the supreme Iranian god, are surely different from the Āditya in the detail of personalities: neither Airyaman nor a 'Baga' appear in them, nor does Mithra; but it remains probable, after much discussion, that the principle of the two groupings is comparable and that, if Ahura Mazdāh has around him this sort of ministerial court, it is not only in imitation of certain Sumerian or Accadian systems, but also because his predecessor the great Indo-Iranian *Asura had around him a group of gods of the type of the Indian Āditya [*Les* Aməša Spənta, *abstractions personnifiées qui entourant le grand dieu iranien, sont sûrement différents des Āditya par le détail des personnalités: ni Airyaman ni un* 'Baga' *n'y figurent, non plus que Miθra; mais il rest probable, après bien des discussions, que le principe des deux groupements est comparable et que, si Ahura Mazdāh a autour de lui cette sorte de cour ministérielle, ce n'est pas seulement à l'imitation de certains systèmes de Sumer ou d'Accad, mais aussi parce que son prédécesseur le grand *Asura indo-iranien avait autour de lui un groupe de dieux du type des Āditya indiens.*]"
3. First edition, p. 131 has a sentence in place of the clause after the dash. "These secondary provinces, Vedic India, which thought in terms of gods rather than heroes, distributed them more simply among the Āditya, around the essential couple of Varuṇa and Mitra. [*Ces provinces secondaires, l'Inde védique, qui pensait par dieux plutôt que par héros, les distribuait plus simplement entre les Āditya, autour du couple essential de Varuṇa et de Mitra.*]"
4. J. Muir, *Original Sanskrit Texts on the Origin and History of the People of India, their Religion and Institutions,* second edition (London: Trübner & Co, 1868), Vol. V, pp. 162–70.
5. A.A. Macdonell, *Vedic Mythology* (Strassburg: Karl J. Trübner, 1897), p. 33.

6. *The Rig Veda: The Earliest Religious Poetry of India*, Vol. I, trans. Stephanie W. Jamison and Joel P. Brereton (Oxford: Oxford University Press, 2014), IV, 53, 6: "the one who impels forth and causes to settle down."
7. *The Nighantu and the Nikukta: The Oldest Indian Treatise on Etymology, Philology, and Semantics*, Sanskrit-English edition, ed. and trans. Lakshman Sarup, second edition (Delhi: Motilal Banarsidass, 1967 [1920]), pp. 188–9.
8. Albrecht Weber, *Indische Studien: Beiträge für die Kunde des indischen Alterthums* (Berlin: Ferd. Dümmler's Verlagsbuchhandlung, 1853), Vol. II, pp. 307–8.
9. *The Vājasaneyi-samhitā in the Mādhyandina and the Kānva-Çākhā, with the Commentary of Mahīdhara*, ed. Albrecht Weber (Berlin: Ferd Dümmler's Verlagsbuchhandlung/London: Williams and Norgate, 1852).
10. This a text for which there is no published translation in a Western European language. See, however, Hukam Chand Patyal, *Gopatha Brāhmaṇa*: English Translation with Notes and Introduction, unpublished dissertation, Department of Sanskrit and Prakrit Languages, Savitribai Phule Pune University, 1969, available at http://hdl.handle.net/10603/151631

Notes to Conclusion

1. Marcel Granet, *La Pensée chinoise* (Paris: La Renaissance du Livre, 1934), pp. 115–48, Chapter II, "Le Yin et le Yang". In the Paris: Albin Michel, 1998 edition, this is found on pp. 101–26.
2. This paragraph and the following one replace a sentence and two shorter paragraphs from the first edition, pp. 145–6: "Ces ressemblances sont compensées par deux graves differences… Il n'est pas exceptionnel d'ailleurs qu'un mythe produise une philosophie." For the full text and translation, see Appendix II.
3. This is a theme throughout Eliade's work. Dumézil may be thinking particularly of Mircea Eliade, *Yoga: Essai sur les origins de la mystique indienne* (Paris: Librairie Orientaliste Paul Geuthner, 1936). Eliade reworked some themes in *Techniques du yoga* (Paris: Gallimard, 1948); itself expanded into *Le Yoga. Immortalité et liberté* (Paris: Payot, 1954); *Yoga, Immortality and Freedom*, trans. Willard R. Trask (Princeton: Princeton University Press, 2009).
4. In some editions this passage appears in XII, 319: "Mitra is Purusha, and Varuṇa is Prakriti."
5. From here the second edition follows the first again.

6. Appendix I of *Flamen-Brahman* is actually entitled "L'Aventure du brahmane céleste," pp. 86–96. The adventure of the celestial brahman, instead of the path of the celestial brahman.

Notes to Appendices

1. "Indra Against the Bonds of Varuṇa," pp. 124–7/75–77 above.
2. As above, in some editions this appears in *Mahābhārata* XII, 319: "Mitra is Purusha, and Varuṇa is Prakriti."

Notes to Afterword

1. Georges Dumézil, *Mitra-Varuna: Essai sur deux representations indo-européennes de la souverainété* (Paris: Presses Universitaires de France, 1940); second edition (Paris: Gallimard, 1948); *Mitra-Varuna: An Essay on Two Indo-European Representations of Sovereignty*, trans. Derek Coltman (New York, NY: Zone Books, 1988). Current critical edition with a new Introduction by Stuart Elden. Subsequent references and page numbers correspond to the current edition.
2. *Mitra-Varuna*, p. xxxix.
3. The evolution of Dumézil's thinking is meticulously tracked in the Introduction to the present edition by Stuart Elden and in Wouter W. Belier, *Decayed Gods: Origin and Development of Georges Dumézil's "Idéologie Tripartite"* (Boston, MA: Brill, 1991), vol. 7.
4. Mitra-Varuna, p. 41.
5. See Veena Das, *Structure and Cognition: Aspects of Hindu Caste and Ritual* (London: Oxford University Press, 2012 [1976]).
6. Louis Dumont, *Homo Hierarchicus: The Caste System and its Implications* (Chicago, IL: University of Chicago Press, 1980).
7. M.N. Srinivas, "Varna and Caste," in *Caste in Modern India and Other Essays* (Bombay: Asia Publishing House, 1962), pp. 63–69.
8. Dumont, *Homo Hierarchicus,* p. 66.
9. Dumont, *Homo Hierarchicus*, pp. 66–67.
10. Veena Das, "*Structure and Cognition*, 'Comments: Axel Michael's article'," *Contributions to Indian Sociology* 54(3), 2020: 388–408.
11. Louis Dumont and David Pocock, "Pure and Impure," *Contributions to Indian Sociology* (1), 1959: 9–39.
12. *Mitra-Varuna*, p. 147
13. Bhrigupati Singh, "The Headless Horseman of Central India: Sovereignty at Varying Thresholds of life," *Cultural Anthropology* 27(2), 2012:

383–407; *Poverty and the Quest for Life: Spiritual and Material Strivings in Rural India* (Chicago, IL: University of Chicago Press, 2015).

14. Singh, "The Headless Horseman," p. 384.
15. Some very nice examples of graded sovereignty and traces of Mitra-Varuna that Singh offers are the pacts with lower-level State officials that villagers make as well as the ever-present possibility of the same officials applying their power to dispossess villagers. See Singh, *Poverty and the Quest for Life*. See also Veena Das, *Slum Acts* (London: Polity Press, 2022), for the upending of local contracts and what she calls the "rogue element" of sovereignty derived from the discussion of the relation between the inside and outside of sovereignty in relation to the first two functions.
16. Gilles Deleuze and Félix Guattari, *A Thousand Plateaus: Capitalism and Schizophrenia* (London: Bloomsbury Publishing, 1988).
17. Deleuze and Guattari, *A Thousand Plateaus*, p. 352.
18. Although Dumézil does not name the king, the story is of Harishchandra, famed for his extreme generosity and his excessive adherence to his word under any circumstances and at any cost.
19. The story of Śunaḥśepa and its variants have been interpreted in many different contexts. For some, the story provides evidence of the conflict between those living within the Brahmanical tradition and those living outside the varna system; for others, it is evidence of the confrontation between different Aryan tribes, those in the Ṛg Veda and those outside it. The integration of new techniques of archeological research and Indo-Aryan Studies has reanimated some of these questions and, without questioning the importance of these issues, it is interesting that the same stories lend themselves to structural interpretations in comparative mythology, which Dumézil pioneered and which shifted attention away from finding the original version. See, in this connection, David Gordon White, "Śunaḥśepa unbound," *Revue de l'histoire des religions* (1986): 227-62. For a critical account of the discovery and development of theories of Aryan origins and the colonial mediation of these stories, see Thomas Trautmann, *Aryans and British India* (Oakland, CA: University of California Press, 1997)
20. I do not doubt that Dumézil is right to stress that the priestly inflections of this story may have emphasized some aspects in this case that give a different tonality to the text as compared to other versions. Indeed Indra is one of the most complex figures of Vedic and post Vedic mythology. My limited issue here is that to detect some kind of humanism in this moment seems to me to have introduced a teleology in the argument that is difficult to defend.
21. *Mitra-Varuna*, p. 77.
22. According to this legend, as Vritra died, struck by Indra's thunderbolt, a ghastly woman emerged from his mouth. She was naked. She had wild

hair and fangs and a terrifying demeanor. She roared as she chased Indra through the three worlds. Eventually she found him hidden in a lotus stalk, and when she enveloped him, he became totally paralyzed. Beseeched by the gods to save Indra from this terrifying female figure, Brāhma intervened and, having identified the woman as brahmhatyā, Brāhma distributed bits of her to the forests and to women, who thus absorbed the sin that Indra had committed. See Nicholas J. Allen, "The Indra-Tullus Comparison," *General Linguistics* 40, 2003: 149–71. In some versions of the story, Indra was advised to pray to the goddess Jagadambā, the mother of the universe, who advised him to perform the horse sacrifice, through which he was purified. In other versions of the Indra legend, Indra is credited with having performed one hundred *aśvamedha* sacrifices to retain his position as the lord of heaven, as one of his names, *śatakrtu*, testifies.

23. See Allen, "The Indra-Tullus Comparison," for a very interesting discussion on the various female characters who appear in this story, including Indra's distraught wife, who beseechs the gods to find him when he goes into hiding, and, one might add, the goddess Jagadambā. The feminine principle is discussed in *The Destiny of the Warrior* with reference to Draupadi, the common wife of the five Pandava brothers, to conclude, following Wikander, that the goddess is not confined to any one function but moves between all three. Georges Dumézil, *The Destiny of the Warrior*, trans. Alf Hiltebeitel (Chicago, IL: University of Chicago Press, 1970). An aspect of Draupadi that goes uncommented is her name as Yajnaseni, which refers to the side story that the earth is tired of the wars among the kṣatriyas and places Draupadi in the ashes of a sacrificial fire, at which point a heavenly voice announces that she would be the cause of the destruction of the Kuru lineage. The many forms and disguises of the warrior goddesses, including grammatical ones, is a possible route to explore for deepening the question of the she-gods in the Indo-European field.